LIKE HUNGRY WOLVES

Culloden Moor
16 April 1746

LIKE HUNGRY WOLVES

Culloden Moor
16 April 1746

Stuart Reid

Colour plates by
Gerry Embleton

WINDROW & GREENE

LONDON

Dedication
To my father

This edition first published in Great Britain 1994 by
Windrow & Greene Ltd
19A Floral Street
London WC2E 9DS

© 1994 Stuart Reid
Colour plates © Gerry Embleton

Design by Victor Shreeve

Printed in China

A CIP catalogue record for this book
is available from the British Library

Standard edition
ISBN 1 85915 080 2

De luxe edition
ISBN 1 85915 041 1

7505678

CONTENTS
INTRODUCTION 7

Introduction

The battle of Culloden is unquestionably one of the most dramatic and evocative episodes in Scottish history, and unsurprisingly the last two hundred years and more have seen a massive outpouring of books and articles on the subject. What is surprising, perhaps, is that so much scholarship and literary endeavour should have left unanswered so many questions about how the battle was actually fought.

It lasted only about forty minutes; and most writers have, understandably perhaps, preferred to dwell less upon the battle than upon its aftermath. Consequently, far more ink has been spent on Prince Charles Edward's escape than has ever been devoted to the battle which turned him into a hunted fugitive in the first place. Nevertheless, it is a story which needs to be told.

In reconstructing the battle I have relied principally upon three sources of information. The first and most important is the mass of contemporary documentation relating to the affair. The Jacobite memoirs are of course well known, but I have also drawn extensively upon the rich and scandalously underused archive of eyewitness accounts to be found in the newspapers of the day.

Similarly useful has been a happy conjunction of Thomas Sandby's contemporary surveys of the battlefield and the modern Ordnance Survey. These are not only compatible, but they also reveal at last the true, horrific significance of that great slew of mass graves stretching southwards from the aptly named Well of the Dead.

Thirdly, information from both sources has been interpreted in the light of a thorough study of the mid-18th century British Army's drill books and tactical doctrines, and the results of tests of the actual effectiveness of 18th century muskets and cannon.

Combining these three sources with the detailed breakdown of the strength of each regiment set down in the "morning state" of the Duke of Cumberland's army for 16 April 1746, it has been possible to plot with reasonable confidence where each battalion stood, how wide a frontage it occupied, and how much damage it was capable of inflicting.

With regard to the conventions adopted for this text, readers should note that in the mid-18th century spelling – even the spelling of proper names – often owed as much to art as to science. Since the text includes much direct quotation, it has seemed pointless to attempt a rigid consistency or to insert [sic] every few lines; wherever the meaning is clearly comprehensible the original variety of spelling has been preserved.

The identification of individual regiments of the British Army was in a transitional stage in the mid-1740s. The old system of identification by the name of the current Colonel was still in general use, but sometimes in parallel with the numerical sequence which became the norm a few years later. Again, the author has preferred clarity to consistency, and both systems are used in the narrative, although direct quotations usually refer by Colonels' names.

Although the conclusions presented here are necessarily those of the author, this study of the battle would not have been possible without the generous assistance of a great many people. The author wishes to record his particular thanks to: Mr. Charles Burnett, Curator of Fine Art, and the other staff of the Scottish United Services Museum in Edinburgh Castle; Mrs. Susanna Ker of the Scottish National Portrait Gallery; Ms. Janice Murray of Dundee Art Galleries and Museums; Ms. Gwyneth Campling of the Royal Collection; the staffs of the National Library of Scotland, the library of the Newcastle Upon Tyne Literary and Philosophical Society, the Scottish Record Office, and the Public Record Office at Kew; Mr. Phillip Elliot-Wright, who provided some useful information on the Irish troops in the service of France; and last and by no means least, the dedicated re-enactors of the 68th (Durham) Light Infantry Display Team, who enthusiastically learned and demonstrated the manual exercise and bayonet fighting techniques practised in 1746.

Stuart Reid
North Shields
April 1994

CHAPTER ONE

Prestonpans

Early on the morning of Wednesday 16 April 1746 a British army began striking their camp on a bleak coastal plain, and preparing for battle. It was a cold morning with a biting, blustery wind bringing occasional flurries of sleet and ice-cold rain out of the north; in the ordinary course of events the redcoats should still have been snug in winter quarters. Ahead of them lay a crucial battle not with their traditional enemies, the French, but against their own fellow countrymen. It would be the last pitched battle between conventional armies ever to take place on British soil; and it would be fought on a rising stretch of moorland above Culloden House, outside Inverness in the Scottish Highlands.

The man they had come there to beat was an Italian-born Prince, the last effective representative of the ancient house of Stuart.

His great-great-grandfather, James VI of Scotland and I of England – once characterised as "the Wisest Fool in Christendom" – had schemed and intrigued his way on to the English throne in 1603, and thereafter very largely turned his back on Scotland (though not before he had outlawed the whole Clan MacGregor). Ever the realist, he was, as Sir Walter Scott put it, fonder of talking about his prerogatives than exercising them. Not so his son, Charles I, whose attempt to destroy the independence of the Scots kirk provoked a national uprising, which in turn led to the yet more ruinous Great Civil War, and to his trial and execution by the English Parliament in 1649.

The beheaded King's son Charles II fared little better, leading Scotland into a last disastrous war with England in 1650; and although he was subsequently restored to the throne by consent in 1660, his brief and unhappy acquaintance with his Scottish subjects discouraged him from ever visiting the kingdom again. Instead he delegated its administration to commissioners with what amounted to viceregal powers. In England he is remembered as politically circumspect; but in Scotland his servants embarked upon a ruthless persecution of the Protestant sects known as the Covenanters. Those "Killing Times" directly and indirectly spawned a series of rebellions throughout Britain, and so eroded support for the Stuarts that in 1689 Charles' successor, his Roman Catholic brother James VII and II, was summarily deposed in favour of his Dutch Protestant son-in-law, William of Orange.

On 4 April 1689 the Scottish Estates, or parliament, roundly declared that King James VII had "forfaultit the Croun", and underlined this announcement a week later on the 11th by the formal adoption of the "Claim of Right". This asserted that by transforming a limited legal monarchy into an arbitrary despotic power, James VII had violated the Scots constitution. The stances adopted by both parties would doubtless have horrified the King's grandfather, James VI, who had done so much to formulate the concept of the

Divine Right of Kings; in effect, by this Claim of Right the Scots stoutly repudiated such high-flown nonsense. The King did not rule by divine right but by the will of his people, and if he misused the powers with which they entrusted him he could be deposed and the crown offered to another.

More practically, the Estates also raised an army to underline their point; and at the battle of Killiecrankie fought against James's supporters on 27 July 1689 only one out of General Mackay's six battalions was English. (Appropriately enough, both it and one of the five Scots battalions, the newly raised Earl of Leven's Regiment, were later to fight in the British line at Culloden as the 13th and 25th Foot respectively.)

When Dutch William died in 1702 he was smoothly succeeded by his sister-in-law, Anne Stuart; and the most significant moment in her 12-year reign was the forcing through in 1707 of an Act of Union, firmly binding together the hitherto still independent kingdoms of Scotland and England.

Objectively, therefore, most Scots could hardly be expected to look back upon the final hundred years of the Stuarts as a golden age. They were characterised by the family's marked reluctance to even clap eyes upon Scotland, and their few interventions in Scottish politics almost invariably had the unhappiest results. Nevertheless, under the Stuarts Scotland had still been an independent country; and it is very hard to escape the impression that 18th century Jacobitism was not primarily an expression of ancient loyalty to the Stuarts, but rather a focus for opposition to the Union.

An attempt by the titular James VIII to capitalise on this opposition by landing in Scotland in 1708 was frustrated by the intransigence of the French Admiral in command of the operation; but Queen Anne's death in 1714, without a natural heir, provided another opportunity. A Protestant heir to the British throne was required, and promptly found in the person of George, Elector of Hanover, a great-grandson of James VI and I. Having served under the Duke of Marlborough the new King George I was assured the support of the Army. This was fortunate, since he very soon had to contend with a full scale Jacobite rising in 1715. After some anxious moments this collapsed, however; and in the 30 years of peace which followed (scarcely disturbed by another minor rising in 1719), Scotland began to realise some benefit from the Union.

The political settlement might be considered highly unsatisfactory; but this was more than counterbalanced by the removal of trading barriers, and in particular by the access which Scots merchants now at last enjoyed to the English colonies in North America and the Caribbean. Glasgow was ideally situated to take advantage of this, and grew dramatically in size, wealth and importance. A combination of stout Protestantism and commercial success ensured that in 1745 the citizens were in no doubt where their best interests lay. It is no coincidence, therefore, that the Glasgow Volunteers were to be one of the more active loyalist units to answer the call.

Although Glasgow was perhaps the most obvious beneficiary, the years which followed the Union were gradually characterised by a growing prosperity in most of Lowland Scotland. It is one of the paradoxes of the Jacobite period that the Stuarts should in the end have come to depend so heavily upon Highland support, given the family's record of repression in that area, culminating most famously in the proscription of the McGregors. Yet it is a paradox easily explained, for the economically backward Highlands gained least from the Union, and nationalist temperament was consequently little tempered by prosperity.

The most superficial reading of Scotland's history in these times will demonstrate, however, that it is far too simplistic to equate loyalty to the British throne with a Lowland commercial class, and Jacobitism with the feudal, agricultural clan communities of the Highlands. The clans were always fiercely divided, and a significant proportion of them remained loyal to the crown. The powerful Clan Campbell of Argyll was only the most prominent and consistent; others included the Grants, Munros, Rosses, Mackays, Sutherlands and, in 1745, Macleods and Mackenzies.

Although a tradition of personal loyalty to the Stuarts was undoubtedly maintained in some quarters, by 1745 it had become increasingly difficult to generate real enthusiasm for a family which had not sat on the throne for over fifty years. The actual incumbent of that throne – by 1745, George II – might have enjoyed no great popularity, it is true; but translating that unpopularity into an armed insurrection on behalf of a virtual stranger, who despite his name was almost equally foreign, was to be no easy matter. Without the still smouldering opposition to the Union it would probably have been impossible; and even this opposition, two generations after the deposing of the Stuarts, was fading in the face of the growing prosperity which Union appeared to have brought.

Moreover, even those who still professed to support the titular King James VIII were adamant that they would not rise without substantial assistance – by which they meant that were King James to land at the head of a French army they would gladly assist him to regain his rightful throne, but they would not, under any other circumstances, enter into a rebellion. Such a rising, when attempted in 1715, had well-nigh ruined them all.

Indeed, after a Jacobite agent named William Drummond (alias MacGregor) of Balhaldy tried to persuade the leaders of pro-Stuart sentiment into rising in 1743 by greatly exaggerating their strength, they formally set out their conditions for raising their men. These were that James's eldest son, Prince Charles Edward, should come to Scotland in person, bringing 6,000 troops, arms for 10,000 more, and £30,000 in gold.

It is not surprising, therefore, that his arrival in July 1745 with next to no money, few arms and, worst of all, not a single French grenadier at his back, inspired more consternation than rapture among his putative followers.

French support had not been forthcoming simply because King Louis XV was unconvinced that the effort was going to be worthwhile. A large scale invasion of England had indeed been planned for early 1744. The necessary troops and shipping were assembled, they were even embarked; but on the

James Francis Edward Stuart (1688-1766), son of King James II and VII and regarded by Jacobites as the rightful King James VIII of Scotland; he is better known as "The Old Pretender". (Author's collection)

night of 6 March a storm arose, dispersing transports and escorts and giving Admiral Norris time to assemble his own fleet. Marshal Saxe, the designated commander of the expedition, thereupon called it off and thankfully began preparing for a conventional campaign in Flanders. During the long drawn out struggle against Britain and her allies in the 18th century the French showed a consistent reluctance to divert significant land forces from the major continental arena in order to gamble on overseas campaigns. In the long term this policy proved costly for France in North America and India, leaving her far behind Britain during the great 19th century scramble for empire; in the case of expeditions to the British Isles themselves, events would prove the prejudice more soundly based.

Thus it was bereft of full-hearted French backing that the 25-year-old Charles Edward Stuart, the "Young Pretender", sailed from Nantes on 5 July 1745 aboard the 16-gun *Le du Teillay* – provided for him, together with her chartered escort the 60-gun *L'Elisabeth*, by an Irish slave-trader named Anthony Walsh. The first carried 1,500 "firelocks" (muskets), 1,800 swords and £4,000 in gold, while the *L'Elisabeth* freighted a further 2,000 firelocks, 600 swords, and – in an almost pathetic gesture towards the 6,000 regular troops demanded by the Scottish Jacobites – a company of 60 Marines clad in blue coats turned up with red.

A hundred miles west of the Lizard this shoestring invasion force ran into Captain Brett's HMS *Lyon* of 58 guns. Unable to outrun her, Captain Dau of the *L'Elisabeth* fought her, and the two ships pounded each other into floating wrecks before night brought the engagement to a close. Walsh, aboard the *Le du Teillay*, kept the Prince safely out of the fight despite Dau's request for assistance. As the shattered *L'Elisabeth*

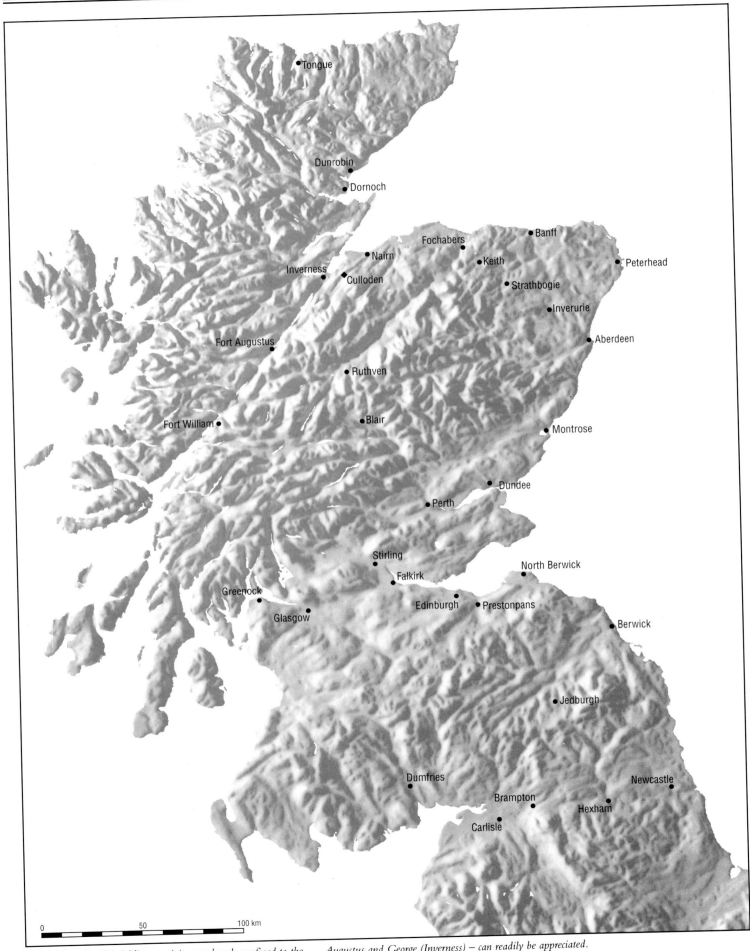

Scotland in the '45. *Military activity was largely confined to the eastern coastal belt, although some minor operations did take place in the interior. The importance of the "chain" – Forts William, Augustus and George (Inverness) – can readily be appreciated. Most French troops were landed at Montrose, but other units also landed at Aberdeen, Peterhead and Tongue.*

limped back to Brest he sailed on northwards; and after a decidedly lukewarm welcome on Eriskay he finally landed the Prince and seven companions on the shores of Loch nan Uamh in Arisaig on 25 July.

Dismayed by the absence of the expected and necessary French troops, the Jacobite clan chiefs were at first reluctant to commit themselves; but eventually support was promised by Ranald MacDonald, younger of Clanranald, by Donald MacDonnell of Scotus, representing Glengarry, and by Alexander Macdonnell of Keppoch. All three raised regiments for the Prince, but without the eventual adherence of Donald Cameron of Locheil it is unlikely that the standard would have been formally raised at Glenfinnan on 19 August.

*   *   *

By that time the Commander-in-Chief Scotland, General Sir John Cope, had word that something was afoot. His problem was what to do about it. In his evidence to the subsequent inquiry, Cope recalled:

"As much as I can remember [he had of course lost his papers at Prestonpans] on the 2nd of July the troops in Scotland were quartered thus;

"Gardener's Dragoons at Stirling, Linlithgow, Musselburgh, Kelso and Coldstream.

"Hamilton's Dragoons at Haddington, Duns and the adjacent places.

N.B.- both regiments at Grass.

"Guise's Regiment of foot at Aberdeen, and the Coast-Quarters.

"Five Companies of Lee's at Dumfries, Stranraer, Glasgow and Stirling.

"Murray's in the Highland Barracks.

"Lascelles' at Edinburgh and Leith.

"Two Additional Companies of the Royals at Perth.

"Two Do. of the Scottish Fuziliers at Glasgow.

"Two Do. of Lord Semple's at Cupar in Fife.

"Three Do. of Lord John Murray's Highland Regiment at Crieff.

"Lord Loudoun's Regiment was beginning to be raised; and besides these, there were the standing garrisons of invalids in the castles."

The more closely this list is examined, the less impressive it appears.

Gardiner's 13th and Hamilton's 14th Dragoons were dispersed in their quarters. Their horses were at grass and consequently soft-backed, while the troopers will have been going through the infantry part of their training cycle – practising platoon-firing rather than cavalry work. Between them, according to the *Scots Magazine*, they mustered 567 rank and file at Prestonpans.

Guise's 6th Foot, who by the time operations actually commenced had taken over the garrisoning of the Highland barracks, were said to have been nearly up to their full establishment of 780 rank and file, but were so scattered as to be ignored in any equations.

Lee's 55th had five of their companies in garrison at Berwick, and therefore outwith Cope's control; but the five remaining, led by Lieutenant Colonel Peter Halkett, younger of Pitfirran, could muster 391 rank and file at Prestonpans, so it too must have been pretty well up to its established strength.

Thomas Murray's 57th, on the other hand, mustered only

Private of the 43rd Highlanders as depicted in the 1742 Cloathing Book. This first Highland regiment of the British line was raised by a Royal Warrant of November 1739, incorporating the Independent Companies previously raised for policing the Highlands. Although the artist has clearly been defeated by the tartan this is otherwise an unusually clear sketch of Highland clothing. (National Museums of Scotland)

580 men at Prestonpans, and having until lately been scattered across the length and breadth of the Highlands their battalion-level training cannot have been of a very high order.

Highland Piper copied from Bowles for Grose's Military Antiquities *and allegedly depicting Donald MacDonald, one of the Black Watch mutineers. The yellow pipe-banner with the red cross is probably a relic of Independent Company days. (Author's collection)*

Peregrine Lascelles' 58th, like Lee's and Murray's, had been raised as recently as 1741, and like the latter appears to have had only about 570 rank and file; moreover two of its ten companies formed part of the garrison of Edinburgh Castle and so were unavailable for field operations.

A fifth battalion, Loudon's 64th Highlanders, had only just commenced recruiting and could not be considered militarily significant. In a similar state were the nine "Additional Companies", no more than depot units supplying recruits for the British Army's Scottish regiments. By Cope's testimony they numbered about 25 wholly untrained men apiece, with the exception of those recruiting for Lord John Murray's 43rd Highlanders (the Black Watch), which he reckoned to be just about complete.

All in all, therefore, he could count on just two and a half weak battalions of infantry, none of whom had ever seen action before, and whose arms, described in 1744 as "indifferent", were now "consequently worse". He also had two similarly untried dragoon regiments who were in any case going to need time to achieve even theoretical readiness for battle. The limitations of the rest were made all too apparent

by the fate of the two Additional Companies of the Royals.

Although in modern times firmly linked with Edinburgh, in the 18th century the 1st of Foot, the Royal Scots, found a fair proportion of their recruits in the Highlands; and for that purpose the Additional Companies were quartered in Perth at the beginning of July and had moved on to Fort Augustus a month later. Aware of the deteriorating situation, the governor of that place took it upon himself to order them south on the 16th in order to reinforce the rather exposed garrison at Fort William. En route they were ambushed at High Bridge and, after a surprisingly determined attempt to fight their way clear, were forced to surrender near Invergarry, having lost two dead and at least one wounded. Militarily of little significance, this affair cannot but have helped to encourage the assembled rebels at Glenfinnan (even though the prisoners, who were forced to watch the raising of the standard, refused all blandishments offered to them to change sides).

Cope meanwhile had been assembling his meagre forces at Stirling.

Charles Edward Stuart (1720-1788). When the exiled King James II of England and VII of Scotland died in 1701, King Louis XIV of France recognised his son James Francis Edward as James III and VIII. After the failure of the 1715 Jacobite rising the French sought improved relations with Britain; in 1717 the Old Pretender was obliged to leave France for Italy, where – following the failure of another attempt to raise Scotland for the Stuarts in 1719, this time with Spanish help – his son Charles Edward was born. When the boy reached adulthood the Old Pretender, tired and disillusioned, appointed him Prince Regent. With Britain and France again at war in opposing alliances fighting over the Austrian succession, Louis XV allowed "The Young Pretender" (also less flatteringly known to his opponents as "The Young Italian") to stay in France after the preparations for an invasion of Britain failed in 1744; and to sail for Scotland in July 1745. This is the only portrait which can reliably be identified as having been produced while he was in Scotland; the artist, Sir Robert Strange, served in his Lifeguards. Prince Charles Edward was said to be handsome, charismatic, and not without personal courage; but he lacked all other qualities necessary to the leader of a military uprising. (National Galleries of Scotland)

His original intention, sensible enough, was to march straight into the Highlands, as General Wightman had done during the abortive rising of 1719, and to nip the affair in the bud. This was, after all, why old General Wade had set in train his famous road-building programme. Finding sufficient men to do the job was far from easy, however. All that Cope could actually muster fit to march were Murray's 57th, Lascelles' 58th (less the two companies in Edinburgh Castle), and the half-battalion of Lee's 55th. The other five companies of Lee's were requested, but failed to materialise. The Additional Companies of Campbell's 21st and Sempill's 25th were left where they were, but two of the Black Watch companies (neither of which had broadswords) were added to his expeditionary force and the third despatched to Inveraray. There was obviously no point in taking his two dragoon regiments into the hills, but once they had rounded up their horses Gardiner's were concentrated at Perth and Stirling, while Hamilton's covered Leith and Edinburgh in Cope's absence. By way of an artillery train he had four obsolete 1½lb. field guns and four Coehorn mortars – but only Major Griffith, the Master Gunner of Edinburgh Castle, and four Invalids to man them.

Although he may by now have been beginning to have his doubts, Cope's orders from the Civil Authorities – the Lords Justices, headed by Lord Tweeddale – left him with no alternative but to march northwards on 20 August. Lascelles' 58th had not yet got their camp equipage in order, so he pushed on to Crieff, leaving them to follow next day with an additional 1,000 "stand of arms" (firelock and bayonet complete) in order to equip the expected loyalist volunteers.

In the event no-one joined him, and he was inclined while waiting at Crieff to postpone the whole attempt; but then, receiving a positive order from Tweeddale (who was safely ensconced in London), he sent 700 stand of the newly arrived arms back to Stirling, and marched deeper into the hills.

His initial objective was Fort Augustus, the central position in the "chain" stretching along the Great Glen; but the rebels too were now on the move and spoiling for a fight. In order to reach Fort Augustus Cope had to lead his men over the seventeen traverses of the Corryairack Pass, and it was there that they elected to meet him.

Forewarned by Captain John Sweetenham, an officer of Guise's who had been captured by the rebels and then released on parole, Cope halted at Dalwhinnie on 26 August and called a council of war. Four options were open to him. He could attempt to force the Corryairack; he could stand fast at Dalwhinnie and offer battle; he could retire to Stirling; or failing these, he could make for Inverness. The first option was rejected unanimously, the pass being too strong a position to be forced with the troops at hand. Nor was there much point in standing around hopefully at Dalwhinnie; there was no guarantee that the rebels would be so obliging as to accept a battle there, and in any case there was insufficient food available to support the army while it waited. The third course was similarly rejected; Cope recognised that this would be seen as a defeat just as decisive as a lost battle, and that a retreat through increasingly hostile territory might well result in disaster. The only realistic option was to make for Fort George at Inverness which, since it was one of the "chain" forts, would at least allow him to fulfil the letter if not the spirit of his orders; but even this course was not without its dangers.

The British intelligence service was still functioning, and

Soldier of the Royals (1st Foot), now the Royal Scots, as depicted in the 1742 Cloathing Book – see caption to Colour Plate A for notes on uniform details. Two Additional Companies of this regiment were the first regular troops to encounter the rebels. (NMS)

on the night of the 27th or very early the next morning Cope received word from one of his agents that the rebels, having been disappointed of fighting him at Corryairack, now hoped to intercept him in the Slochd Mor pass between Carrbridge and Tomatin. There was no time to lose. The Laird of Grant promised to secure the pass with his men, but then almost at once announced that he was himself in danger of attack and consequently unable to assist. If he was to avoid the trap Cope was going to have to march hard and fast. On the 28th he therefore made for Ruthven Barracks and added Captain Sweetenham's company of Guise's 6th to his little army, leaving behind in their place "a very good Serjeant and twelve men, with a good quantity of Ammunition." Outpacing the rebels, he thankfully arrived in Inverness on the 29th. There he was at last joined by three incomplete companies of Loudon's 64th Highlanders, and a 200-strong loyalist battalion led by Captain George Monro of Culcairn.

That same day a party of Camerons, led by Locheil's brother Archy and an Irish professional soldier named John William O'Sullivan, attacked Ruthven. Tiny though his garrison was Sergeant Molloy of the 55th refused to surrender, replying that "I was too old a Soldier to surrender a Garrison of such Strength without bloody noses". When the rebels responded by threatening to hang them all if put to the trouble of storming the building, Molloy stoutly "told them I would take my Chance", and proceeded to beat off the assault which followed. (Cope subsequently recommended him for a commission, and it is pleasant to record that he is next heard of as Lieutenant Molloy.)

Cope's abrupt departure from the scene, without fighting, momentarily left the Jacobites at something of a loose end. Some were for pursuing him or at least trying to head him off at the Slochd pass, though this particular idea did not get beyond the abortive attack on Ruthven Barracks. Instead, an immediate advance southwards into Perthshire appeared a more attractive proposition. In the short term large numbers of recruits could be expected, and beyond lay the glittering prize of an apparently undefended Edinburgh. It was too good an opportunity to miss.

By the time the rebel army reached Perth it was high time to sort out its hitherto rather haphazard command structure. Until then the army had more or less been run by committee, with John O'Sullivan looking after the everyday details as Adjutant General, a post for which he had been recommended by old Colonel John McDonnell, an officer of France's Irish Brigade and one of the original "Seven Men of Moidart" who had landed with the Prince. O'Sullivan, a stoutly built 45-year-old Kerry man, had originally been intended for the priesthood but instead went soldiering, serving on Marshal Maillebois's staff in Corsica and Italy — experience which stood him in good stead in Scotland.

Now, however, two Lieutenant Generals were appointed. The Prince's original choice was James Drummond, titular Duke of Perth; but "though brave even to excess, every way honourable, and possessed of a mild and gentle disposition, [he] was of very limited abilities and interfered with nothing." His compliant nature might have suited the autocratic Prince; but unfortunately he was also openly Roman Catholic, and it was therefore thought politically expedient to appoint a second General, the unimpeachably Protestant Lord George Murray.

The fifth son of John, Duke of Atholl, Lord George was nearly 50 years old. He had been an Ensign in the 1st Battalion of the Royals in 1712-15, but in the latter year had joined the rebels and commanded a battalion at Sherriffmuir. He was "out" once more in 1719, being wounded at Glenshiel but escaping abroad. He was pardoned in 1726; and thereafter lived on friendly terms with his brother James, 2nd Duke of Atholl. This gave rise to suspicions over his loyalty

Simon Fraser, Lord Lovat (1667-1747). Lovat was an inveterate schemer whose guiding principle appears to have been personal advancement. After a scandalous career he was too old for campaigning in 1745; but after professing neutrality he attempted to kidnap the loyalist Lord President, Duncan Forbes of Culloden, before finally throwing in his hand with the rebels and sending out his son to fight. Captured after Culloden, Simon the elder was executed in 1747. (Private Scottish collection)

to the cause, which were exacerbated by his character. Although he was to prove a far more capable officer than Perth he was not without his faults, as one of his aides de camp, a bumptious Edinburgh snob named James Johnstone, admitted:

"Lord George was vigilant, active, and diligent; his plans were always judiciously formed, and he carried them promptly and vigorously into execution. However, with an infinity of good qualities, he was not without his defects: proud, haughty, blunt and imperious, he wished to have the exclusive disposal of everything and, feeling his superiority, would listen to no advice."

Not surprisingly, he and O'Sullivan the Adjutant General clashed almost at once. The latter has generally been cast as an incompetent, but in fact the evidence suggests the opposite. He was an experienced staff officer and, had he and Murray been able to get on, they might have made a formidable team combining the former's instinctive ability with the latter's technical expertise. Unfortunately Murray's arrogance on the one hand, and an unfounded belief on the part of O'Sullivan and some of the other Irish officers that Murray was not to be trusted, resulted in a bitter feud. Murray charged O'Sullivan with incompetence, and it is plain from O'Sullivan's narrative that he for his part regarded Murray as an over-excitable amateur. It was hardly a sound basis for a good working relationship, but in the early days at least they managed to tolerate one another.

The Jacobite force, now mustering over 2,000 men, left Perth on 11 September, and two days later crossed the River Forth some way above Stirling Castle by the Fords of Frew. No attempt was made to stop them by Colonel James Gardiner and his 13th Dragoons, who fell back steadily to Edinburgh. On 15 September Gardiner rendezvoused with Hamilton's 14th Dragoons and a loyalist volunteer unit from Edinburgh at Corstorphine. That evening, probably much to his relief since he was in poor health, Gardiner was superseded by Brigadier Thomas Fowke. A Dutch infantry regiment, although expected hourly, had not appeared; and after conferring with Lieutenant General Joshua Guest, the governor of Edinburgh Castle, Fowke judged it expedient to retire eastwards in the hope of joining up with General Cope. Thus abandoned, the capital — though not its castle — fell to the rebels without a fight.

Having reached Inverness safely, the Commander-in-Chief Scotland was well aware that he then had to return to Edinburgh as quickly as possible. Leaving behind a company each of the 43rd and 64th Highlanders to hold Fort George, he picked up Captain Pointz's company of Guise's 6th and two more cannon and marched hard for Aberdeen, which he reached on 11 September. If necessary he was then prepared to march down the east coast, but by the time he reached the burgh sufficient shipping had been arranged to carry his army south by sea. Dismissing Culcairn's loyalist battalion, and picking up a fourth company of Loudon's 64th, he promptly embarked his regulars and arrived off Dunbar on the 17th. Brigadier Fowke joined him there that evening with the dragoons — and the unwelcome news that Edinburgh had already been captured by the rebels.

Undaunted, Cope set off on the morning of the 19th with the intention of bringing the rebels to battle. Marching first to Haddington, Cope pushed on towards Prestonpans on the 20th, but a reconnaissance party then discovered the rebels approaching Musselburgh. At the time his men were standing on a flat and fairly featureless area of stubble-covered ground just to the north of Tranent; and judging it to be a good battle-site, Cope elected to stand and wait for them there.

Lord George Murray, meanwhile, had decided to seize the high ground of Falside Hill which overlooked Cope's position from the south, and promptly embarked on a brisk cross country march to reach it. The effort turned out to have been made in vain, for despite Murray's claim to know the area well, upon reaching the brow of the hill the Jacobites discovered to their dismay that a stretch of marshy ground known as the Tranent Meadows lay at the foot of it. James Johnstone afterwards commented:

"We arrived, about two o'clock in the afternoon, within musket shot of the enemy, where we halted behind an eminence, having a full view of the camp of General Cope, the position of which was chosen with a great deal of skill. The more we examined it, the more we were convinced of the impossibility of attacking it; and we were all thrown into consternation, and at quite a loss what course to take. ... The camp of the enemy was fortified by nature, and in the happiest position for so small an army. The General had on his right two enclosures surrounded by stone walls from six to seven feet high, between which there was a road about twenty feet broad, leading to the village of Prestonpans. Before him was another enclosure, surrounded by a deep ditch filled with water and from ten to twelve feet broad, which served as a drain to the marshy ground. On his left was

James Drummond, Duke of Perth (1713-1747). Memorably dismissed as a "silly horse-racing boy", Perth was appointed a Lieutenant General in the Jacobite Army. Although he was personally popular, his inexperience and overt Catholicism relegated him to a supporting role. In poor health throughout the campaign, he died at sea while escaping to France. (Grimsthorpe and Drummond Castle Trust)

a marsh which terminated in a deep pond, and behind him was the sea, so that he was enclosed as in a fortification . . . we spent the afternoon in reconnoitring this position; the more we examined it, the more our uneasiness and chagrin increased, as we saw no possibility of attacking it without exposing ourselves to be cut to pieces in a disgraceful manner."

At length Murray proposed that the army should march around the eastern end of the marsh, in order to attack Cope from the direction of Seton, and across a field even more flat and open than the one which he later criticised at Culloden. This was immediately agreed, and the chances of success were considerably increased when a local volunteer, Robert Anderson of Whitburgh, pointed out a shortcut by way of a narrow footpath crossing the marsh near Riggonhead Farm.

It was thought best to make the move under cover of darkness, but any hope of catching the British army unawares was lost when every dog in Tranent set up a furious barking. Any remaining uncertainty as to the rebels' intentions was decisively dispelled when the head of their column was bumped by a dragoon picquet posted at Riggonhead.

First light was now only minutes away, and a thick mist hampered visibility as both armies raced to get into position. Far from being rudely awakened by the rebels (as the jaunty song would have it), the evidence presented at the subsequent inquiry showed that Cope was able to swing his army around to face the east and have it fully formed and ready before the rebel assault began. Sir John Cope was a "neat, fussy little man", whose career had benefited from wealth and interest; he had risen from Cornet to Lieutenant Colonel in the 1st Dragoons in just three years (1707-10), and subsequent service in the Guards had sped his further advancement; but he was not without energy or ability. He had already been ill-served by his political masters; now his soldiers were to let him down too.

The morning states for 21 September were mislaid after the inquiry held into the debacle, but the *Scots Magazine* seems to have had sight of a copy at the time, and its September issue allowed Cope a total strength of 2,191 rank and file exclusive of officers, sergeants and drums (which to judge by Cumberland's morning states for Culloden ought to add about another 16%, or around 350 men, to make about 2,500 in all).

On the left of the line stood Hamilton's 14th Dragoons, with two squadrons up and one in reserve. As Cope was reliably informed that the rebels had no cavalry he ordered both them and Gardiner's Dragoons, on the right, to draw up in two ranks rather than the usual three in order to make the most of his superiority.

Next came Murray's 57th Foot; then a composite battalion comprising eight companies of Lascelles' 58th and two of Guise's; then five companies of Lee's 55th. According to the *Scots Magazine* they mustered 580, 570 and 291 men apiece, but in fact all three were slightly weaker since about 300 men had been drawn from them to form the outward picquets, and in the hurry to form it was thought expedient to fall them in as an ad hoc battalion on the right of Lee's instead of returning them to their parent units. In addition a further 100 men, commanded by Captain Cochrane and Lieutenant Cranston of Murray's 57th, were assigned as an artillery guard and posted on the extreme right of the line.

On the immediate left of this last detachment were placed four Coehorn mortars, and the six 1½lb. guns; these were

Trooper, 13th Dragoons, 1742. Red coat with green cuffs and light buff turnbacks, white waistcoat and breeches. Red cloak with white lining rolled outermost. Light yellowish saddle housings with mixed red, green and black embroidery. This style of saddle housing had almost certainly been replaced by the more modern one shown on Colour Plate D by 1746. (NMS)

described by Lieutenant Colonel Whitefoord as "gallopers", so presumably they were curricle guns – light two-wheeled carts with the gun barrel mounted on the flat bed. Cope was afterwards criticised for keeping his guns together on the right, but although he had requested that two of them be moved to the left wing just as the battle was beginning he actually had little option. Both the civilian drivers and the few sea-gunners whom he had borrowed from the Royal Navy deserted before the battle started, leaving Lieutenant Colonel Whitefoord and Major Griffith with only their four

Invalids to man all ten pieces.

It was originally planned that sufficient room should be left between the guns and the right flank of the infantry for two squadrons of Gardiner's 13th Dragoons to form up, but with the picquets thrust into the line next to Lee's there was only room for one of Gardiner's squadrons, commanded by Lieutenant Colonel Whitney, to stand in the front line. Gardiner's own squadron was ordered by Brigadier Fowke to post itself behind the guns. Between them, if the *Scots Magazine's* source was correct, the two dragoon regiments mustered 567 troopers, or say 650 all ranks.

In addition, Cope had a company of the 43rd Highlanders commanded by Captain Sir Peter Murray, and four and a half companies of Loudoun's 64th Highlanders commanded by Captains Alexander Mackay, John Stuart, Henry Monro and John Murray respectively, the remainder being part of his own company under Captain Lieutenant Archibald McNab. None of these companies was very strong, and the *Scots Magazine* allowed a total of 183 rank and file. Sensibly, they were posted out of harm's way in Cockenzie to act as a baggage guard. The previous day Cope had also been joined by 80 loyalist volunteers led by a Mr. Drummond, but these had been allowed to sleep in their own beds and consequently most of them missed the battle.

Not surprisingly in the circumstances, the Jacobite deployment on the other side of the field was rather a scrambling affair. In the race to form before Cope's men the Duke of Perth, commanding the leading division, led his men too far northwards. Under his immediate command he had the three MacDonald regiments under Clanranald, Glengarry and Keppoch; the first mustered about 200 men, the second as many as 400 including the Glen Urquhart and Glenmoriston

men, and the third some 250 or so, or perhaps more if the Glencoe Macdonalds are not included in that total. Sufficient space was to be left between this division and the marsh to allow room for the second division, commanded by Lord George Murray, to form up, but Perth misjudged the distance so that a wide gap was left between them.

Murray for his part also had three battalions: Perth's, seemingly commanded in his absence by Major James More Drummond (or Macgregor), mustering about 200 men; the Stewarts of Appin, also 200 strong; and slightly more than 500 Camerons under Locheil.

By way of a reserve, under the Prince himself, there were about 250 Athollmen led by Lord Nairne, 100 or 150 MacLachlans and, well to the rear, about 50 cavalry commanded by Lords Elcho and Strathallan. These men to some extent covered the gap in the front line; but so precipitate was the ensuing attack that they were quite unable to catch up. The total Jacobite strength was thus some 200 or 300 less than that of Cope's command.

The attack began as soon as Murray's division was formed up – or rather, Murray went forward as soon as he was ready and the others followed as soon as they realised what he was doing. Loudon, evidently unable to tell his right from his left, saw them come on:

"By this time the Highlanders appeared in the Front, coming from our Left, running (not marching) towards our Right, in order to form their Front. When they had cover'd

Prestonpans. Based on contemporary maps and the evidence presented at the inquiry into Cope's defeat, this shows the dispositions of the two armies at the commencement of the battle. Cope's guns are omitted for the sake of clarity, but were posted on the left of the artillery guard. All unit frontages are to scale.

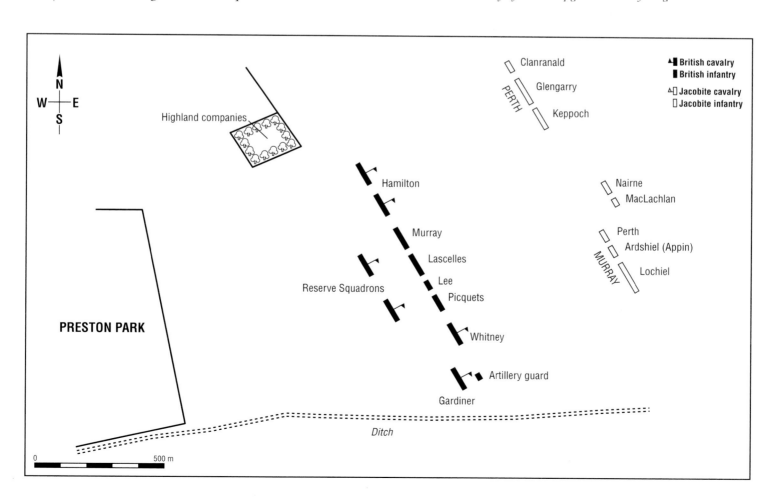

Colonel James Gardiner, 13th Dragoons (1688-1745). One of the many Scots officers serving in nominally English regiments, Gardiner was born in Linlithgow, the son of a professional soldier, and died within sight of his home – Bankton House, near Prestonpans. (NMS)

about two Thirds of our Front, there seemed to be a great Confusion amongst them, but still kept on, and in a few Seconds were form'd into five square Bodies or Columns, that on the Left the largest, and about twenty deep; I myself saw but three of those Bodies from the Situation I happen'd to be on the Right."

As the Highlanders approached, the four Invalids supposedly manning the guns took to their heels; but Whiteford managed to fire five of the six cannon and Griffith fired all four Coehorns. Positioned on the extreme right, they were able to partially enfilade the oncoming Highlanders and had the satisfaction of seeing their rounds take effect. After the first cannonade the two officers could do no more. Major Griffith afterwards testified that he had provided 40 rounds apiece for the guns, but when the Invalids bolted they took the powder horns with them so that he and Whiteford were unable to prime, let alone reload the guns after the initial discharge.

Captain Cochrane's artillery guard also "gave a very irregular fire"; and when Lieutenant Colonel Whitney tried to lead his dragoons forward they at first refused to follow him, and then made off, along with most of Gardiner's and the reserve squadron. Exactly what happened to Gardiner himself is uncertain. Only about 15 of his troopers stood by him, and he is said to have been wounded and unhorsed. He may then have been cut down almost at once by some of the MacGregors in Perth's Regiment, but a report current at the time claimed that he had actually dismounted to place himself at the head of an infantry unit lacking officers – pre-

sumably the picquets – and that he was killed while leading them. If it was indeed men from Perth's Regiment who killed him this is perhaps the likeliest explanation, since they were on the right of Lord George Murray's division.

On Cope's left flank a similarly dismal story unfolded with equal speed. Hamilton's Dragoons made no attempt to charge the MacDonald regiments to their front, but remained where they were until a few "dropping shots" brought down a couple of men and horses, whereupon they broke and ran. Captain Clark, commanding the reserve squadron, shouted to his men to stand fast, intending to charge the rebels as soon as the fugitives cleared his front; but to his consternation his men melted away with the rest.

At this point Lord Drummore, a judge who had been accompanying the army as an interested spectator, correctly "concluded all was lost and that it was full time for a Pen-and-Ink Gentleman to provide for his Safety, which I did by riding off, but I hope with more Discretion and Deliberation than the Dragoons did."

Cope's infantry, commanded by Colonel Lascelles, held for a moment or two longer, but when a party of Locheil's Camerons and some other men belonging to Murray's division began rolling up their right flank they too gave way. Lieutenant Colonel Halkett of Lee's 55th, with five other officers and 14 men, made a brief stand within the ditched enclosure surrounding Bankton House (Colonel Gardiner's home); but when Lord George Murray brought up a formed body of about a hundred men and offered them terms they sensibly capitulated.

In seven or eight minutes it was all over. The official Jacobite account admitted to the loss of five officers and about 30 men killed, and another 70 or 80 wounded. Four of the officers and nine out of eleven wounded men arrested when the Jacobite army evacuated Edinburgh belonged to units of Murray's division.

Lacking any returns apart from a note that Hamilton's Dragoons lost 87 horses, it is impossible to put a precise figure on the British casualties. Some Jacobite sources put them as high as 500 dead, although John Murray of Broughton, the Prince's secretary, reckoned that 300 were killed. Andrew Henderson, a contemporary historian, quoted a figure of 200; and the *Newcastle Journal*, employing "the Utmost Care and Industry", arrived at the yet lower but altogether more convincing total of 150 dead.

John Home, who had been one of Mr. Drummond's loyalist volunteers, stated in his *History* that only 170 of Cope's infantry (besides Colonel Lascelles) escaped from the field. If these are added to the 150 dead claimed by the *Journal* then 1,300 remain to be accounted for – a figure which, allowing for a few dragoons, equates more or less exactly with the number of prisoners held by the Jacobites.

Notwithstanding this large haul of prisoners, which included 78 officers, there was an ugly side to the battle of Prestonpans which is too often glossed over by writers of Jacobite sympathies. Many, if not most of the British soldiers killed that day were actually "knocked on the head" while they were trying to make good their escape; and it was certainly an article of faith among many of the British officers present that a number of their men, trapped amongst the walled parks surrounding Preston House, were murdered in cold blood.

It was an ominous precedent, which the British army was not to forget at Culloden.

CHAPTER TWO

Civil War

The Jacobites naturally made the most of their victory at Prestonpans, and were quick to claim that the whole country was now theirs. In reality, besides the garrisons of Edinburgh and Stirling Castles, eight companies of Guise's 6th still held Forts William and Augustus, Molloy and his stout-hearted platoon held Ruthven, and two companies of Campbell's 21st were in Dumbarton Castle. Although posing no direct threat to the rebels, these all served to show the flag, and the latter kept the Clyde open to the Royal Navy.

More important still, Inverness was held for King George by the Lord President, Duncan Forbes of Culloden. Cope left two weak companies there at the beginning of December, and now they formed the nucleus of a loyalist army. Authorised to raise 18 Independent Companies, Forbes distributed the commissions with great care. Some, obviously, went to known supporters of the Government, such as Captain George Monro of Culcairn; but others were successfully dangled as bait before waverers undecided whether to support King or Pretender.

Similarly, General John Campbell of Mamore was ordered to raise "eight Independent Companies, each of 100 men with the proper officers; and likewise to arm 16 companies more, without the charge of commissioned officers, who are to serve without pay, and are to be raised from the Duke of Argyll's and the Earl of Breadalbanes' Countrey" – this was the beginning of the Argyll Militia. Besides these "regular" levies, yet more men were raised by the Laird of Grant, the Earl of Sutherland, and by the Skye chieftains Sir Alexander MacDonald of Sleat and Norman McLeod of McLeod.

Eventually as many clansmen took arms against the Prince as came out for him; but organising them, equipping them, and persuading them to undertake an offensive role was going to take time and a better commander than the Earl of Loudon, who arrived in Inverness on 14 October. In the meantime the Jacobites had important decisions to make.

A counter-attack across the border was only a matter of time; but to hold Edinburgh they would have to maintain a standing army in southern Scotland while simultaneously fighting loyalist troops in the north and west. Therefore, although many favoured settling for a Stuart restoration in an independent Scotland, an invasion of England appeared to offer the chance of forcing a decisive result. Remaining doubts were overcome by the Prince's confident declaration that he had firm assurances of English support and of an imminent French landing.

During October 1745 the strength of the rebel army grew steadily. Lord Ogilvy, the eldest son of the Earl of Airlie, brought in 300 men from Forfarshire, and a similar number were raised among the Duke of Gordon's tenantry by his factor John Hamilton. Some 200 followed Lord Pitsligo from Aberdeenshire. Old John Gordon of Glenbucket – an inveterate Jacobite who had commanded a battalion at Sherriff-

muir in 1715, and who was probably out with Dundee in 1689 – brought out 200 more; he had a considerable reputation as a recruiter in the north-east, but being about 72 years old and infirm he did not otherwise actively exercise his commission as a Major General. Some recruits were even found in Edinburgh, although the regiment which rather hopefully bore that title, commanded by Colonel John Roy Stuart, actually drew most of its men from the north of Scotland. Some of the regulars taken prisoner at Prestonpans were also enlisted both in this regiment and the Duke of Perth's, but so many subsequently escaped that in December a composite battalion composed of the survivors of Lee's, Murray's and Lascelles' was organised at Newcastle.

About 500 cavalry were also raised, organised in three squadrons each about 150 strong, besides a small troop of "Hussars". During October, too, French ships landed six guns, and a badly needed supply of small-arms and ammunition.

Forbes of Culloden's efforts on behalf of the Government ensured that there was no corresponding increase in the number of Jacobite recruits from the Highlands, however, although the Atholl Brigade was expanded to form three battalions, and Ewen MacPherson of Cluny, a sometime Captain in Loudon's 64th Highlanders, raised 300 of his clan in Badenoch. Another renegade officer from the 64th, Donald McDonnell of Lochgarry, raised only a few reinforcements for Glengarry's Regiment, while John MacKinnon of MacKinnon brought in just 120 men from Skye.

In all the Jacobite army mustered some 5,000 infantry and 500 cavalry by the end of October; but although they had 13 cannon of various shapes and sizes, not one of them was fit for battering walls. The Prince was for marching this host directly on Newcastle Upon Tyne, and either fighting or frightening off the Anglo-Dutch army assembling there under Field Marshal Wade. Lord George Murray, on the other hand, proposed marching by way of Carlisle instead; and this was agreed to, as was his suggested deception plan.

On 3 November the rebels left Edinburgh and headed southwards in two divisions, parting company at Dalkeith. The first, commanded by the Duke of Perth, then went by way of Peebles and Moffat. Lord George Murray's division marched through Lauder to Kelso, halted for a day to ensure that Wade received reports of their heading towards Newcastle, and then moved westwards through Jedburgh and Liddesdale to rendezvous with Perth's division just north of Carlisle on 9 November.

This was staff work of the highest order, and Captain Johnstone admiringly remarked: "This march was arranged and executed with such precision that there was not an interval of two hours between the arrival of the different columns at the place of rendezvous." The credit for this was undoubtedly due to the march tables drawn up by the much-maligned Colonel John William O'Sullivan, particularly in view of Sir John McDonnell's comment that John Gordon of

Glenbucket was "the only Scot I ever knew who was able to start at the hour fixed."

Having thus arrived in front of Carlisle the Jacobites were then faced with the problem of how to capture the place. The garrison comprised just two companies of Invalids (superannuated soldiers no longer fit for service in marching regiments), 500 Militia, and some volunteer companies of townsmen; but the walls of the old border fortress were solid enough.

The siege which followed was remarkable for the lack of enthusiasm displayed by both parties. Well aware that their artillery was wholly inadequate for the task, the rebels mounted a blockade and went through the motions of raising a battery in the snow. Lieutenant Colonel Durand, the governor, was unimpressed; but an ambiguously worded letter from Wade arrived on the 13th, which seemed to suggest that he was unable to mount a relief operation. George Wade, famous for his patient construction of a network of roads and forts in the Highlands, was now 72 years old, and an indecisive and ineffectual field commander. In point of fact he did march from Newcastle on the 16th, but by that time the Militia and volunteers at Carlisle had cravenly voted to surrender and Durand, in the castle, was forced to follow suit.

An unedifying quarrel then broke out among the Prince's staff officers, which first saw Lord George Murray's resignation as junior Lieutenant General and then his reinstatement as the senior in place of Perth, the chief result of which was to further exacerbate the increasingly strained relationship between Murray and the rest of the senior officers.

Once it became clear that Wade had turned back at Hexham and no longer posed an immediate threat, Murray agreed to press on southwards, and despite the wintery weather the rebels made good speed, reaching Manchester by 30 November without encountering any opposition. This was about to change.

Wade's army was no further south than Piercebridge, but in the Midlands another Government force was assembling near Coventry under Sir John Ligonier; and a loyalist volunteer unit, Colonel Graham's Liverpool Blues, had broken most of the Mersey bridges. On the approach of the rebels he prudently fell back on Chester to join Lord Cholmondley's newly raised 73rd and five companies of Blakeney's 27th, but this action effectively ruled out a Jacobite move westwards into Wales.

In point of fact this may never have been a realistic option, and instead they headed south-eastwards, reaching Derby on 4 December. Finding no signs of substantial English support, or for that matter of the promised French landing, the crucial (and in the Prince's view mutinous) decision was then taken to turn back rather than to risk a battle with Ligonier's force, now commanded by William Augustus, Duke of Cumberland.

The retreat began early on the 6th, and although they had a head start over Cumberland the Jacobites were now in some danger inasmuch as they were moving closer to Wade's army. During the march south they had successfully kept the Government guessing as to their intended route; but that uncertainty was now ended, and there was a chance that Wade could throw his army into the rebels' path while Cumberland came up from behind. A more vigorous commander might have achieved this, but the slow-moving Wade only reached Wakefield on the 10th, by which time the Jacobites

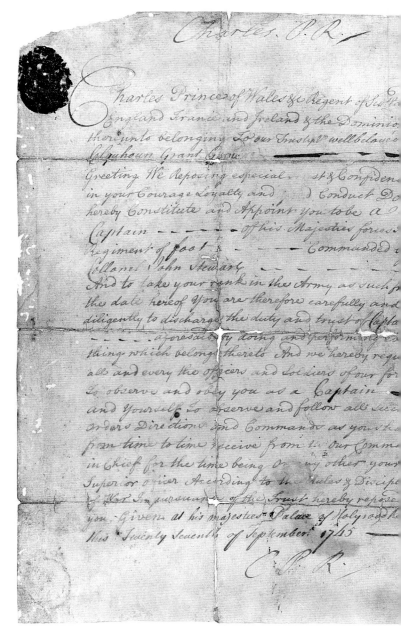

Commission given to Captain Colquhoun Grant of John Roy Stuart's Regiment, 27 September 1745. An Edinburgh "writer" (solicitor), he appears to have survived the campaign. (NMS)

were at Wigan. At this point Wade gave up and marched most of his forces back to Newcastle, but ordered General Oglethorpe to make a final attempt to get in front of the rebels at Preston, with an exotic collection of cavalry regiments: St. George's 8th Dragoons, Montagu's newly raised 9th Horse, the blue-coated Yorkshire Hunters, and Oglethorpe's own green-coated Georgia Rangers. (This last, a mounted infantry unit raised for North American service, was reported by contemporary newspapers to be accompanied by an "Indian king".)

On 13 December elements of Cumberland's cavalry met Oglethorpe's brigade at Preston. For a short while they were only hours behind the Jacobites, but the bulk of Cumberland's men were still too far away, and it was not until the night of the 18th that he and his cavalry finally caught up with them at Clifton.

Both sides knew that a fight was imminent and there had earlier been some skirmishing between rebel cavalry and the Georgia Rangers. Lord George Murray was ordered to with-

Contemporary etching of Jacobite troops parading outside Holyrood House, Edinburgh. Judging by the fact that they wear hats rather than bonnets, the cavalrymen on the left would appear to be the Prince's Lifeguards. Note that all the Highlanders have firelocks and bayonets. The gatehouse in the immediate background was demolished in 1792. (NMS)

draw but, realising that it would be necessary to make a stand in order to break contact, he waited until three of Cumberland's regiments dismounted and began feeling their way forward through the hedgerows before he launched a local counter-attack. The dragoons refused to be intimidated, and tactically the night ended in a draw, with Cumberland left in possession of the field and the Jacobites getting clean away. In time-honoured fashion both sides claimed to have killed prodigious numbers of their opponents; in fact the rebels admitted to losing a dozen men, while Cumberland lost six men of Bland's 3rd, three of Cobham's 10th and one of Kerr's 11th Dragoons, besides four officers of Bland's and an unknown number of men wounded.

Next day the Jacobite army reached Carlisle, where the Prince took the unfortunate decision to leave a garrison in the castle, which surrendered to Cumberland on 30 December.

At the beginning of November Lord Strathallan had been left behind at Perth charged with the task of assembling reinforcements to be sent on south after the rebel army. Encouragingly, Lord John Drummond arrived from France on 22 November with his own regiment, the Royal Ecossois (the contemporary spelling), and a weak composite battalion made up of "Picquets" from the French army's Irish regiments. However, having then assumed command of all the Jacobite forces in Scotland, Drummond was quite unable to join the Prince.

On 14 November General Handasyde re-occupied Edinburgh with two battalions – Price's 14th and Colonel Francis Ligonier's 59th; and two regiments of cavalry – Ligonier's (formerly Gardiner's) 13th and Hamilton's 14th Dragoons. Following their arrival a loyalist battalion was raised in the city by Lord Home, a pistol-wielding Guardsman who had stopped some of those dragoons from running away at Pre-stonpans. Home also commanded another loyalist battalion recruited in Glasgow, and this was soon joined by a third from Paisley under the Earl of Glencairn, and a fourth formed at Stirling.

Learning of the French landing Handasyde moved fast, and leaving the Edinburgh Regiment to guard the capital he moved forward to Stirling at the beginning of December with the cavalry, his regular infantry and the other loyalist battalions, blocking any attempt by Drummond to move south.

In the west the Argyll Militia was taking shape, and by 22 December, when General Campbell finally arrived in Inveraray, his son Lieutenant Colonel John Campbell of the 64th Highlanders had raised something in the region of 2,000 men, although at that stage they were still lacking clothing, arms and equipment. In the north Loudon and Forbes had been equally successful, despite a spirited attempt by the supposedly neutral Lord Lovat to kidnap Forbes on 27 October.

After a lifetime of prevarication and double-dealing, Lovat finally committed himself by sending his son to join Drummond at Perth, and in retaliation Loudon resolved upon a punitive expedition. Never a man to take unnecessary chances, he assembled no fewer than 800 men, some of them from his own 64th Highlanders and others from the newly raised Independent Companies. Lovat, of course, was nowhere to be found, and the 800 men would have been better employed in reinforcing the detachment sent off the same day to recapture Aberdeen.

This expedition, initially led by the Laird of MacLeod, numbered little more than 400 of his own men and a company commanded by John MacLeod of Geanies; and it turned into one of those fiascos so typical of Loudon's exercise of command. As the Aberdeen rebels, under Lord Lewis Gordon, were just as strong and able to call upon substantial reinforcements, Loudon (or more likely Forbes) soon had misgivings about the size of MacLeod's force, and on the 13th Monro of Culcairn was hurried forward with two more companies. Arrangements were also made for a rendezvous at Keith with 500 men under the Laird of Grant, but Loudon's orders were sufficiently ambiguous for him to wriggle out of it with an appearance of good faith.

Nevertheless MacLeod pressed on; and Culcairn finally caught up with him at Inverurie, a small town just ten miles short of Aberdeen, on 20 December. On the night of the 23rd the Jacobites counter-attacked. With ample warning of the loyalists' approach, they assembled 150 French regulars of the Royal Ecossois under Captain Cuthbert, two battalions of Lord Lewis Gordon's Regiment under John Gordon of Avochie and James Moir of Stonywood, and a part of the second battalion of Lord Ogilvy's Regiment, making about 1,000 men in all.

The engagement, fought under bright moonlight, began badly for the rebels when most of their men hid in bushes and ditches, and ended farcically when the rest engaged in a fierce but one-sided firefight with an inoffensive earth bank; but by that time MacLeod and Culcairn were on their way back to Inverness, leaving behind six dead and 30 prisoners. For their part the Jacobites lost about a dozen, mainly from among the Royal Ecossois.

Meanwhile, the unwelcome reappearance of the Jacobite field army in the south led to a flurry of activity. They had reached Moffat before anyone realised the danger; but then Guest, who superseded Handasyde as Commander-in-Chief Scotland early in December, recalled the regiments from Stirling. The rebels avoided an engagement, however, and instead of trying to retake Edinburgh they marched to Glasgow.

After retaking Carlisle the Duke of Cumberland had been called south again to face a threatened French invasion; but General Henry Hawley superseded Wade at Newcastle. A gallant and successful commander of cavalry in Flanders, Hawley, now in his mid-60s, had been a soldier since the age of 15; he was an unpopular officer, with a reputation as a fierce disciplinarian, but certainly did not lack energy. He immediately began moving his troops northwards. The bad weather and a lack of suitable quarters meant that no more than two battalions could move together and each pair therefore marched a day apart. The first two battalions only arrived in Edinburgh on 2 January 1746, the day before the rebels left Glasgow, and it was the 10th by the time the last of Hawley's battalions closed up.

In theory, until that date Edinburgh might have been vulnerable to a Jacobite offensive. But the decision to retreat from Derby, justified and sensible though it was, seems to have deprived the rebel leaders of their earlier sense of purpose, and far from seeking to regain the initiative they drifted northwards to rendezvous with Drummond's forces at Bannockburn and besiege Stirling Castle.

First they had to capture the burgh, and even this went less than smoothly. On 7 January the magistrates agreed to surrender, and that evening the loyalists and most of the militia shut themselves up in the castle with the governor, General Blakeney. Although now in his seventies this gallant old officer, the Colonel of the 27th Foot, showed no lack of military vigour. Despite the magistrates' decision it appeared that there were men of Blakeney's kidney among the burghers, too; led by Walter Stephenson and William Wright, they repudiated the surrender and stoutly manned the walls. The rebels retaliated by opening fire from a three-gun battery; and Blakeney, "observing the bravery of the inhabitants", authorised Captain McKillop of the loyalist battalion to reinforce them with as many volunteers as he could muster. Next morning, however, receiving assurances that

they would not be plundered or have contributions levied on them, the townspeople agreed to surrender after all (though not before they had deposited all their arms in the castle). Not for the first time in the story of this rebellion, one is left with a strong impression of unexcitable calculation, rather than partisan enthusiasm, on the part of Scotland's townspeople.

Like Edinburgh, Stirling Castle is perched on the summit of an outcrop of volcanic rock rising sharply from the surrounding plain, and the biggest obstacle to any besieging force without the time or patience to starve the garrison was to find a suitable position on which to raise a battery. First, however, they had to get Drummond's big guns down to Stirling. Two were dragged with difficulty across the Forth by the Fords of Frew, before someone suggested loading the others on to a ship at Alloa and floating them up to Stirling. Attempts by a local customs officer named Walter Grossett to intercept these guns, with the aid of the Royal Navy and a party of the 27th led by Lieutenant Colonel Francis Leighton, came to nothing, although a rebel battery at Elphinstone was badly shot up in the process.

By that time General Hawley was on the move. Grossett returned to Edinburgh on 12 January, and next day went scouting ahead of Major General John Huske, who had been ordered to Linlithgow with a division comprising four regular battalions, the loyalist Glasgow Volunteers, and the 13th and 14th Dragoons. Huske, who had covered himself with glory and had been badly wounded at the battle of Dettingen in 1743, was a brave, blunt, veteran infantry officer whose care for his redcoats had earned him the fondest nickname the British soldier could bestow – "Daddy".

As it happened, Lord George Murray was already in the burgh with five battalions – Glengarry's, Clanranald's, Keppoch's, the Stewarts of Appin and Cluny's McPhersons – and Elcho's and Pitsligo's Horse. He had no intention of fighting, however, and withdrew across the bridge at the western end of the burgh, much to the disappointment of Huske who had hoped to take him by surprise. Feeling himself secure, Murray then organised an ambush, hoping to tempt Huske's dragoons across the bridge; but they were having none of it, and the affair petered out in what Elcho called "very abusive language."

With a major battle impending, Hawley was determined to feel his way forward as carefully as possible. His artillery train was still delayed at Newcastle, but ten assorted pieces were assembled by Captain Archibald Cunningham and manned by an equally miscellaneous collection of Royal Artillerymen and some sea-gunners rounded up in Bo'ness by the energetic customs officer Grossett. The guns and the rest of the infantry were pushed forward to Linlithgow on the 15th, and next day Hawley himself came up with the newly arrived Cobham's 10th Dragoons and pressed on to Falkirk.

The defeat at Inverurie provided Loudon with sufficient excuse to remain inactive at Inverness, but young Mamore marched his Highlanders across from Dumbarton to join Hawley at Falkirk early on the morning of 17 January. His arrival was timely, for the rebels had decided to go on to the offensive.

Lord George Murray proposed that they should begin by seizing the Hill of Falkirk, a bare open ridge on the south-west of the town which overlooked Hawley's camp. As usual a deception plan was also arranged, and Lord John Drum-

I Solemnly promise and swear In the presence of Almighty God That I shall faithfully and diligently serve James the Eighth King of Scotland England France and Ireland against all his Enemies forreign or domestick And shall not desert or leave his service without leave asked and given of my officer And hereby pass from all former alledgeance given by me to George Elector of Hannover So help me God

Oath of Abjuration signed by members of the Duke of Perth's Regiment while it lay at Edinburgh. A significant number of the names appear to be English; presumably these were survivors of Cope's army who had been persuaded to enlist. Only one of the deserters on this roll, William Lillie of Murray's 57th, is known to have been picked up after Culloden. (NMS)

23

Eyre Coote (1726-1783). An Ensign in Blakeney's 27th Foot, he ran away very quickly indeed at Falkirk; but having had the foresight to carry the regimental colour to safety with him, he was acquitted at his subsequent court-martial. This inauspicious start to his military career was more than atoned for later in India, where he showed himself brave and energetic, and rose to the highest command. (Author's collection)

A satirical print emphasising Jacobite links with the Catholic Church, and by implication with the Devil. The group on the right wear "English" clothes with tartan sashes, and may be intended to represent members of the Manchester Regiment, which was captured at Carlisle. In a contemporary history of the rebellion Andrew Henderson declared that they were dressed in "blue cloathes, Hangers, a Plaid Sash and white Cockade". (NGS)

mond ostentatiously headed off down the main road with the cavalry and French regulars while Murray swung southwards, covered by the thick Torwood.

Drummond's force was seen, as it was intended to be, and the redcoats briefly stood-to until the Jacobites headed back to Plean. Shortly afterwards, however, their midday meal was interrupted by a loyalist scout who rode into the camp to report that the rebels' main body was approaching. General Huske promptly formed the army again and sent word to Hawley, who was dining at Callendar House. By this time the Jacobites' objective was obvious, and a race began to gain the summit of the hill. The dragoon regiments led the way, and came face to face with the Jacobites near the crest, whereupon both sides paused and hastily formed on a line running very roughly north-south.

Deployed from left to right in the Jacobite front line were Locheil's Regiment (about 800 men), the Stewarts of Appin (300), the Master of Lovat's Regiment (300), Lady MacIntosh's Regiment (200), Farquharson of Monaltrie's battalion (150), Lord Cromartie's Regiment (200), Cluny's MacPhersons (300), and the three MacDonald regiments – Clanranald (350), Glengarry (800), and Keppock (400).

The second line comprised only three bodies of men covering the left, right and centre: the two battalions of Lord Lewis Gordon's Regiment (400), two battalions of Lord Ogilvy's Regiment (500) and the three-battalion Atholl Brigade (600).

Finally, a third line was formed comprising the cavalry and the French regulars under Lord John Drummond. The former, according to Lord Elcho, numbered about 360 in total, though it is less clear how many French regulars were present. Only the Irish Picquets are mentioned in contemporary narratives, which suggests that the Royal Ecossois were left in Stirling.

In all, the Jacobite army appears to have numbered something in the region of 5,800 infantry and 360 cavalry – rather less than the strength with which they are usually credited.

Facing them, again from left to right, were three dragoon regiments: Ligonier's 13th, Cobham's 10th and Hamilton's 14th. Ligonier's and Hamilton's were both much depleted by desertion and mustered about 180 men apiece, while Cobham's 10th was about 300 strong. Hawley's morning states do not appear to have survived, but using the Culloden figures as a guide it is possible to arrive at an estimate of about 4,100 regular foot and 1,500 loyalists, exclusive of officers and NCOs. Again, these are lower than the figures quoted in secondary sources, although if 16% is added to them to allow for officers, NCOs and drummers the total rises to something in the region of 6,500 infantry and 770 cavalry.

Apart from the dragoons, the rest of the front line, from left to right, comprised: Wolfe's 8th (300), Cholmondley's 34th (400), Pulteney's 13th (300), the 2nd Battalion of the Royals (400), Price's 14th (300) and Ligonier's 59th (300).

The second line was made up of Blakeney's 27th (300), Monro's 37th (400), Fleming's 36th (350), Barrell's 4th (300) and Battereau's 62nd (350); while Howard's 3rd (400), lagging behind, formed a reserve.

Hawley also had a fair number of loyalist troops; Home's Glasgow and Paisley Regiments mustered about 650 men between them, although an Edinburgh company and some of the Stirling volunteers were also present which might have raised the total to something over 700 men. These units were posted amongst some houses and walls at the foot of the hill behind the dragoons. Mamore's men, comprising one company of the 43rd and three of the 64th Highlanders, together with 12 companies of the loyalist Argyll Militia, totalling about 800 men, similarly formed in the rear of Hawley's right wing, but unlike Home's loyalists they played very little part in the battle.

The battle of Falkirk was a confused, scrambling affair, latterly conducted in pitch darkness and a wild storm. It is hardly surprising that both sides afterwards claimed victory; and while there is no doubt that a substantial part of Hawley's army fled incontinently, other units stood fast. The battle began at about four in the afternoon when the three British dragoon regiments launched an unsuccessful frontal assault on the MacDonald brigade. A well-disciplined volley stopped most of them, and the rest were beaten off with some loss after a brief struggle. Most of Ligonier's and Cobham's retired in fair order to the right, but Hamilton's went straight back down the hill, where they were shot up in the confusion by the Glasgow Volunteers.

Suitably elated by their success, the MacDonalds then set off down the hill in pursuit and got in amongst Home's loyalist battalions, who were still disordered after being ridden over by the fleeing dragoons. The rest of the Jacobite front line followed their example, under the cover of a heavy rainstorm driven by an equally strong wind blowing in the faces of the British infantry – a serious impediment to troops armed with flintlock muskets, guaranteeing a high proportion of misfires.

Most of the British left wing battalions panicked and fled down the hill: but over on the right wing Barrell's 4th and Ligonier's 59th, led by Brigadier General James Cholmondley, stood fast behind a ravine and fired into the rebels' flank. This brought them to a confused halt, and gave time for Cholmondley to get together about a hundred of Cobham's and Ligonier's Dragoons. Encouraged by the Jacobites' obvious confusion, he then attempted a local counter-attack, and "got them to the top of the hill, where I saw the Highlanders formed behind some houses and a barn (I was forced to fire a pistol amongst them, before I could get them to do this), I then returned to the two battalions to march them up, here General Huske joined me, and I told him, that if we could get some more battalions to join us, we might drive them".

Huske for his part had rallied at least two other battalions – Price's 14th and Fleming's 36th – on Howard's 3rd (Buffs) who had also stood fast, and somewhere to his rear Brigadier General Mordaunt was trying to round up the others; but he was less keen than Cholmondley on counter-attacking in the failing light. Indeed, one problem was finding any formed bodies of the enemy to fight. Lord George Murray had led the Jacobites up the hill, but then rather perversely decided that having done so, he was to command only the right wing; and the resultant problems were compounded by the fact that Murray had elected to fight on foot, thus rendering it impossible for him to exercise any meaningful command function at all.

At any rate, when the Jacobite front line regiments charged off down the hill, most of those in the second line followed after them and were caught up in the confusion caused by Cholmondley's stand. Eventually O'Sullivan managed to bring up the Irish Picquets; at this Cobham's Dragoons retired, and Huske too fell back with his infantry. On the way back to their camp they were surprised to find the artillery train, which had been abandoned by Captain Cunningham (not surprisingly, he was subsequently cashiered); the grenadiers of Barrell's succeeded in dragging one gun away with them, and two others were recovered later.

The storm was now at its height, and as one correspondent wrote: "The weather was so severe that he (Hawley) chose rather to abandon his camp, and retire to Linlithgow, than to destroy the Men by lying on their Arms all Night, wet to the Skin, subject to continuall Alarms." This gave the rebels suf-

Contemporary plan of the battle of Falkirk, showing the British approach march. (NMS)

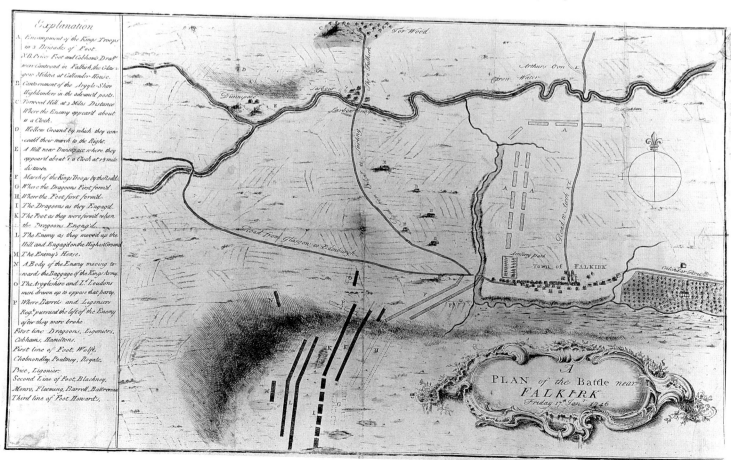

25

to 50 killed and 60 to 80 wounded, while Hawley returned 12 officers and 55 men killed and 280 others missing. The latter figure was reduced when 170 of the missing officers and men turned up in a ship which they had enterprisingly commandeered at Bo'ness, and other runaways were also rounded up. Hardest hit, according to contemporary reports, were the Glasgow Volunteers, but even they lost only 22 killed, 11 wounded and 14 prisoners.

Afterwards Hawley's officers were quite candid in admitting that so few men were lost simply because they had run away so quickly, and that a relatively high proportion of officers were killed because they had been abandoned by their men. This was particularly true of Monro's 37th which lost its Colonel, Lieutenant Colonel and three Captains – a fact which they were to remember on Culloden Moor three months later. There was an ugly rumour that Monro himself, whose body was particularly mangled, had first been wounded and subsequently murdered, together with his brother Dr.Monro, as his injuries were being treated.

At Linlithgow it was soon found that all the ammunition remaining in the men's cartridge boxes was soaked, and as the burgh was overcrowded anyway it was decided to retire on Edinburgh to reorganise and resupply them in some security. For their part the rebels, in no good humour, returned to their rather futile siege of Stirling Castle; and were still there on 30 January, when the Duke of Cumberland arrived in Edinburgh to supersede Hawley.

He found the army in surprisingly good heart, for (with the dismal exception of Hamilton's Dragoons) it did not consider itself beaten. Although Hawley at first talked ferociously of hanging or shooting dozens of the runaways, his bark as usual proved to be worse than his bite: only four were actually executed, and these were deserters who had joined the French service after Fontenoy.

The stand made by Cholmondley's and Huske's battalions was obviously partly responsible for this mood; but another boost to morale was provided by the indefatigable Walter Grossett, who launched a daring raid deep into rebel-held territory only the day after the battle. With the aid of loyalist partisans and a covering force provided by the Argyll Militia he succeeded in rescuing 31 officers who had been captured at Prestonpans and convoyed them safely back to Edinburgh.

At the same time reinforcements were coming in almost daily. Sempill's 25th marched into Edinburgh on 17 January and Campbell's 21st followed the next day, together with the long-awaited Royal Artillery detachment. With 14 regular battalions now at his disposal Hawley very graciously dismissed the Glasgow Volunteers; and the arrival of Lord Mark Kerr's 11th Dragoons on the 25th meant he no longer had to rely on the disgraced 13th and 14th Dragoons.

There was thus no reason for Cumberland to linger in Edinburgh, and he marched for Linlithgow on 31 January. Once again the Prince was faced with what he regarded as a mutiny staged by Lord George Murray and his supporters. Rightly judging their depleted regiments to be incapable of fighting a second battle, they announced their decision to retire northwards, sugaring the pill with the confident assertion that they could spend the winter in reducing the various loyalist-held posts before taking the field again 10,000 strong in the spring.

On 1 February Falkirk was evacuated only hours ahead of the British army, and with Stirling Bridge still broken down the Jacobites streamed away next morning to the Fords of

Private, 37th Foot (Monro's), 1742. Red coat with yellow lapels and turnbacks. The small collar patches are shown as red and the old-fashioned cuffs are also red. All lace on the coat and the red waistcoat is plain yellow. Although it is possible that this uniform was still being worn in 1746, it is much more likely that it already had the yellow cuffs shown by Morier in ca.1748. (NMS)

ficient excuse to claim a famous victory; but their true feelings are apparent from their failure to follow it up by pursuing Hawley, and their subsequent retreat northwards rather than face another battle.

Casualties on both sides were light. The Jacobites admitted

Frew, abandoning their heavy guns and other equipment and blowing up a magazine established in St.Ninian's church.

On the 3rd the Lowland units and French regulars reached Perth, while the clans straggled into Crieff. An extremely heated council of war was held there that night, fuelled by the realisation that the scale of desertion was not as bad as had been supposed. There was no question, however, of making a stand; and having agreed to make for Inverness the two divisions parted on the next day. The clans set off to march directly over the hills while Lord George Murray took the rest round by Aberdeen.

Having occupied Perth on 6 February and seeing little profit in pushing his men on through the snow, Cumberland halted and waited to see whether or not the rebels intended to disperse, as their predecessors had done in very similar circumstances in 1716.

In the meantime six battalions of British-allied Hessian infantry accompanied by a regiment of hussars and a small train of artillery landed at Leith on 8 February. Their arrival followed French protests over the employment by the British of Dutch auxiliaries. The Dutch regiments in question had been released by the French on parole after their capture at Tournai, and as there was now a substantive French presence in Scotland their continued employment was held to be a breach of that parole. In the event the Hessians proved to be of rather more practical value. At a conference held in Edinburgh on 16 February Cumberland decided to march his men northwards as far as Aberdeen, while his line of communications was covered by Hessian units posted at Stirling and Perth, by St.George's 8th Dragoons at Bridge of Earn, and by the remnants of the 13th and 14th Dragoons at Bannockburn. Edinburgh itself was to be held by its loyalist battalion, and by five companies of Lee's 55th called up from Berwick.

Cumberland's advance was unopposed and he entered Aberdeen on 27 February, being joined there by Bligh's 20th Foot; but in the Highlands it was a different matter. Gordon of Glenbucket had opened hostilities on 11 February by using a couple of guns to persuade Lieutenant Molloy finally to surrender Ruthven Barracks in return for safe passage to Perth.

On the 16th Loudon, displaying uncharacteristic energy, riposted with an enterprising attempt to kidnap the Prince from Moy Hall near Inverness. A failure of security led to their quarry bolting in his nightshirt while a loyalist scouting party ran into a minor ambush. As all too frequently happens in such circumstances, Loudon's men ended up shooting at each other in the dark while the greater part of them took to their heels and ran. As it turned out the Prince's nocturnal excursion brought him down with something akin to pneumonia, but this can have been of small comfort to Loudon as he evacuated Inverness and retreated northwards across the Kessock Ferry on 18 February.

It took the rebels just two days to capture Fort George – then simply a fortified barrack on the castle hill – and the governor, Major George Grant of the 43rd Highlanders, was afterwards cashiered for his feeble defence. Buoyed up by this minor success the Jacobites then set about destroying the rest of the "chain". Fort Augustus, defended by three companies of Guise's 6th under Major Hu Wentworth, surrendered on 5 March after an explosion in the magazine; but Fort William held out until its besiegers were recalled to Inverness on 3 April.

Private, 36th Foot (Fleming's), 1742. Red coat, sea green facings. White lace with green chain. (NMS)

In Perthshire part of the Argyll Militia had occupied a number of posts forward of the Hessian brigade at Perth, and on 17 March Lord George Murray launched an ambitious series of raids which snapped all of them up except the main detachment at Blair Castle. Three days later his colleague the Duke of Perth struck northwards in a well-planned amphibious operation against Loudon at Dornoch. The burgh was

"Advocates' Colour": this relic of the Great Civil War, originally a fifth captain's colour as evidenced by the five red roses in the centre, was carried by the Edinburgh Volunteers at Falkirk. The roses in the centre of the white saltire are depicted in their natural tinctures, while the inscription is picked out in gold on the blue field. (NMS)

Highland officer and sergeant, after Van Gucht. Unlike the rankers, both men have their hair tied back and clubbed. (Author's collection)

defended only by 120 men of the 64th Highlanders under Major MacKenzie, and the rest of Loudon's men were scattered along 12 miles of the River Shin. Not surprisingly, the whole lot retreated in some disorder. Loudon fled to Skye, but some of the 64th retired northwards.

These latter were afterwards involved in the seizure of a consignment of French gold landed at Tongue on 26 March. This gold was desperately needed by the Jacobites, and after the Duke of Perth returned to Inverness the Earl of Cromartie was sent in quest of it; but on 15 April his men were ambushed and effectively wiped out at Dunrobin by three companies of the Earl of Sutherland's loyalist battalion. At the time they were making their way back to Inverness, for Cumberland's army was fast approaching. The battle of Culloden was to be fought the very next day.

CHAPTER THREE

The British Army in 1745

At the outset of the rebellion in the late summer of 1745 Britain was at war with France, and most of her army was serving overseas in the Caribbean, in North America and in Flanders. But now the motley collection of raw recruits so easily routed at Prestonpans was being replaced by regiments of seasoned professionals recalled from Flanders and the Irish garrisons.

Like Kipling's "Tommy Atkins", the 18th century British soldier might easily have been excused for suspecting that he had very few friends except in times of national crisis. To some, perhaps most politicians the Army was no more than an unwelcome necessity in wartime and an unjustifiable extravagance in peacetime. Indeed, just a hundred years after the hated regime of Cromwell's Major Generals the very concept of a standing army was regarded as abhorrent by many. Partly as a consequence of this historical prejudice, it was starved of the money needed for such an apparent necessity as proper barracks; investment in such facilities would have been an unwelcome sign of acceptance of the Army's permanence. With a few exceptions, largely in the form of crumbling fortresses, regiments were lodged up and down the country in dispersed and temporary billets, usually inns – with predictably disastrous effects both on their military efficiency and on their good relations with the local civil population (and with publicans in particular).

Nevertheless, the overall impression which is to be gained from a close study of the Army's own records, and from the surviving letters and diaries of most officers (and occasionally from those of their men) is that by and large the British army which fought on Culloden Moor on 16 April 1746 was little different in character or in spirit from that led by Wellington sixty years later – or perhaps even, in some respects, from today's British Army. It was, above all, an army which was led, not driven into battle.

In the middle years of the 18th century the Industrial Revolution and the coincidental unemployment created by agrarian reform had yet to swell the ranks of the urban poor to any notable degree. Consequently most of the Army's recruits were still countrymen or discontented tradesmen picked up at markets or hiring fairs. In 1740 one critic of the Government (the Duke of Argyll, no less) claimed, perhaps a little too harshly, that they were for the most part men who were "too stupid or too infamous to learn or carry on a Trade"; but their behaviour rarely bears out the frequently flung charge that the Army was the last refuge of the desperate and the criminal classes.

To cite only one from among many recorded instances of courage and devotion to duty: during the fighting at L'Orient in 1746 a party of grenadiers crept on their hands and knees behind a wall under fire to rescue the badly wounded Major Samuel Bagshawe, and subsequently carried him on their shoulders eleven miles through the night to safety.

The written instructions which were regularly issued to all recruiting parties invariably included solemn warnings against enlisting Roman Catholics (technically illegal, though often winked at), foreigners, boys, old men, idiots, the ruptured and the lame. Besides these rather obvious categories of undesirables, there was also an understandable reluctance on the part of recruiting officers to entertain "strollers, vagabonds, and tinkers" – a sometimes unpopular scruple, since these were, of course, exactly the sort of *mauvais sujets* whom magistrates were all too keen to dump on the Army. Indeed, the instructions issued to recruiters for the 93rd Foot in early 1760 ruled that they should only take such men "as were born in the Neighbourhood of the place they are Inlisted in, & of whom you can get and give a good Account". These and similar injunctions, repeated time and again, clearly contradict the casual view of the 18th century Army as some form of penal repository.

The majority of recruits also seem to have been comparatively young men when they enlisted – service generally being at that time for life, or in other words until such time as they were too "crazy" or worn out to soldier any longer. Out of the 67 men who joined Captain Hamilton Maxwell's company of the 71st Highlanders during the winter of 1775-76 the oldest was aged 40, while two others, including a sergeant, were 38 and 39; but the overwhelming majority of the recruits were aged between 17 and 25 years. In other words, most of them were young men who had not yet settled down to a trade or calling, and were without family or other ties.

As to their backgrounds, most of Captain Maxwell's recruits were agricultural labourers, but they also included some tailors and other clothworkers, carpenters, gardeners, shoemakers, a mason, a tobacconist, a brickmaker, a butcher, and even a 15-year-old fiddler (who promptly deserted). There might well, of course, be some regional and seasonal variations on this sample, and the preponderance of agricultural labourers in Maxwell's company might perhaps be explained by the inevitable laying off of casual workers after the harvest. At other times, slumps in trade were notorious for producing a considerable increase in the numbers of weavers and other clothworkers coming forward to join the Army. Nevertheless, Maxwell's company roll appears to show a fairly representative sample of the sort of men who joined the Army voluntarily; but not all of the recruits gathered into the ranks of the infantry were willing volunteers.

Suitably alarmed by the apparent strength of the Jacobite uprising, the Government rushed through two Acts in 1745 encouraging magistrates to impress all "able-bodied men who do not follow or exercise any lawful calling or employment" and "all such able-bodied, idle and disorderly persons who cannot upon examination prove themselves to exercise and industriously follow some lawful trade or employment, or to have some substance sufficient for their support and maintenance".

Private, 3rd Foot (The Buffs), 1742. Red coat and waistcoat, ochre coloured facings and very pale buff accoutrements. The lace is white with a red chain and a yellow line; the line is on the outside on cuffs and lapels, and inside on the button-loops and waistcoat. (NMS)

For each reluctant recruit thus patriotically delivered up to the Army the parish officers received the not inconsiderable reward of £1, and a further £3 was also paid at the same time into the vestry account. Theoretically this sum was intended to provide for the upkeep of any dependants of the impressed man who might thus be left behind as a burden on the parish.

By way of an incentive to voluntary enlistment, however, the whole of the £4 was payable directly to the man concerned if he managed to offer his services to a regular recruiting party before the sexton and his mates got their rapacious hands on him.

This measure was a typical politician's response to a crisis, whereby His Majesty's Government might immediately be seen to be "doing something" positive, while in reality actually achieving very little, or even in fact making matters worse. Whether voluntary or not these particular recruits – known as "Vestry men" – were probably something of a liability to the Army, since both Acts also considerately provided that unless regularly enlisted, the men thus caught up were entitled to be discharged again within six months, or at the end of the rebellion. They were therefore to all intents and purposes penal detachments.

Those Vestry men who actually served at Culloden probably did not join their regiments until a large draft of recovered sick and other reinforcements joined the army in Aberdeen at the end of February 1746. Needless to say there was very little point by that date in the army wasting too much time in training up those unfortunates who actually reached their battalions, and perhaps there might also have been a certain reluctance to go to the expense of properly clothing and equipping them. They are likely in fact to have spent most of their service in performing all the unpleasant jobs which nobody else would touch.

At any rate, the regimental returns for those battalions still quartered in Scotland in September and October 1746 show that those Vestry men who had not already been discharged by their units were employed in the undemanding and unpopular job of prisoner handling.

Notwithstanding the pious hopes of those sending out the recruiting parties, the antecedents of some soldiers might not bear much examination, and even without the despised Vestry men every regiment undoubtedly had its share of hard cases. Nevertheless, examination of the crimes recorded in surviving regimental orderly books shows little that cannot be found in their modern equivalents. Generally they are minor disciplinary offences, and the charges are brought not by the "sadistic" officers beloved of modern legend, but rather, as in the modern British Army, by those NCOs responsible for the everyday administration of their companies.

It is true that the Army emerged from the Culloden campaign with something of a reputation for brutality; but while this was not unjustified, it must be emphasised that it was the wretched, untrained Vestry men, not the regulars, who were responsible for mistreating prisoners, and probably for a great deal worse besides.

The extent to which ordinary "crime" in the Army was punished by flogging is hard to assess. A wide range of less formal punishments were evidently employed without recourse to the awful majesty of a court martial, such as confinement (with or without irons), and that favourite standby in all armies throughout history – the award of extra duties. The practice obviously varied very considerably from regiment to regiment; and while Lieutenant Colonel Robert Rich of Barrell's 4th Foot was a renowned flogger, Major Matthews Sewell of the 39th Foot was able to write in July 1750 that he had ordered a cat-o'-nine-tails to be bought "in terrorem, but hope we shall have no Occasion to use them". Flogging, in short, seems to have been regarded, in the

"Push your bayonets" — a grenadier of Pulteney's demonstrates the posture, pushing the end of the butt with the heel of his right hand. This is one of the important drawings of members of his recruiting party made and engraved by Lieutenant William Baillie of the 13th Foot in 1753, in this case showing "John Golding of Capt Turyl's Company" at Birmingham. Although they show uniforms of some years later than 1746, their great value lies in their confirmed date, and the fact that they were certainly made from life. The small shoulder wings on the coat, worn here and in many of Morier's grenadier studies, almost certainly post-date Culloden. Note that this drawing does not show the grenadier's belly-box familiar from the Morier series. (Photograph Michael Robson; courtesy the Trustees, Somerset Military Museum)

Two of Lieutenant Baillie's 1753 drawings show Corporal Jones, of a battalion company of the 13th; neither shows a corporal's shoulder knot. In this sketch of Jones loading his firelock note the butt held clear of the ground; and the hair swept upwards under the hat, apart from a curl at the side. (Courtesy the Trustees of the British Museum)

better-run units at least, as a punishment of last resort. Sergeants no doubt casually threatened anyone and everyone with it in the ordinary course of military conversation, but it is likely that only a small minority of soldiers actually "felt the cat".

Ideally, training ought to have occupied a good deal of a regiment's time, but in practice it was often surprisingly difficult to find that time, or even for that matter the space in which to conduct it. Assuming that an infantry battalion was sufficiently concentrated to permit such exercises — and this was seldom the case in peacetime, with companies dispersed in billets over a wide area — some 300 to 400 rank and file (the average strength of the battalions at Culloden) required a field 200 metres broad simply in order to be able to draw up in a straight line, let alone to find enough room in which to carry out their required repertoire of manoeuvres. Consequently, although small arms drill — the "manual exercise", as it was termed — was generally practised to a high standard, the overall level of training in many units was abysmal. In one of his more vitriolic outbursts James Wolfe, a Brigade Major

at Culloden and later the celebrated, albeit posthumous victor at Quebec, wrote:

"I have but a very mean opinion of the infantry in general. I know their discipline to be bad, & their valour precarious. They are easily put into disorder, & hard to recover out of it; they frequently kill their Officers thro' fear, & murder one another in their confusion. . . ."

Although Wolfe was a notably efficient battalion commander in his time, his youth and highly-strung temperament must be taken into account when judging the ascerbic outbursts to which he was prone — though the Vestry men could doubtless provoke a saint; and as ever, the standard of training actually depended very much on the quality and professionalism of the officers in a particular regiment.

The British Army's officers came from a wide variety of backgrounds, but by and large it was only the aristocrats and landed gentry who reached the most senior ranks. They had both the money to purchase promotion and, much more importantly, the "interest": that is, they could rely upon patronage and the influence of friends and relations in high places to facilitate their upward progress.

By far the greater number of ordinary regimental officers, however, were simply "private gentlemen" (a rather elastic term in the 18th century) of good family, but seldom possessed of very much in the way of either money or prospects. Captain Robert Bannatyne, for example, wrote shortly before his death at Conjeveram in 1759: "My Father had no great Estate and dying whilst his Children were young you May guess whether five of us did not find use for small inheritance."

Not unnaturally, a substantial number of them were themselves the sons of Army officers; but clergymen (Robert Bannatyne's father was minister of Dores in Inverness-shire), doctors and other professionals and substantial tradesmen contributed their sons as well. A quite disproportionate number of officers, perhaps at times as many as a third of them, were Scots, and Anglo-Irishmen were nearly as common.

Finally, a far from negligible group of officers were promoted rankers, given free commissions in recognition of their ability. One such, of course, was the intrepid Sergeant Molloy of Lee's 55th Foot, whose defence of Ruthven Barracks won him instant promotion to Lieutenant. Usually such officers were employed as Adjutants, since they knew the workings of the Army inside out; but some, like Molloy, did occasionally serve as line officers, and in time often obtained commissions for their own sons. Nor was it unusual for Quartermaster Sergeants to become commissioned in the course of time, although they enjoyed a lower social status and had rather less opportunity for advancement.

In peacetime the majority of commissions were purchased, though it is hard to say what the true cost to the individual actually was. Although there was an officially regulated scale, prices sometimes varied from regiment to regiment (and no doubt according to their current proximity to London); and the actual sums which changed hands tended in practice to be less than a superficial reading of the official scales might suggest. Samuel Bagshawe explained it thus in a memorandum written some time in 1742:

"...When a Capt. has leave to quitt the Service & dispose of his Commission 'tis generally done in this manner, the Lieutenant recommended either gives him his (own) Commission and the difference between the Commissions of a Capt. & Lt. or a certain sum of money in which last case the Lt. has the disposing of his own Commission which if sold to an Ensign, that Ensign acts in the same way that is, gives the Lieutenant his Ensign's Commission and the difference or else a certain Sume & sells the Colours himself, So that the price of a Captain's Commission is either a certain Sume, or is compos'd of the difference between a Capt. and a Lieutenant's Commission, the difference between a Lieutenancy and a pair of Colours & the Colours. Now suppose a Company is dispos'd of in this last way & sold for eleven hundred pounds the Case stands thus

The Difference between the Captains & the Lt's Commission	£600
The Diff. between ye Lieutenancy & ye Colours	£100
The Colours	£400
	£1100 "

Once the initial investment had been made in an Ensign's commission (and, of course, in the not inconsiderable cost of his uniforms and sundry equipment) it was therefore relatively easy to make Lieutenant, and in time Captain. If an officer died in harness, or was dismissed from the service by the sentence of a court-martial, his successor, normally the

Private, 21st Royal North British Fuziliers, 1742 (the spelling varied). See caption to Colour Plate B for uniform details. The cap and its frontlet ("little flap") are blue. The star is white with a gold garter enclosing a red thistle on a green roundel. On the frontlet the title ROYAL FUZILIERS is picked out in black on a white backing, edged red. The thistle is depicted in natural colours. (NMS)

most senior officer in the rank below, stepped into his boots gratis.

Although further promotion was certainly not barred to the holders of free commissions (whatever their source), it was obviously much more difficult for them subsequently to proceed up the ladder, as they could not offset the value of their commission against the cost of the next step. Nevertheless, meritorious officers could and did rise quite high in their profession, presumably because their commanding officers ensured that they stepped into any non-purchase vacancies which might arise.

The purchase system is frequently attacked by its many critics as being a wholly bad practice which denied promotion to those deserving officers who lacked the necessary cash, but in fact it is remarkable how well it actually worked in practice. To the politicians, of course, the great virtue of the purchase system was that it was self-financing and, just as importantly, that it kept the Army firmly in the hands of "men of family and fortune" who might be relied upon to preserve liberty and property, rather than in the grubby hands of unreliable "mercenaries" who might be rather more prone to destroying or making off, respectively, with these pillars of the social order.

Not surprisingly, most officers advanced in rank fairly slowly in peacetime, and on average it seems to have taken about ten years to achieve promotion to Captain and thus to

Front and back of a surviving example of a grenadier ranker's mitre cap of the 49th Foot, which appears to be dateable to 1747-48; this is probably typical of those worn by grenadier companies at Culloden. The front (bearing the Royal Cypher or sometimes a traditional badge), and the rear turn-up (bearing the number, and often martial emblems), were in regimental facing colour, the coarse fabric in this case retaining small traces of buff. The back and the "little flap" at the front were red, the latter bearing the motto and white horse badge of Hanover. Missing here is the tuft of white and coloured drawn threads displayed at the apex of the cap. The grenadier cap was handsome, but gave little protection from the sun or bad weather; no doubt this, as much as concern for their much more expensive bullion embroidery, was the reason that grenadier officers seem often to have preferred cocked hats on campaign. (Courtesy of the Director, National Army Museum, London)

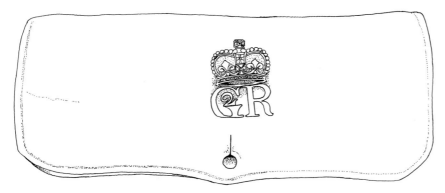

Leather flap covering cartridge belly-box of the type issued to Highland units. The crown and cypher are embossed, though it is possible that officers may have had metal badges. (Author's drawing)

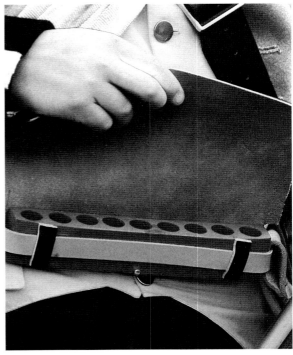

Interior of a reconstruction of the same cartridge box. Essentially it comprises only a red painted wooden block, drilled to take nine rounds, with a leather flap to retain them and provide minimal protection from the weather. (Photo: Neil Leonard)

take command a company or troop. During the long peace which followed Queen Anne's War and the Jacobite Rising of 1715 there was considerable stagnation, and most of those officers "in post" in 1740 had taken nearly twice as long to climb each rung of the ladder. The massive expansion of the Army which followed the outbreak of the War of Austrian Succession naturally speeded up the general run of promotions quite considerably, but nevertheless most of the officers who fought at Culloden had significant peacetime service behind them.

There were, of course, some spectacularly quick promotions, and as Captain-General (Allied commander-in-chief) at the tender age of 25 the Duke of Cumberland himself is an obvious example. These were far from common, however, and as in Cumberland's case they can generally be attributed to the judicious application of "interest" rather than to the mere availability of hard cash.

On the other hand, the fact of accelerated promotion through interest did not of itself prove unsuitability. Though Cumberland, as the younger son of King George II, was a Major General at 21, he distinguished himself at Dettingen the following year. While he was beaten at Fontenoy in May 1745 he certainly did not disgrace himself – indeed, it was never a disgrace to be beaten by Marshal Saxe; and the nickname "Butcher" thrown at him by his enemies tends to conceal a competent officer, possessed of real administrative talents and a genuine regard for the welfare of the common soldier.

Perhaps an even easier example to justify is the 19-year-old James Wolfe. The son of a general, he had served at Dettingen as a 16-year-old regimental officer in the most heavily engaged battalion, and by 1746 was a staff Major. His later career hardly suggests that his promotions were premature.

In times of crisis there was often a certain amount of "raising for rank". A commission would be offered free of charge to a would-be officer who had the right connections and could raise the requisite number of recruits – or afford to buy them from a "crimp". This was not necessarily the bargain it might at first appear, since most of the not inconsiderable expense of recruiting fell upon the aspirant, and he could not always count upon getting half-pay for himself when the crisis ended and his company was disbanded. Whole regiments might be also raised in this way; in fact no fewer than 12 regiments of infantry and two of cavalry were recruited by patriotic individuals in England during the rising, and a number of volunteer militia regiments in Scot-

land. Two of them – the Duke of Kingston's Light Horse, and the Argyllshire Militia – fought at Culloden.

At the end of his service an officer would normally provide for his retirement by selling his commission (always assuming he had had the foresight to purchase it in the first place), or he could exchange on to the Half Pay List. This pension had originally been granted as a concession to the officers of disbanded regiments, since it would clearly be impossible for them to recover their original investment by finding buyers for their now empty commissions. However, if an officer from a disbanded regiment wished to stay on the active list there was nothing whatever to prevent his exchanging with an officer in a standing regiment who wished to retire, but for one reason or another could not find a suitable buyer for his commission.

Artillery officers were in some measure a law unto themselves since they came under the control of the Board of Ordnance rather than the Horse Guards. This distinction was pointedly emphasised by the wearing of blue uniforms rather than the red coats worn by the rest of the Army. Moreover, since their branch of the service naturally demanded a level of technical competence somewhat above that commonly required of infantry and cavalry officers, commissions could not be purchased. Instead, an aspiring gunner had first to join the Royal Regiment of Artillery as a cadet and learn the intricacies of his craft before being let loose on the world. Once he did achieve commissioned rank promotion came strictly by seniority and was in consequence ponderously slow.

Infantry

The British infantryman of the day was clothed surprisingly comfortably. He wore a fairly generously cut double-breasted red woollen coat – effectively an overcoat – over a long-skirted waistcoat and woollen breeches. Stockings and shoes were protected from wet and mud by a pair of thigh-length canvas gaiters, and a black tricorne hat trimmed with white braid was crammed on his head.

Regiments were distinguished one from another by the "facing" colour used to line their coats and displayed on the broad lapels, cuffs and turned-back skirts. Only a limited variety of these facing colours were available; blue was reserved for Royal regiments, and most of the units which fought at Culloden had buff or yellow facings. Regiments displaying the same facing colour were therefore further distinguished by the pattern woven into the white worsted lace decorating the coats.

Thus far the redcoat was largely spared the worst of the sartorial fancies which were to afflict soldiers in future years, and linen "rollers" were still worn around the neck rather than the infamous leather stocks in use by the end of the century. Grenadiers, the battalion's elite, marked their superior status not only by their tall, embroidered cloth "mitre" caps, but also by wearing their hair in an elaborate plait at the back; the ordinary battalion company men on the other hand merely had to brush theirs up under their hats.

Their accoutrements comprised a waterproofed leather cartridge box or pouch holding anything from nine to 24 rounds (the latter was the number ordered to be carried by Cumberland's men at Culloden), suspended by a broad buff-leather belt slung over the left shoulder. Around his waist went another, equally broad belt supporting a light sword and bayonet on his left hip. This may conveniently be termed "fighting order", and on the march the individual soldier was also slung about with a leather or canvas knapsack, often resembling a duffle-bag. He also carried a linen haversack or bread-bag for his rations, and a tin canteen (in which water tended to be magically transformed into gin, or even New England rum). There seems to have been a degree of variation in the details of these items of marching kit.

The regular infantry regiments which fought at Culloden each comprised ten companies with an average strength of around 30 to 40 effectives apiece, besides officers, sergeants and drummers, making up something over 300 or 400 men in total. One of the companies was the grenadier company, formed of picked men and distinguished by their tall mitre caps. It is possible that the Vestry men, too, were formed into

an additional company of their own rather than dispersed throughout the battalion.

Three of the battalion companies were notionally commanded by field officers. The senior of these was the Colonel himself, who gave his name to the regiment; often a General officer and not infrequently aged and infirm, he was in consequence rarely to be seen with his regiment – only four out of 15 Colonels fought at Culloden. Most regiments were in fact commanded on a day-to-day basis by their Lieutenant Colonel, or even by the Major. The latter, assisted by the Adjutant, was also particularly responsible for training and discipline.

The seven remaining companies were commanded by Captains, each, like the field officers, assisted by a Lieutenant and an Ensign (except for the grenadiers, who had a second Lieutenant instead of the Ensign, since a greater degree of self-reliance was expected of that company). Because the Colonel, whether present or not, generally had more important things to worry about, his company was actually commanded by the regiment's senior Lieutenant. For his considerable pains this officer received the curious title of "Captain-Lieutenant", but was addressed and treated as a Captain in almost every particular except his pay.

Two Highland units served with the British Army at Culloden: a single company of regulars belonging to Loudon's 64th Highlanders, and a weak volunteer battalion, the Argyllshire Militia. Both wore Highland dress, and Loudon's men may have had broadswords, but they were otherwise conventionally equipped and organised.

Companies were merely administrative sub-units. The tactical organisation of infantry units – that is, the manner in which they were actually arranged for fighting – was quite different. Just how they were organised depended both on the strength of the individual battalion and on the particular system of drill favoured by the Colonel.

Most regiments conducted themselves more or less in accordance with the King's regulations of 1728; these were in turn largely cribbed from Humphrey Bland's *Treatise of Military Discipline*, first published in the previous year and going

The Land Pattern bayonet: 17ins. of steel, ground to a shallow triangular section, which after some uncertainty on the part of its users generally proved itself at least the equal of the broadsword if wielded with determination. (Author's collection)

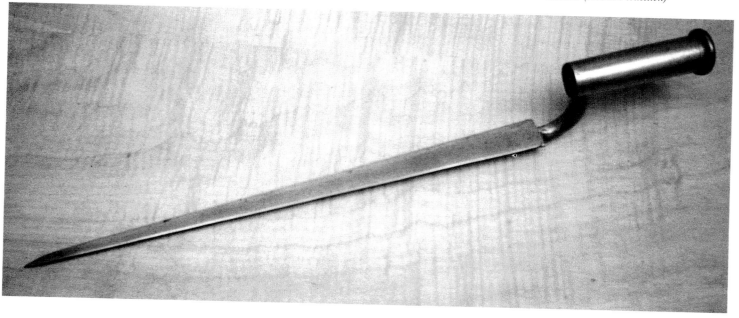

through several editions until 1762. These regulations were very much open to individual interpretation, however; and as late as 1782 the satirical *Advice to the Officers of the British Army* cheerfully recommended to Colonels: "When promoted to the command of a regiment from some other corps, show them that they were all in the dark before, and overturning their whole routine of discipline, introduce another as different as possible."

Nevertheless, the basic principles involved were quite straightforward. When preparing for action the whole battalion was lined up in three ranks and the men evenly told off into four grand divisions by the Major and his assistant, the Adjutant. These grand divisions were then in turn divided into three or four platoons apiece, depending on the number of men available – around 30 being reckoned the minimum required for each platoon.

The grenadier company, however, formed no part of the grand divisions, but was itself divided into two small platoons; one of these was posted out on each flank of the battalion to act independently as circumstances required.

The reason for this seemingly complicated arrangement

One of the series of studies of grenadiers of the British Army painted at the Duke of Cumberland's instruction by the Swiss artist David Morier. They are usually dated to ca.1751 but, as mentioned elsewhere in this book, close analysis of differences in presentation, quality and background suggests that they may in fact have been painted, in London and Flanders, in three separate groups over a period of perhaps a year commencing in winter 1747-48. At least one of the complementary cavalry series cannot post-date 1748, since it shows a regiment disbanded in that year.

It is notoriously difficult to reconcile the facings and lace of some of the regiments painted by Morier with other sources such as the 1742 Cloathing Book and those listed in the 1751 Warrant, due to changes in the numbering of the line between 1739 and 1749; however, in this plate showing the 34th, 35th and 36th Foot of ca.1748 the 34th and 36th can be identified with Cholmondley's and Fleming's which fought at Culloden.

The Morier paintings show some details which post-date Culloden, but are nevertheless valuable for their general impression. Here we see (left) the waistbelt supporting the hanger and bayonet worn instead as a second crossbelt; (right) a hairstyle with hanging sidelocks; and two casual ways of carrying the musket. (The Royal Collection © 1994 Her Majesty The Queen)

Another painting from the Morier grenadier series, showing the 46th to 48th Regiments, which is of interest in showing men with marching equipment. Note at left the fabric haversack, and at right an unshaven cowhide knapsack, slung from the left and right shoulders respectively; at right, a tin canteen; the belly-boxes for extra cartridges which appear throughout this series; at centre the linen "roller" or stock is either removed or worn unfastened; at left its rear buckle is visible. There was probably considerable variation in the detail of items of marching equipment due to local manufacture and procurement. In this series Morier invariably shows white gaiters; elsewhere he, and other sources, suggest that black, grey or brown were seen on campaign. (The Royal Collection © 1994 Her Majesty The Queen)

was to permit the employment of platoon firing, a system which in theory allowed an infantry battalion to maintain a steady and effective fire in battle.

Almost all infantrymen were armed with the Land Pattern firelock, a fairly sturdy muzzle-loading flintlock smoothbore musket with a 46in. barrel. It fired a .75 calibre (12 bore) soft lead ball weighing one and one-third ounces, which produced a terrible wound. A well-trained individual could comfortably fire his weapon twice in a minute, and in

extremis might manage to do even better over short periods. The musket was reasonably accurate in the hands of a good shot up to 50 yards or so, but could still be effective beyond that distance against the massed targets provided by infantry battalions. It is easy to compare it unfavourably with more modern weapons; but the fact remains that almost all battles of the period were decided one way or another by the application of infantry firepower rather than by the somewhat overrated qualities of cold steel. Culloden was to be no exception.

Should every man in a battalion discharge his firelock at the enemy upon a single word of command, the effect – as on the Plains of Abraham before Quebec on 13 September 1759 – might be suitably devastating. On the other hand, if the immediate results were less than impressive – and the great Marshal Saxe acidly commented that he had seen battalion volleys which killed no more than four men – then the battalion was clearly going to be in deep trouble if the enemy continued to advance while they frantically reloaded their firelocks. Platoon firing was intended to obviate such a danger.

When the decision was taken to commence firing, normally well within 100 metres of the enemy (General Hawley reckoned in 1746 that 60 yards – or 50 metres – was a "large Musket shot"), the three ranks were tightly locked up; that, is the front rank went down on one knee, the second rank closed up to fire over their heads, and the third moved half a pace to their right in order to avoid blowing the heads off the men in front of them.

On the command actually being given to open fire, only the right hand platoon in each of the four grand divisions initially did so. As soon as they had fired the platoon on their immediate left followed suit, and then the next, and so on until by the time the last platoon in the division had fired the first was reloaded and ready to begin the cycle again.

There were a surprising number of minor variations on this basic theme; for example, the outermost platoons in each division could fire first, and then the next inwards, steadily working in towards the centre of the battalion. It was also quite common to keep some kind of reserve in addition to the grenadiers. This reserve might be a single platoon posted in the centre of the line under the commanding officer's personal charge; or in exceptional circumstances the whole of the front rank might sometimes be preserved to blast one desperate volley at close range. It is more than likely that this was done by at least some of the front line battalions at Culloden.

Such at least was the theory; in practice it was rarely so neatly done. After the first couple of volleys had been fired in their proper sequence, each platoon – and ultimately, if the firefight lasted long enough, each individual – usually ended up loading and firing as fast as possible without much regard to precedence. Even Humphrey Bland, whose *Treatise of Military Discipline* formed the basis for all these drills, recognised that controlled platoon fire was something that British soldiers were only "with difficulty brought to, from a natural Desire and Eagerness to enter soon into Action". As one account of the battle of Dettingen in 1743 recalled:

"They were under no command by way of Hyde Park firing, but the whole three ranks made a running fire of their own accord, and at the same time with great judgement and skill stooping as low as they could, making almost every ball take place."

Whether the musketry was strictly controlled or simply allowed to degenerate into a running fire, the end result was the same: a relentless, meatgrinding barrage of fire.

Consequently, infantry swords were generally more decorative than useful and were not always carried by battalion company men, although grenadiers invariably had them. If cold steel was called for it was almost always the bayonet which was used, though its effects were generally more psychological than physical. It comprised a 17in.-long triangular section blade fixed to an iron tube which slotted over the muzzle of the firelock. The blade was offset to the right and slightly angled outwards so that the weapon could still be loaded and fired with the bayonet locked on. It was not, therefore, a particularly handy weapon, and its usefulness was also rather undermined by its usual loose fit on the end of the barrel. As a result, the individual soldier probably found it as easy and effective to simply butt-stroke rather than to stab his opponent in a hand-to-hand skirmish.

Contemporary bayonet fighting drills consequently reflected and stressed the need for soldiers to act in concert rather than individually. Essentially these drills were no more

Trooper, 14th Dragoons, 1742. Red coat with white cuffs and light buff turnbacks, white waistcoat and breeches; cloak and saddle-housings as for Gardiner's. (NMS)

than an adaptation of the old pike fighting drills employed in the Great Civil War of a hundred years before.

On the command being given to "Charge Bayonets", the soldier took a half turn to his right and levelled his firelock breast high, with the point of balance resting in his left hand up under the chin and his right hand grasping the end of the butt. On the further command "Push your Bayonets", he did just that – stamping forward in unison with his comrades on either side and thrusting the firelock forward by means of a vigorous push on the butt-plate with the right hand. A barking shout was of course a recommended accompaniment to this rather impressive movement.

During the six weeks while the army was quartered at Aberdeen a small but significant refinement to this drill was introduced. Allegedly inspired by classical precedents, the officers of Barrell's Regiment suggested that instead of thrusting directly forwards, each soldier in the front rank was to alter his point of aim in order to attack the next Highlander along to his right. The idea was that a Highlander so assaulted would be unable to protect himself with the targe held in his left hand. Whether this actually worked in the heat of battle is at best debatable, but it does seem to have given the soldiers some badly needed confidence, and at least one account from Culloden does stress its effectiveness.

Cavalry

Cumberland had two regiments of dragoons at Culloden, and one of light horse. Dragoons had originally been no more than mounted infantry, and although they were now only seldom employed in this role – the skirmish at Clifton being something of an aberration – they were still equipped for it, and trained both for mounted action and in the 1728 platoon exercise.

They were dressed very similarly to infantrymen, although neither dragoons nor light horse wore lapels on their coats. They also wore heavy knee-length boots in place of the infantryman's canvas gaiters.

Dragoons were heavily armed. Each carried a basket-hilted broadsword which was not so very different from the weapon carried by many Highlanders, and a pair of pistols holstered on the saddle. Either sword or pistol could be used on horseback according to circumstances; and the dragoon also carried a Short Land Pattern firelock strapped to his saddle in case he should be called upon to fight on foot. Except for having a 42in. barrel it was virtually identical to the musket carried by infantrymen.

Kingston's Light Horse, being intended to act as hussars, had a slightly curved sword or sabre, a pair of pistols and, instead of the dragoon's heavy firelock, a light .69 calibre carbine which could be fired from horseback.

Dragoons and light horse were organised slightly differently. Both Cobham's 10th and Kerr's 11th Dragoons mustered slightly less than 300 men on the day besides officers, and each was divided into six troops. The Duke of Kingston's regiment, a non-regular volunteer unit, appears to have had only some 200 men, divided between four troops.

The battlefield organisation and tactical handling of the cavalry was rather more straightforward than that of the infantry. They too normally formed in three ranks, unless – as at Prestonpans – there was no expected danger of running into hostile cavalry. However, while foot soldiers locked up tightly in order to be able to fight all three ranks, a minimum distance of six feet had to be preserved between each rank of cavalrymen in order to prevent their horses stumbling over one another.

Depending upon the number of riders actually available, troops were generally paired up into squadrons each commanded either by a field officer or the senior Captain. At Culloden, however, both regular dragoon regiments simply formed up in their troops, while Kingston's, being rather weaker, formed two squadrons. Although a single pace served to mark the interval between each platoon or tactical grouping within an infantry regiment, a much greater interval was required in order to let cavalrymen manoeuvre properly; the rule of thumb was that each tactical unit should be separated from the next by a distance equivalent to its own frontage.

As for the tactics employed, the British Army had by now firmly fixed upon the use of the sword and a steady advance at a good round trot. Shock action in the popular sense was unknown, since horses are too intelligent to charge straight into one another head-on. Instead, should the enemy stand firm, both sides tended to open their ranks and engage in a vigorous if not very bloody combat. Use of the pistol, in the British service at least, was to be reserved for the pursuit, though once fighting had actually begun this injunction was probably more honoured in the breach than the observance.

Artillery

The guns which Captain-Lieutenant John Godwin commanded at Culloden were of two types, both of them rather lightweight by continental standards, although no doubt the best that could be dragged along what then passed for roads in the north of Scotland.

There were six Coehorn mortars – short, stubby cast-bronze pots, set in a solid wooden block, which lobbed spherical explosive shells or "bombs". Looking remarkably like those wielded by cartoon anarchists, these bombshells can have had only a limited effect at Culloden since the mortar was designed to provide indirect fire, dropping the shells over walls to explode in confined, built-up spaces. Little could be done to correct the fall of shot; and even if the length of fuse was calculated accurately enough to allow of its bursting at the right moment, it is likely that most of the bombs will simply have buried themselves in the spongy soil of the moor. Perhaps significantly, Cumberland made no mention of the Coehorns in his account of the battle, though they do appear in at least one contemporary print.

Far more effective were the ten 3lb. cannon, placed in pairs in the intervals between the front line regiments and levelled directly at the Jacobites. They were capable of firing two or three solid iron roundshot (of 3lbs. weight) every minute, though once again the softness of the ground must have limited their effective range. Unlike modern artillery rounds they skipped and bounced like flat stones skimmed across a pond, smashing anything and everything in their path. On soft ground, however, they tended to bury themselves and did not bounce so far. Nevertheless it is clear that a number of casualties were inflicted by the artillery; and once the clans charged forward the gunners switched from ball to case or "cartridge" shot. This was a linen or even a paper bag, tightly packed with musket balls, which burst on firing, turning each cannon into a huge shotgun with murderous effect.

Important though the artillery's role in the battle may have been, in the end it still came down to the regiments of infantry and cavalry to win it.

CHAPTER FOUR

The Jacobite Army

The Jacobite army which faced Cumberland's redcoats on Culloden Moor on 16 April 1746 drew its personnel from four principal sources. First there were those men, mainly Highlanders, who joined in the rebellion – in the language of the time, "came out" – because they were told to do so by landlords, employers, feudal superiors or clan chiefs. The bulk of the men standing in the clan regiments clearly fell into this category, but it is difficult to assess the actual enthusiasm of their participation.

Many of those who were taken prisoner during or after the rebellion testified that they had been forced out by the Jacobites, either by means of threats that their homes would be burned and their cattle taken, or even because they were simply beaten up if they held back. Typical evidence of this was advanced, on behalf of some of his imprisoned parishioners, by James Robertson, the minister of Lochbroom in Ross-shire. He testified that on 17 March 1746 MacDonald of Keppoch and some of his men:

"...unexpectedly surprized the poor people, snatching some of them out of their beds. Others, who thought their old age would excuse them were dragged from their ploughs ... while some were taken off the highways. One I did myself see overtaken by speed of foot, and when he declared he would rather die than be carried to the rebellion, was knock'd to the ground by the butt of a musket and carried away all bleed."

The frequency with which this perhaps predictable defence was advanced suggests that the practice was indeed fairly widespread; indeed, some men from Glen Urquhart were pressed into the ranks of Glengarry's Regiment only a day or so before the battle of Culloden. Nevertheless the courts almost invariably declined to admit evidence of coercion unless it could also be shown that the individual had subsequently made every effort to escape. The situation was evidently regarded by the authorities as being not unlike that of the "Vestry men" conscripted into the British Army, or indeed of the thousands of men pressed into the Royal Navy. The material fact considered by the courts at the end of the day was not the manner of their recruitment, but the question of whether or not they were taken in arms – whether they were actually serving as rebel soldiers when they were captured.

A second, and rather similar category of recruits were those men who were raised in the Lowlands of Scotland as fencibles or militiamen. Using the existing tax records, the Jacobite authorities demanded that landowners should supply an able-bodied man, suitably clothed and accoutered, for every £100 (Scots) of valued rent. Alternatively they could simply pay £5 sterling in lieu of a man; and allegations were rife at the time that the Jacobites were more interested in getting the money than in gaining recruits. Notwithstanding these understandable suspicions a considerable number of men appear to have been raised by this means; and old John

Gordon of Glenbucket, for one, refused offers of money instead of men.

In a confidential letter to one of his officers Lord Lewis Gordon, the local Jacobite commander in the north-east of Scotland, wrote in December 1745:

"Although I have got some voluntiers, I assure you that att least two thirds of the men I have raised is by the stipulation att first agreed on, and all those that have not as yet sent their quotas, have been wrote to in very strong terms."

Equally strong deeds were also required to reinforce words from time to time and, just as in the Highlands, there was a certain amount of "forcing" to fill the required quotas. After a brief experiment with quartering Highlanders on the refractory, Lord Lewis Gordon took to naked threats of burning, and as a contemporary remarked:

"This soon had the desired effect, for the burning of a single house or farm stack in a Parish terrified the whole, so that they would quickly send in their proportion, and by this means, with the few that joined as volunteers, he raised near 300 men called the Strathboggy Battalion in the country thereabouts."

Many landlords were understandably unwilling to send their tenants off to join the rebellion, but rather than defy the Jacobites and incur the threatened penalties they often turned to the third category of recruit: men hired on the open market. Most lists of rebels compiled for the Government after the rebellion fail to distinguish between the various categories, but the record for the Banff area is quite revealing. It shows that officers aside, no fewer than a third of the rebels were mercenaries "hired out by the county"

Although these hired men might be considered willing recruits as opposed to pressed men, it is important to distinguish between them and the fourth category: the volunteers. The latter formed a far from negligible group who not only provided the officers, the cavalry, and many of the men in the Lowland units, but who also did most of the fighting. After the skirmish at Inverurie just before Christmas 1745 even the Jacobites themselves admitted that the greater part of their men had hidden amongst bushes and in ditches until it became clear to them that they were on the winning side.

The reasons why men volunteered were many and varied. Some, like Lord Pitsligo, genuinely believed in the justice of the Pretender's cause and were prepared to risk everything in his service. Another such was John Daniel, a Lancashire gentleman who served in the Prince's Lifeguard at Culloden:

"The lessons of loyalty, which had been instilled into me from my infant years, had made a deep and indelible impression upon my mind; and as I advanced towards maturity, and my reasoning faculties were developed, I became so firmly convinced of the solidity of the principles which I had been taught, that, when i arrived at the age of Twenty-two, I resolved never to deviate from them, but to act to the best of my power the part of a good and faithful subject, notwithstanding the customs of an unhappy kingdom to the contrary. Nor was it long before an opportunity presented itself of proving my fidelity to my lawful Sovereign; viz., when the Prince entered triumphantly into Lancashire on the 24th of November 1745, attended by about four thousand armed men. The first time I saw this loyal army was betwixt Lancaster and Garstang; the brave Prince marching on foot at their head like a Cyrus or a Trojan Hero, drawing admiration and love from all those who beheld him, raising their long dejected hearts, and solacing their minds with the happy prospect of another Golden Age. Struck with this charming sight and seeming invitation *'Leave your nets and follow me'* I felt a paternal ardor pervade my veins, and having before my eyes the admonition *'Serve God and then your King'* I immediately became one of his followers."

Many others, however, joined the rebellion hoping to repair shattered fortunes. One was John Hamilton, Factor to the Duke of Gordon, of whom it was said that although he was long suspected of being a Jacobite, "the reason of his commencing adventurer was generally imagined to be owing to the disorder of his affairs". A very similar case was James Moir of Stonywood: "This gentleman very early imbibed the Jacobite principles and was entirely educated in that way; his fortune also was greatly embarrassed so that his going off was no great surprise."

Also found amongst the volunteers were a number of deserters from the British Army, though it is easy to overestimate their importance. A considerable number appear to have been enlisted from amongst the prisoners taken at Prestonpans, particularly into the Duke of Perth's and Colonel John Roy Stuart's Regiments. By Culloden, however, most of these had evidently escaped, for only a very few can be identified amongst the prisoners taken there.

Substantial numbers of men also deserted from the 64th (Loudon's) Highlanders early in the rising, including some officers such as Captain Donald MacDonnell of Lochgarry, who was to command Glengarry's Regiment at Culloden. A number of other deserters from Loudon's 64th were also found in the ranks of Lord Cromartie's Regiment when it was captured at Dunrobin; but the largest single group out of the 98 deserters actually recorded as retaken at Culloden belonged to Guise's 6th Foot. These men were captured for the most part at Fort Augustus, and afterwards they were enlisted in the French regiments – the Irish Picquets and Royal Ecossois.

The French Army provided the Jacobites with two weak infantry battalions; a squadron of cavalry (without horses) drawn, like one of the battalions, from its famous Irish Brigade; and a number of artillerymen, engineers and assorted volunteers.

The French Army's Irish Brigade – the "Wild Geese" of legend – had its origins in the Jacobite War of the 1690s, when James VII and II exchanged some battalions of Irish recruits for French regulars to assist him in his fight against Dutch William. By 1745 there were six Irish infantry regiments and one Scottish one, well assimilated into the French Army but commanded by British officers or their French-born sons. Service with the Irish Brigade was traditional in certain Catholic families; the Nugents, for example, were particularly associated with the cavalry regiment, Fitzjames's Horse. The men for the brigade were recruited more or less clandestinely, both in the British Isles and from deserters on the continent, where the regiments were also able to draw

Lord Lewis Gordon (1725-1754). A younger brother of the Duke of Gordon, he had entered the Royal Navy and was third lieutenant in the Dunkirk in 1744. In 1745 he declared for the Prince and acted as Jacobite commander-in-chief in north-east Scotland. He raised a three-battalion regiment which fought at Culloden, though apart from a false report that he had been captured there is no evidence that he was present. After Culloden he escaped to France, dying after a prolonged illness in 1754. (Goodwood Estate Co. Ltd.)

upon men "run" from the Scots Brigade in the Dutch service. A surprising number of recruits were also found from amongst captured merchant seamen.

When the possibility of invading England came under discussion in 1744 and again in 1745, the Irish Brigade was naturally considered; but in order to provide direct assistance for the Jacobites permission was given to form "picquets" of 50 volunteers drawn from each regiment for service in Scotland. These quotas generally appear to have been exceeded, for in the middle of November 1745 some 400 men were embarked at Ostend. The composition of this force is a little unclear; Jacobite accounts refer to five picquets having landed in Scotland on or about 22 November, but the Royal Navy appears to have captured the whole of the contingents from Bulkeley's and Clare's Regiments, and a substantial part of Berwick's picquet. Nevertheless three officers from Bulkeley's were taken at Culloden (and a fourth shortly afterwards), together with Captain John Burke of Clare's. A second picquet from Berwick's certainly landed safely at Peterhead at the end of February 1746, and a third had the misfortune to be captured shortly after landing in Sutherland.

In addition to the red-coated Irish Picquets Lord John Drummond, the commander of the French troops, also brought some 400 men of his own regiment, the Royal Ecossois. This was a Scottish unit raised in 1744, for which Drummond was given permission to raise a second battalion in Scotland. A couple of officers and some men can certainly

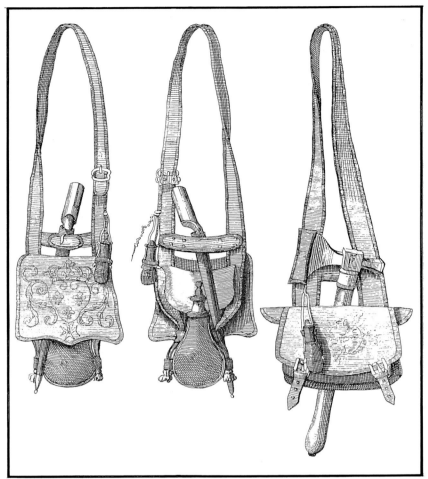

French infantry accoutrements: these *gibernes were obsolete by 1745, but this would not have prevented their being off-loaded on to the Jacobites. Note the separate powder flasks; the pouch with the hatchet was a special pattern for grenadiers. (Author's collection)*

Arthur Elphinstone (1688-1746). A man of firm principles but poor judgement, he deserted from the British Army to the Jacobites in 1716, was pardoned in 1733, but joined them again in 1745 when he commanded a troop of the Prince's Lifeguards. Succeeding to the title of Lord Balmerino in January 1746, he escaped from Culloden, but after Ruthven surrendered to the Laird of Grant's men and was subsequently executed. Horace Walpole, who watched him die, recorded that he walked calmly to the block "treading with the air of a general." (Author's collection)

be identified as having joined the regiment after its arrival in Scotland, but this projected second battalion never materialised. Unlike the Irish regiments there was no polite fiction that these Scots soldiers were merely "on loan" from the British Army and consequently, instead of the full-skirted red coats worn by the Irish, the Royal Ecossois had a rather dashing blue uniform.

All of the Jacobite army's recruits, whether they were serving willingly or otherwise, were enlisted into regiments which were at least notionally ·organised on conventional lines, even to the extent (in at least two recorded cases – Lord Ogilvy's and Macdonnell of Glengarry's regiments) of mustering grenadier companies.

One of the Jacobite army's besetting problems prior to Culloden had been an overabundance of officers and a proliferation of small and militarily useless regiments. To an extent this was a result of granting commissions to anyone with pretensions to being a gentleman, as much perhaps in order to gratify their vanity as for any better reason; but it was perhaps inevitable that with a pressing need to recruit men the net had to be cast very widely indeed. While some officers might be successful in bringing in sufficient volunteers to justify their commissions others, perhaps with the best will in the world, were markedly less successful. Some Highland units in particular appear to have been over-officered to a remarkable degree; but there are clear indications that by April 1746 the Jacobite leaders were beginning to address the problem by

amalgamating some of the smaller units, or even simply absorbing them into larger formations.

A good example of this sensible process can be seen in Lord Kilmarnock's Footguards. Originally this had been a cavalry regiment, but in February 1746 the remaining troopers gave up their horses in order to mount the newly arrived Fitzjames's Horse. Kilmarnock then proceeded to recruit an infantry regiment around a nucleus of his old troopers and some other soi-disant cavalrymen from Lord Pitsligo's Horse. By far the greater number of the new Footguards were enlisted in the Buchan district of Aberdeenshire, where Kilmarnock had family connections – not the least of whom was the formidable Lady Forrester. A small and badly disciplined company raised some time earlier in Aberdeenshire by James Crichton of Auchengoul also seems to have been joined with the Footguards; at any rate a Jacobite soldier named William McKenzie, from Bruntbrae in Aberdeenshire, confessed after Culloden that "he did bear Arms in a Company of Kilmarnock's Rebel Regiment, commanded by James CRICHTON of Auchingowl, Captain." It is possible that Crichton may have actually commanded the regiment at Culloden.

Judging by the considerable diversity of units represented at the battle, the process does not, however, appear to have done very much to reduce the numbers of officers, or to have entirely removed the anomaly of Colonels commanding what were little more than independent companies.

The officers themselves naturally varied considerably in the experience and expertise which they brought to the army. Very few of them had actually seen much service in either the British or the French armies, and fewer still had advanced beyond subaltern rank.

In Highland units in particular military rank was often simply a reflection of social standing, and it is doubtful if many of the officers were really equal to the tasks which faced them. They were no doubt brave, and possessed of at least some leadership skills – after all, they ran families, farms and sometimes small businesses – but this did not always fit them for military command. The surviving Jacobite orderly books are full of complaints of routine orders being disregarded or neglected, and punctuality appears to have been an alien concept to many.

Discipline was poor, and generally speaking the picture which emerges is of officers who were brave and willing enough to lead their men into battle, but who were unable or disinclined to apply themselves to the more mundane aspects of soldiering. Given that hardly any of them had any previous military service this is perhaps not surprising; but while a newly commissioned subaltern in a regular regiment could look to his fellow officers (and probably more importantly, to his sergeant) for advice and assistance, no such support was available to most Jacobite officers.

Nevertheless some attempt was made to "discipline" or train the men, and there is no question of the Jacobite army having been little more than the howling mob of clansmen so beloved of film-makers and romantic novelists. Lord Ogilvy's Regiment, a Lowland unit largely raised in Forfarshire, had a French regular officer (Lieutenant Nicholas Glasgoe of Dillon's Regiment) attached to it to "discipline" the men and act as what would now be called an operations officer. This particular regiment also benefited from the experience of a Chelsea out-pensioner named James Webster, who acted as a drill instructor and taught the men the firelock exercise.

Such efforts were not limited to the Lowland regiments, as one witness, Allan Stewart, testified:

"Some days before the battle of Culloden I remember to have seen said Colonel Francis Farquharson with a big blue coat on, at the head of his own regiment which was then drawn out with Ardshiel's regiment and some of the McLeods upon a plain about a mile from Inverness, and that they went through their exercise and were reviewed by the pretender's son."

Ardshiel's Stuarts of Appin seem to have had a reputation for being well-disciplined, for the same witness recalled that Colonel Ker of Graden had complained of some Highlanders firing too soon in an ambush and that he had "wished Ardshiel's regiment had been with him because he knew that regiment would obey orders."

Infantry

The Jacobite infantry were organised in two divisions, a Highland and a Lowland, of which the former was rather stronger and regarded itself as the elite of the army. Despite a policy of attempting to clothe the whole army in Highland dress, contemporary observers on both sides were usually able to distinguish between the two readily enough. Whether there was in fact very much to choose between them is perhaps a moot point.

The Jacobite leaders were certainly in no doubt as to how their men were to be clothed and equipped. On 6 December 1745 Lord Lewis Gordon issued the following instructions: "All men are to be well cloathed, with short cloathes, plaid, new shoes and three pair of hose and accoutred with shoulder ball gun, pistolls and sword."

While this might have been regarded as the ideal, and is certainly how Jacobite soldiers are commonly envisaged as being dressed and equipped, the available evidence suggests that most Lowlanders wore breeches, and that on the whole all Jacobite infantrymen, both Highland and Lowland, were fairly conventionally equipped. In 1927 Sir Bruce Seton drew attention to the fact that the traditional picture was not supported by the relative quantities of arms actually surrendered by parties of clansmen after Culloden.

For example, on 15 May 77 of Glengarry's men handed in 65 firelocks, 26 swords and four dirks, while 98 of Keppoch's men turned in a firelock apiece, but only 22 swords and a dirk. Two days later, on the 17th, 44 men surrendered 27 firelocks, three swords and six pistols, and a fourth group gave up ten firelocks, four swords and two pistols. Twenty of the Appin men surrendered with 16 firelocks and two swords, and 20 Camerons also gave up 16 firelocks but only one sword. Only in one instance, a party of 23 Mackintoshes who also surrendered on 17 May, was there anything like parity between the numbers of firelocks and swords handed in: 16 to 13.

William Boyd, Earl of Kilmarnock (1704-1746). Joining the rebels in 1745, Kilmarnock raised a troop of Horse Grenadiers; these were dismounted in February 1746 to supply mounts for Fitzjames's Horse, and he raised a regiment of Footguards instead. Captured at Culloden, he was executed together with Lord Balmerino. (Author's collection)

EARL of KILMARNOCK

With the exception of this last group, rather less than a third of all the men concerned had broadswords. It is of course possible that while they were ready enough to surrender firelocks, swords which might have a sentimental or even mystical value were hidden; but this is not borne out by the return of weapons actually recovered by Cumberland's men from Culloden Moor itself.

On the day after the battle Cumberland reckoned that the Jacobites had lost some 2,000 men, including nearly 600 taken prisoner. Not surprisingly, therefore, 2,320 firelocks were reported picked up from the moor; but in contrast to this only 190 broadswords and blades were found. Even if a certain allowance is made for casualties among Lowland units and for French regulars who are known not to have been armed with broadswords, this suggests that out of something like 1,000 Highlanders slain on the moor or on the road to Inverness, only about one in five had a broadsword – a figure entirely consistent with the later surrenders. It is also consistent with General Hawley's remarks, made shortly before his debacle at Falkirk: "They Commonly form their Front rank of what they call their best men, or True Highlanders, the number of which being allways but few, when they form in Battalions they commonly form four deep, & these Highlanders form the front of the four, the rest being lowlanders & arrant scum."

Making due allowance for hyperbole, Hawley's description matches both the evidence quoted as to the relative numbers of weapons recovered, and other accounts of clan warfare. The front rank of a Highland regiment was comprised of "gentlemen", armed with the full panoply of weapons – firelock, pistols, broadsword and targe. But those standing behind, the ordinary clansmen, the tenants, servants and dependants of the gentlemen, were armed only with firelocks and bayonets. In the Lowland regiments broadswords were probably confined to the officers (those belonging to Lord Ogilvy's Regiment were ordered to provide themselves with targes at Edinburgh); and most contemporary accounts certainly refer only to firelocks and bayonets.

The firelocks themselves appear for the most part to have been French or Spanish weapons. The author of the Woodhouslee Ms. described how the Highlanders who took Edinburgh were armed with a startling collection of antique weapons: "they were guns of diferent syses, and some of innormows length, some with butts turned up lick a heren, some tyed with puck threed to the stock, some withowt locks and some matchlocks." The rebels had of course subsequently captured numbers of British Land Pattern firelocks, and Murray of Broughton states that Gordon of Glenbucket's Regiment and the first battalion of Lord Ogilvy's were both equipped with arms captured from Cope's army at Prestonpans; but other evidence suggests that by the time Culloden was fought the rebels had largely discarded these in favour of the foreign arms. At any rate, three days after the battle Cumberland issued an order to the effect that: "French or Spanish firelocks or bayonets and cartridge boxes to be delivered by the Train to Ensign Stewart of Lascelles' Regt.; he is to distribute them to the Prisoners of our Army released here." Had British Land Pattern firelocks been recovered in any number there would obviously have been no need to re-arm the released prisoners with French or Spanish muskets.

Large numbers of French firelocks and bayonets were in fact supplied to the rebels in the course of the campaign, and 1,500 to 1,600 stand of arms (firelocks and bayonets complete) were landed at Montrose in October alone. These were probably the Model 1717 (rather than the more modern Model 1728) which superficially resembled the Land Pattern in appearance save in that there was a single iron barrel-band half way between lock and muzzle, and that the sling was fastened to the side rather than the underside of the weapon. The important difference lay in its calibre of .69in. (16 bore); the decision to standardise on this weapon, and the very similar Spanish firelocks – also of .69 calibre – landed at Peterhead, must have been made in order to avoid any problems arising from two different calibres of small-arms ammunition being required.

Similarly, most infantrymen serving in the Lowland regiments at least were equipped with French cartridge boxes. Since the arms and equipment supplied by foreign powers to client insurgents are traditionally the cast-offs from the previous generation, it is more than likely that most of these were "gargoussiers" or bellyboxes worn on a waistbelt, though it is possible that some men received the larger and more modern "giberne" worn like British cartridge boxes on a shoulder belt. Even as late as the 1740s the French Army was not entirely convinced that ready made-up paper cartridges containing both powder and ball speeded up loading, and therefore both types of cartridge box were worn in conjunction with a large powder flask.

As for the more mundane articles of military equipment: 6,000 canteens were requisitioned while the army was in Edinburgh, and the ever-observant John Bisset noted in his diary that when the Jacobites marched out of Aberdeen to fight McLeod at Inverurie a few days before Christmas 1745, they all had on their "wallets and pocks in a posture of marching".

The tactical doctrines adopted by the rebel forces were very different to those practised by the British Army. In the Lowland units at least the available evidence suggests that French teaching prevailed. This generally called for manoeuvring in column (O'Sullivan referred to "Stonywood & the other Regimt yt is in Colloum behind you"); stressed the use of a four-deep fighting line (as described by Hawley); and preached reliance upon shock action with the bayonet rather than upon firepower. This, of course, accorded well with Highland notions of how to fight a battle.

The old Highland way of fighting was to advance quickly towards the enemy without paying much regard to preserving a line, firing a hasty volley at fairly close range and then running in under the smoke, led by the swordsmen. Popularly they are also said to have thrown themselves flat when the enemy fired, before springing up and attacking as the latter struggled through the flintlock musket's lengthy reloading drill. However, since the regular army's drills stressed the importance of maintaining a steady rolling fire rather than all firing at once, the likelihood of such a ruse actually succeeding in battle can only be guessed at.

The Highland charge succeeded, when it did succeed, by intimidating the opposition in exactly the same way that the French revolutionary armies were to do in the 1790s: that is, by storming forward in deep columns (indeed, accounts from the "receiving end" of Highland charges invariably describe the clansmen coming forward in columns or wedges). For these tactics the fixed bayonets carried by the majority of Jacobite soldiers worked just as well as the broadswords brandished so frighteningly by the gentlemen in the front rank. At Prestonpans General Cope's raw Scots recruits had indeed

William Drummond, Lord Strathallan (1690-1746). An early adherent of the Prince, Strathallan commanded a troop of horse at Prestonpans, and was afterwards left in charge of the Jacobite forces in Scotland during the rebel army's march to Derby. He was killed at Culloden. (Private collection)

equal, and that a body of regular troops was absolutely necessary to support them, when they should at any time go in, sword in hand; for they were sensible, that without more leisure and time to discipline their own men, it would not be possible to make them keep their ranks, or rally soon enough upon any sudden emergency, so that any small number of the enemy, either keeping in a body when they were in confusion, or rallying, would deprive them of a victory, even after they had done their best."

A couple of interesting points stand out from this realistic analysis. Firstly, and despite the successes which they had gained at Prestonpans and (partially) at Falkirk, the commanders of the Highland regiments were evidently well aware of the limitations of their men, and apparently considered that if there was the time for it they should be properly trained or "disciplined". Secondly, aware that this was not in the circumstances a practical proposition (although, as we have seen, a number of regiments were observed drilling just before Culloden), more regular troops were required – presumably, though it is not explicitly spelled out, French troops.

Cavalry

The Jacobite cavalry has never enjoyed a particularly good reputation, and there is no doubt that even at their peak they were incapable of fighting most regular cavalry on equal terms. Indeed, two regiments – Lord Pitsligo's Horse and Lord Kilmarnock's Horse Grenadiers – were dismounted a couple of months before the battle and their remaining horses turned over to Fitzjames's Irish regulars. Although it is easy, therefore, to dismiss their contribution as insignificant, this is to misunderstand their actual role, which was confined to providing reconnaisance and security patrols.

Lord Strathallan's Perthshire squadron was the senior of the three Jacobite cavalry units standing on the moor. It was first raised shortly before the battle of Prestonpans, and a surviving muster roll dated 7 February 1746 lists 82 officers and men serving in two troops. For some reason the designations or occupations of the officers and troopers are recorded in this roll. Apparently some 25 of them could be considered as being gentlemen, since they either bore the prefix Mr., or were described as being "of" a particular place. Six others were professional men, mainly writers (lawyers), while another 20 were servants, presumably attending upon the gentlemen in the troop. The remainder were small tradesmen such as tailors, wrights (carpenters), slaters and shoemakers; and there was a solitary labourer.

The Prince's Lifeguards, perhaps predictably, appear to have taken the view that their principal role lay in lending some tone to the proceedings. The names of some 112 Lifeguards are known – a high proportion of the total; and where Strathallan's men were gentlemen of small estate, with a heavy admixture of tradesmen, the Lifeguards were very largely young men drawn from Edinburgh and Dundee "society". A surprising number were identified as being gentlemen's sons, while the greater part of them were merchants and writers – and, of course, their servants.

The Lifeguards' superior social status was underlined by their blue coats turned up with red, by their gold-laced hats and waistcoats, and by a marked reluctance to undertake such menial duties as patrolling, much to the exasperation of Lord John Drummond, who had them for a time under his command on the Spey.

been intimidated and stampeded into a rout, and much of Hawley's army at Falkirk had similarly panicked. Significantly, however, those regular units which did not run away were left well alone.

Considering the resultant confusion, Lord George Murray afterwards decided that effective though Highlanders might be in launching the first onset, the Jacobite army required more regular troops if their successes were to be properly exploited:

"... the best of the Highland officers, whilst they remained at Falkirk after the battle, were absolutely convinced, that, except they could attack the enemy at very considerable advantage, either by surprise or by some strong situation of ground, or a narrow pass, they could not expect any great success, especially if their numbers were no ways

in Ober Officier der Berg-Schotten zu Pferd.   Ein Fähnrich der sel.

Officer and ensign of a Highland regiment, by
J.C. Schmidhamer. The device on the colours appears to be
imaginary, but the officer wearing trews and riding boots is
interesting. (NMS)

In complete contrast, the third of the rebel mounted units at Culloden – Bagot's Hussars – seem to have gone out of their way to cultivate a distinctly raffish air. This troop had originally been raised in the Edinburgh area by John Murray of Broughton; but he remained no more than a titular commander, and after a less than distinguished record during the march into England the Hussars were taken over by Major John Bagot, an officer in the Franco-Irish Régiment Roth, and given a thorough re-organisation. The original aristocratic troop leaders either conveniently got themselves captured or found staff appointments, being replaced by other Irish officers. Under their professional leadership the Hussars' performance improved quite dramatically.

Major Bagot, of course, had no illusions about their fitness to stand in the line of battle, and instead he trained them very effectively as light cavalry or hussars in the continental manner. Their primary role was intelligence-gathering, often in small patrols and, according to the admiring Lancashire Jacobite, John Daniel:

"A set of braver fellows it would be very hard to find; many of them having mounted themselves on horses which

they had taken from the enemy. Their Commander also was a wise, courageous virtuous man, and behaved himself in his station to the admiration of all, regulating his corps with such order as to make our enemies and the country, even fifty miles distant from us, have more fear of them than almost the whole army. In fine, he was of infinite service to the Prince, as also were his horse; for their conduct was daring, and their courage was steeled, and few of them there were, who would have scrupled to go, if possible to hell's gates to fetch away the keys."

Lord George Murray was less impressed. On the subject of plundering he wrote: "As to plundering our men were not entirely free of it; but there was much less of this than could have been expected, and few regular armies but are as guilty. To be sure there was some noted thieves amongst the Highlanders, (those called our Huzzars were not better;) what army is without them?" By and large contemporary opinion bears him out; the Hussars had a great name, in Aberdeenshire at least, as looters.

As for the matter of arms and equipment: the Jacobite cavalrymen naturally carried swords, but were also liberally provided with firearms. An Edinburgh engraver named Robert Strange, who served in the Lifeguards, afterwards recalled that at Culloden one of his comrades named Austin ("a worthy fellow") had his horse shot from under him, but undaunted picked up his firelock, took his pistols from the holsters, and stepped forward to join the infantry.

David, Lord Ogilvy (1725-1803). Son of the Earl of Airlie, he raised a regiment after Prestonpans and marched with it to Derby. In his absence a second battalion was raised, and he led both at Falkirk and Culloden. Escaping to Norway, he was imprisoned for a time in Bergen but eventually reached France and the command of a regiment. A Lieutenant General in the French Army, he received a pardon in 1778, having in the meantime succeeded to the Earldom.

The same or very similar black and red tartan is worn in a portrait of another of the regiment's officers, and it is possible that there was some kind of common purchase of clothing. (Private Scottish collection)

The English and Irish regulars of Fitzjames's Horse were even more heavily armed. When they landed at Aberdeen on 22 February 1746 their equipment even included cuirasses; and when writing to Lord Pitsligo on 23 March to request some cavalry to carry out reconnaisance along the Spey, Major Hale of the Royal Ecossois remarked: "But as for Fitz-james's Horse they will be of no use to us here as they are too heavy and besides we must not wear out their horses at that exercise but keep them for a better occasion."

They were to find that occasion at Culloden.

Central portion of the colours of Lord Ogilvy's second battalion. This colour measures 5ft.1in. by 5ft.9ins. and is made of silk poplin, strengthened along the edges with a linen strip. Although now faded to a light blue it was originally much darker. The central device of a white saltire surmounted by a thistle in its proper tinctures, and the old Scots motto NEMO ME IMPUNE LACESSET (sic) in gold on a white scroll, are all painted. (Dundee Art Galleries & Museums)

Artillery

In contrast to the British army's deployment of ten 3lb. light cannon and six Coehorn mortars, the Jacobite artillery appears to have been a rather heterogeneous collection of pieces. Cumberland afterwards reported that he had recovered a total of 22 assorted guns at Culloden: three 1½lb., eleven 3lb. and eight 4lb. cannon.

The first three guns were rather obsolete British cannon captured from General Cope at Prestonpans. The 3lb. pieces were also British, some of them captured from Hawley at Falkirk, while the others were shipped over from France, having originally been taken from Cumberland's army at Fontenoy in 1745.

All eight of the 4lb. pieces were French; four were brass (like the British guns), but the other four were so-called "Swedish" cannon with iron barrels. These had recently been introduced into the French service and were shorter and much lighter in weight than their brass counterparts. With an effective range of 600 metres, the "Swedish" gun was reckoned to be capable (in theory) of firing at the astonishing rate of about eight rounds per minute in contrast to the three rounds per minute normally expected from the older brass 4lb. cannon.

In practice this advantage was quite meaningless without trained artillerymen to fight the guns, and it is one of the minor mysteries of Culloden that most of the Jacobite guns were fought by untrained men even though a number of presumably expert French artillerymen were taken prisoner afterwards in Inverness, apparently without having taken part in the battle. This may presumably have been because they had not been required for the abortive night attack on Cumberland's camp at Nairn, and were afterwards simply forgotten.

Contrary to the suggestion made in a number of modern accounts, the poor performance of the Jacobite guns at Culloden would not appear to have been caused by any supply problems arising out of a multiplicity of calibres. Most of the guns taken by Cumberland had actually been left behind in Inverness, and were not found on the moor. The Jacobites began the battle of Culloden with the eleven 3lb. cannon only; a twelfth gun, a 4lb. piece crewed by a French engineer and some gunners, only came up some time after these had already been silenced.

CHAPTER FIVE

Advance to Contact

While the greater part of Cumberland's army rested at Aberdeen a number of security outposts were established around the burgh. Some of these were only small cavalry picquets, but Major General Humphrey Bland was pushed forward with a rather more substantial force of four battalions and two regiments of cavalry.

Initially he took his infantry no further out than the small towns of Inverurie and Old Meldrum, but Cobham's Dragoons were quartered in the parish of Udny, and 50 of Kingston's Horse went the length of Fyvie. No reference is made in the quartering returns as to the whereabouts of the Argyll Militia, but to judge from subsequent events at least some of them must have been attached to Bland's force and a company sent with the detachment of Kingston's Horse at Fyvie.

On 17 March 1746 Bland pushed forward as far as Strathbogie. As it happened a rebel detachment led by Colonel John Roy Stuart was also in the area, intending to attack the Laird of Grant's men at Clatt. In this they were unsuccessful, and no sooner had they returned to Strathbogie and ordered dinner than they received the unwelcome news that Bland was approaching. A hasty retreat then followed, covered by the Hussars and some of the Prince's Lifeguards.

As he was in unknown (and temporarily fogbound) territory Bland judged it best to let them go, and thereupon lodged the 2nd Battalion of the Royals in the castle and his other three regular battalions – Barrel's, Price's and Cholmondley's – in the town. He also considered it prudent to establish a system of patrols; and on the night of the 20th one of them came to grief at Keith, a small town some six miles west of Strathbogie and lying halfway between that town and the rebel base at Fochabers.

The commander of this detachment, Lieutenant Alexander Campbell of Loudon's Highlanders, had earlier shown some aptitude for outpost work, but unfortunately he now came up against one of the rebel army's more professional officers: Nicholas Glasgow, a Lieutenant in Dillon's Irish regiment in French service, and now a Major of Lord Ogilvy's. According to Bland's subsequent report, Campbell's 70 Argyll Militia and 30 troopers of Kingston's Horse were merely supposed to make a reconnaissance, but: "Being determined to do something that should transmit his name to future ages, he took upon himself to act quite contrary to my orders. He formed a wild project of his own to surprise Fochabers and lay all night at Keith, where he was surprised."

A rebel officer, Captain Robert Stewart of Colonel John Roy Stuart's Regiment, subsequently wrote a detailed and remarkably honest account of the affair which reveals that such operations have changed little over the years:

"... the Colonel gave orders for five men of a company to be turned out, (which accordingly was done) the whole fifty to be commanded by Captain Robert Stewart, younger ... and, upon his examining the men's arms and ammunition, and finding them in very indifferent order, was obliged to disperse the most of all his own powder and shot. ... Then, throwing away his plaid, he desired that every one might do the like, &c.; then ordered by the Colonel to march his men to the Cross of Fochabers, there to wait for farther orders from Major Glasgow, who was to command the whole party in chief. Upon his marching back to the Cross again, the inhabitants seemed a little surprised; but, to prevent further conjectures, Captain Stewart called out, pretty loud, to get the keys of the guard-house, for he was come to take the guard of the town that night: but, at the same time, desired his soldiers, quietly, if they inclined to take any small refreshment, by half dozens, they might.

"He had not been a quarter of an hour at the Cross, when a small body of huzzars came riding down the street in haste, and told him that Cumberland's light horse was in the Fir Park, within rig length of the town; that they had been firing on one another for some time; that they wanted a party of his men to line the horse, and would go into the Park and attack them. ... This detachment had waited upon the street about three quarters of an hour, when, in the dusk of the evening, the Major came up with a detachment of Lord Ogilvie's men, about sixteen of the French [probably from Berwick's] and about twenty or thirty horses of different corps. Upon seeing the party before them, the French officer challenged, Who was there? Captain Stewart answered, it was Colonel Stewart's men. The French officer replied, he was well pleased to see them there, – that was the brave men. The Major called Captain Stewart, told him to allow the French to go in the front, and that they would shew them the way; that Lord Ogilvie's was to follow him in the rear, which accordingly was done. Away they marched, and entered the Fir Park, the horse commanded by Lieutenant [John] Simpson [of Bagot's Hussars], surrounding the same, and searching it out to the other end. Finding none of the enemy, they sat down very quiet, till such time as the horse had patroled the whole bounds, and returned again, finding none of the light horse.

"Then they began their march again towards Keith; at the same time, Major Glasgow told Captain Stewart, that the French was to form the advance guard with the horse; that he was to march at a hundred paces distance, (which was pointedly observed). Then, upon their way, they got intelligence of their enemy's patrol having passed before them. After five miles marching, they parted from the Keith road, eastward, and passed by Taremore. They searched it; but found none of their enemies there: then passed the water of Illa, at Mill of Keith; made a circle round the town, to the tents of Summer-eve's Fair, as if they had been from Strathbogie. Then Captain Stewart was ordered to close up with his party to the advance guard. As twelve o'clock at night struck, they came near the town.

"The Campbell's sentry challenged, Who was there? It was

finding the guard in the school, and their main body in the kirk, the French began the action with a platoon on the guard; and a general huzza was given, with these words, 'God save Prince Charles!' The action continued very hot on both sides, about half an hour, (the fire from the Campbells coming very hard from the windows of the kirk). . . . At the surrendering of the kirk and guard, the Major sent to Captain Stewart, desiring that he might come with a party of his men, for he was like to be overpowered in the streets, (for Kingston's light horse was quartered in the town). Captain Stewart immediately came down the street with a party, where there was a pretty hot action for some time in the street. He vanquished them, and made the whole of them prisoners, carried them over the bridge, and sent back a party to assist in bringing up the rest of the prisoners. . . .

"In this action, there were nine of Cumberland's men killed, a good number wounded, about eighty taken prisoners, and betwixt twenty and thirty horses, which Major Glasgow, with his party, delivered at Spey, a little before sunrising.

"Of the Prince's, there was only one Frenchman killed; but a good many wounded, particularly Lord Ogilvie's men, as they happened to stand in the south side of the kirk-yard, by the firing from the windows of the kirk."

Bland initially claimed that all 70 of the Argylls were lost, but the actual returns record 53 of them killed or missing together with 31 of Kingston's.

Cumberland was understandably furious about the affair, especially as some of his favourite Light Horse had been lost, but it is hard to entirely blame Campbell – "the mad-headed Highlander who commanded the party." Such affairs are the ordinary small-change of outpost warfare; Campbell was simply unlucky, and paid for it by being badly "mangled" and left for dead when he subsequently tried to escape.

Thereafter the countryside between Strathbogie and Fochabers became something of a debatable ground occasionally scoured by patrols, who generally met at Keith and fired at each other across the river, but made no attempt to cross.

On 21 March, two more battalions – the Scots Fusiliers and Monro's 37th – arrived to reinforce Bland, and two days later the Earl of Albemarle arrived to supersede him. All was now ready for the final advance.

The operation was extremely well planned, reflecting a high degree of staff work. Albemarle's detachment became the 1st Division, comprising Cobham's Dragoons and Kingston's Light Horse, and the 1st and 3rd Infantry Brigades – respectively the 2/Royals, Cholmondley's and Price's; Barrel's, Monro's and the Fusiliers. Their task was to remain at Strathbogie until 10 April, covering the movement of the three other divisions. Owing to a lack of suitable quarters and a shortage of forage each had to move northwards independently, and there was obviously some danger of a rebel spoiling attack.

Brigadier Mordaunt with the 5th Infantry Brigade (Pulteney's, Battereau's and Blakeney's) and four cannon, marched off first to their jumping-off point at Old Meldrum on the 23rd, but the operation did not properly begin until the morning of 8 April.

Mordaunt's brigade then marched north to Turriff, while Cumberland left Aberdeen with the 3rd Division to take their place at Old Meldrum; this comprised Kerr's Dragoons, the 2nd Infantry Brigade – Howard's, Fleming's and Bligh's –

Private, 4th Foot (Barrell's), 1742. Red coat with blue facings, blue waistcoat and breeches. White lace with blue vandyked line. (NMS)

answered, Friends – the Campbells. He replied, you are very welcome; we hear the enemy is at hand. On their coming up to him, they seized his arms, griped him by the neck, and threw him to the ground. Then he began to cry: they told him if he made any more noise they would thrust a dirk to his heart. Then Lieutenant Simpson surrounded the town with the horse. The Major, with the foot entered the town, marched down the street, and up to the church-yard; when, and six guns. Lord Sempill's 4th Infantry Brigade – Wolfe's, Ligonier's and Sempill's – also marched that day, but their destination was Inverurie.

On 9 April Mordaunt's 5th Brigade moved on to the coastal town of Banff; and as it would have been difficult for Albemarle to support them there and to cover the other divisions at the same time, Cumberland took the decision to force-march the 3rd Division some 20 miles to join them there that same night. Sempill followed at a more normal pace; and, with no sign of movement from the rebel camp, Cumberland called up Albemarle's men and concentrated the whole army at Cullen on 11 April.

Next day the army marched on Fochabers in the confident expectation that the rebels would stand and fight there in order to defend the Spey crossings. This was indeed the Jacobites' intention. Lord John Drummond had established a hutted camp on the west bank from Rothes to the river mouth, known as "the barracks". This was occupied by some 2,000 men, made up of the cavalry, the Lowland regiments and about half of the French regulars.

Unfortunately for the rebels neither the Highland Division nor the artillery train were in position; had they been, the decisive battle in the campaign might have been fought on the Spey rather than outside Inverness. But the Jacobites were already finding it hard to feed their men, and a degree of dispersion was therefore necessary. Although it was planned that the Highland Division would close up on this position if a battle became imminent, the speed of Cumberland's advance took the rebels by surprise. Some of the Highlanders were in the far north in search of the missing French gold lost at Tongue; others were in Lochaber, and the rest in Badenoch or the Braes of Atholl under Lord George Murray. The artillery, perhaps with less excuse, was also at Inverness. The news that Cumberland had left Aberdeen resulted in the Highland Division's beginning to concentrate at Inverness, but they were to be too late to reinforce Drummond.

The Jacobite failure to contest the crossing of the Spey – if one excepts a few ineffectual pistol shots fired by some of the Prince's Lifeguards – led Cumberland's men to speculate that the rebels were deliberately drawing them into a trap; but in fact it was simply due to inadequate reconnaissance. Drummond seems to have had some inkling of trouble, for patrols had been stepped up since the affair at Keith. Nevertheless, despite repeated orders, in the last few days any proper system of reconnaissance began to fall apart.

Fitzjames's Horse were being kept in reserve and were ordered not to exhaust their horses in patrolling. Elcho's troop of the Lifeguards, perhaps deeming outpost duty to be beneath their dignity or too much like hard work, followed suit, to his considerable annoyance; and in consequence the remaining cavalry were soon far too tired to do their job properly.

On the night of the 11th a ten-man patrol led by John Daniel of Balmerino's troop picked up a messenger heading for the Duchess of Gordon's house with a letter ordering supplies to be gathered, and advising her that Cumberland intended to force the river that day (the 12th). Instead of sending this important intelligence back at once Daniel continued with his patrol, and found the British army drawn up in order of battle two miles further on. At this point, by his own account: "after seeing all we could see, and some bravadoes and huzzas, we retired with all speed, leaving them to wonder what we meant."

Private, 59th Foot (Ligonier's), 1742. Red coat, buff facings, white lace with green chain and yellow line – line outwards. (NMS)

Although he subsequently claimed to have reported all of this on his return to the rebel camp, the upshot of his behaviour was that Drummond, his elder brother the Duke of Perth, and Colonel John Roy Stuart were still sitting in the minister's house at Speymouth after breakfast when a countryman burst in with the news that the Enzie (the parish on the other side of the river) was all in a "Vermine of Red Quites". At first, despite Daniel's earlier report, they found

The Right Honble the Earl of Loudoun
in the Regimentals of His Highland Regt.

A Ramsay pinxt 1747

John Campbell, Earl of Loudon (1705-1782), after Alan Ramsay and depicted as Colonel of the 64th Highlanders — see caption to Colour Plate C for notes on the regiment's uniform. A capable enough subordinate, Loudon proved irresolute when in independent command; he was slow to make up his mind, quick to change it, and glad to seize any excuse to do nothing. Nevertheless, he did much to curb a Jacobite take-over of the north of Scotland. (NMS)

Print by J.S. Muller dated 4 November 1746 and depicting members of the 43rd Highlanders. There are obvious similarities with the well-known "mutineer" prints by Bowles. (NMS)

this hard to believe, and somebody flippantly suggested that the dark masses of soldiers seen in the distance were only muck-heaps; whereupon the countryman observed that that might very well be so, but he had never seen muck-heaps moving before.

As Kingston's Horse, who formed the British advance guard, came within half a mile of the river they could see the rebels drawn up on the other side and James Ray, a volunteer from Whitehaven, particularly noted their white colours. Accordingly Kingston's halted in a ploughed field and waited for orders; but as the infantry came up in their turn the rebels set fire to their barracks and guardhouse, which was correctly interpreted as a sign that they did not intend to fight.

"At this Time his Royal Highness gave Orders for the Duke of Kingston's Horse to advance. Accordingly we marched through the Town of Fochabers, which consists mostly of one long Street, where I observed several good Houses, and People of Fashion standing looking at us; but not one Person to wish us good Success. . . ."

John Daniel was also in Fochabers at the time and sound asleep, which rather suggests that he himself had attached no great urgency to the report which he gave to Drummond:

"When fast asleep, a servant came in to tell me that the enemy was in the town, and that it was too late to think of escaping, almost all of our party having already passed the river. However starting up in great confusion, I resolved to risk all rather than fall into their hands, and mounting my horse escaped by a back road."

Just how he managed to get himself across the river is not explained, which is a pity given that the ford was a notoriously difficult one – a point emphasised by James Ray of Kingston's:

"We entered the River with a Guide, wading on Foot, to shew where the Ford lay; which was bad enough, having loose Stones at the Bottom, which made it very difficult for Man or Horse to step without falling; the Water Belly-deep, and very rapid; the Ford not lying right across, we were obliged to go Midway into the River, then turn to the Right and go down it for about sixty yards, then turn to the Left, inclining upwards to the landing Place. In this Situation had the Rebels stood us here, it might have been of bad Consequence to our Army, they having a great Advantage over us, and might have defended this important Pass a long Time, to our great Loss."

As their barracks burned the Jacobites fell back towards Nairn. The Highland Division still had not come up from Inverness by the time they reached it, but in any case the decision had already been taken to fight in the Culloden area.

Two experienced officers were sent to reconnoitre a suitable battlefield on the morning of the 14th, and pitched on a site just south of the Water of Nairn and hard by Kilravock Castle. In the meantime the news of Cumberland's rapid approach led to the rebel Adjutant General, O'Sullivan, riding out to Nairn to have a look for himself. On the way he naturally stopped to have a look at the proposed battlefield, and to his dismay found it to be quite unsuitable. Having then examined an alternative site, a likely-looking stretch of moorland some distance to the south-east of the Jacobite headquarters at Culloden House, he continued on his way to Nairn; and there became caught up in what soon threatened to become a precipitate retreat.

Drummond and Perth were actually in the process of pulling their men out of Nairn just as O'Sullivan arrived. Apparently suspecting that they were over-reacting, and knowing that the Highland Division was still marching up from Inverness and had not yet reached Culloden, he ordered them to halt and take up a covering position.

At this critical point, by his own admission, he abruptly fainted; having been bled and purged only a few days earlier he was still feeling anaemic. Within half an hour, however, he had recovered sufficiently to take the cavalry out on a reconnaissance across the river. Hardly had they ridden clear of the town than he saw the British army in full march towards them. This evidently came as a shock, but he ordered Lord Balmerino to form his little troop of Lifeguards, with the Hussars and Captain Robert Shea's squadron of Fitzjames's Horse, in a single line in order to make as brave a show as possible, then waited to see what happened next.

"The Duke [of Perth] & Sullivan waited on a hight neer the bridge until the enemy was very neer them, the Duke and Ld John retired with the foot. Sullivan kept Berwick's piquet with him composed of three officers & twenty-five men; he got the sergeant & some of those men to set two or three little Turf carts on the bridge and set fire to them. This done, the enemy just over against, Sullivan retired, joyned the horse & formed them on the high road, about two musquet shots from the Town and marched. A moment after the enemy's horse appears in the plaine ford & march against us. Sullivan fires his little cavalry likewise, but made a poor figure over against nine squadrons, & sends to the Duke of Perth to pray him, to leave him five hundred of foot.

"Sullivan continued his retraite making volte face from time to time alternatively with the small number of horse he had & those five and twenty men of Berwicks. Four battaillons of the enemy joyns their horse, they continu to pursue Sullivan, firing from time to time but were not near enough to do any hurt. Sullivan sent again to the Duke of Perth to pray him to leave a hundred and fifty men, or even fifty but the Duke and Ld John went to meet the Prince yt was in march towards them with the rest of the Army, & not a soul would wait for Sullivan. He continued his retreat so, for four miles, before he joyned the foot with nine squadrons & four bataillons at his heels, haveing alwaise part of this little Cavalry faceing towards them, & had in all yt time but a trooper & two horses of fitz James wounded."

Cumberland actually had only eight squadrons of cavalry, not nine, but the mistake is pardonable enough in the circumstances. John Daniel, who had been serving with the rearguard since his escape, backs up O'Sullivan's version, and reckoned that the action lasted about three or four hours, although he also suggests that Perth himself may have stuck with the cavalry:

"And here it was his Grace the Duke of Perth and Colonel O'Sullivan gained immortal honour by their bravery and conduct in bringing us off in good order from under the very nose of the enemy; for notwithstanding all their firing upon our rear, and though we were much inferior in numbers, we lost not one man."

Having seen the rebels off the premises, as it were, Cumberland encamped his infantry at Balblair, just outside the town; and, knowing that a battle was imminent, ordered a day of rest for the army.

The Jacobites meanwhile were faced with two questions: whether or not to fight at once, and if so, where was the best place to fight?

The popular impression, largely gained both from Lord George Murray's papers and Lord Elcho's published journal, is that the decision to stand and fight on Culloden Moor was taken precipitately, and that despite the manifest disadvantages of the site Prince Charles Edward and the rebel Adjutant General O'Sullivan perversely refused to consider more suitable alternatives. The reality was rather different.

Edward Harvey (1718-1778), an ADC to the Duke of Cumberland at Culloden. Harvey entered the Army as a Cornet in the 10th Dragoons in 1741 and became a Captain in the 7th in 1747. It is not clear with which of these regiments he served in 1746, though the 10th seems likeliest. He is depicted here in the uniform of the 6th (Inniskilling) Dragoons, of which he became Colonel in 1760. He died in 1778 while simultaneously holding the posts of Adjutant General, Governor of Portsmouth, Colonel of the Inniskillings, and MP for Harwich. (NMS)

As to the first question facing them: most of the Jacobite chroniclers are agreed that it was considered absolutely necessary to fight in order to protect the ammunition, stores and transport assembled at Inverness. In particular it was necessary to preserve the magazine of oatmeal, since a desperate shortage of ready cash meant that the rebel army was unable to obtain any other food. If Inverness were abandoned to the British army the rebels would either starve or would be forced to disperse in search of food. It is sometimes suggested that the rebel army ought to have retired and conducted a guerrilla campaign instead, but this is unlikely to have been a viable operation without the firm prospect of an eventual French landing.

A retreat from Inverness would also, inevitably, have been regarded on all sides as a major defeat, leading to widespread desertion. Although it was subsequently claimed that the rebels might have subsisted on sheep and cattle taken from the hillsides, without gold to pay for them they would very soon have lost any support from the uncommitted civilian population. In any case, British intelligence reports gathered that summer consistently cited a shortage of oatmeal as being the principal obstacle facing those rebel officers trying to reassemble their forces.

William Augustus, Duke of Cumberland (1721-1765) at Culloden, by David Morier. In this important portrait Cumberland wears a scarlet coat faced with a very dark blue, and considerable quantities of gold braid. The saddle housings are also red and gold. Rather more interestingly, the battalion in the middle distance appears by its position and yellow facings to be Pulteney's 13th. Close examination shows both officers and men wearing black gaiters, and the grenadier officer on the flank wearing a hat and carrying a fusil. The depiction of the Jacobite army appears to be based upon Sandby's watercolour sketch. (NMS)

Most crucially of all, the regular army's ability to penetrate into and operate among the hills has probably been underestimated by partisan historians. In deciding what course to follow the Jacobite leaders must have reflected uneasily on a raid by a mixed force of British infantry and dragoons which had penetrated deep into upper Strathdon and captured a magazine of Spanish arms and ammunition stored at Corgarff Castle. Lord Ancrum had marched from Aberdeen on 28 February with 300 foot and 100 of Kerr's (11th) Dragoons, and late the next day arrived at Corgarff where, according to Captain Alexander Stewart of Kerr's, "I dare say never Dragoons were before, nor ever will be again. ..." Although a false report that Gordon of Glenbucket was in the area led to their dumping most of the ammunition and all but a few hundred firelocks and bayonets in the river, the expedition was undoubtedly a success.

If the British army was capable of mounting such a bold incursion in the depths of a Highland winter, there would clearly be little to prevent their repeating it in the summer.

The Jacobite army therefore assembled on Culloden Moor on 15 April, and Lord George Murray described the situation thus:

"On Sunday morning, the 13th, it was confirmed that the enemy were coming on, and passed the Spey. Many of our people, as it was seed time, had slipt home; and as they had no pay for a month past, it was not an easy matter to keep them together. On Monday, the 14th, Locheil came up, and that day his Royal Highness went to Culloden, and all the other men as they came up marched there; and that night, the Duke of Perth came back with all the men he had on Speyside. The Duke of Cumberland . . . encamped this night at Nairn. Many were for retiring to stronger ground till all our army was gathered; but most of the baggage being at Inverness, this was not agreed to. Early on Tuesday morning, we all drew up in a line of battle, in an open muir near Culloden. I did not like the ground: it was certainly not proper for Highlanders."

Useful as this summary is, Murray omits to mention that he had earlier been ordered to find a suitable battlefield, and that he had sent two of his aides out to look for one on Sunday 13 April. The site which they chose was an odd one, and as he has consistently been condemned for electing to fight on the open moor O'Sullivan's own reasons for rejecting this previously considered ground are worth quoting in full:

"Lord George sent yt same day his Aide de Camp Ker, a very honest man & Kennedy, Aide Major in Buckley's Regiment to Reconnoitre a field of Battle, wch they did & Ld George looked upon it to be the finest thing in the world. Sullivan parted early the next morning to joyn the Duke of Perth & had orders to examine the field of Battle wch was in his way. Sullivan having examined this famiouse field of Battle, found it was the worst that could be chosen for the highlanders & the most advantagiouse for the enemy. I leave yu to judge of it this field of Battle was near the old Lady MccIntoshes Castle yt is at the right hand of the road from Invernesse to Nairn, over against the five mils house. There is a Ravin or hollow yt is very deep & large yt goes in zig zag, formed by a stream yt runs there, just near the castle so yt we were fortified, no enemy could come to us, having this Ravin before us. The enemy was to occupy the other side of the Ravin where the Castle is, wch is a rissing ground & commands altogether the side we were to occupy. The Castle is within musquet shot of this Ravin, wch the enemy was to be in possession of.

"I ask yu now yt knows the highlanders whither a field of Battle, where there is such an impediment as yt Ravin was, wch is impractical for man or horse, was proper for highlanders whose way of fighting is to go directly sword in hand on the enemy? Any man yt ever served with the highlanders, knows yt they fire but one shot & abandon their firelocks after. If there be any obstruction yt hinders them of going on the enemy all is lost; they don't like to be exposed to the enemy's fire, nor can they resist it, not being trained to charge [load] as fast as regular troops, especially the English wch are the troops in the world yt fires best. If I was to chuse a field of Battle for the English, or if they were to chouse it themselfs they could not chuse a better, for there are no troops in the world but what they overcome in fireing, if yu don't go in Sword in hand, or the bayonett among them."

O'Sullivan was mistaken as to the identity of the castle: the Dowager Lady MacIntosh's house was Dalcross Castle, but its situation does not fit his description. He must therefore have actually been talking about Kilravock Castle. This lies five miles short of Nairn, and unlike Dalcross is indeed within

musket-shot of the river.

In all other respects O'Sullivan, so frequently dismissed as an incompetent, was absolutely right. The site at Kilravock proposed by Lord George Murray on the 14th might have been an ideal one on which to fight a defensive battle – if the defending force was well supplied with ammunition, well trained in musketry, and facing an enemy obliging enough to attack on that ground.

In the first place there was of course no guarantee that Cumberland would be so rash as to oblige them by attacking such a strong position head on. The likelihood is that he would either have first taken Inverness – and the rebel magazines there; or else would have fought a defensive battle, obliging the Jacobites to attack him across a ravine which, as O'Sullivan points out, would have made it impossible for the Highlanders to charge.

Lord George Murray himself must have appreciated this. Of the two aides whom he sent to reconnoitre, Major Kennedy of Bulkeley's Regiment had recently arrived from France, but Colonel Ker had been with the rebels from the very beginning and was just as alive to the Highlanders' requirements as Murray and O'Sullivan. The conclusion must therefore be that Murray, firmly convinced as he was that a battle outside Inverness would be disastrous, had impressed upon them the need to find a battlefield from which it would be possible to execute a successful retreat, rather than one on which to win a decisive victory. O'Sullivan, on the other hand, was intending to fight.

Even without taking all these factors into account, the actual choice of Culloden Moor as a battlefield has been roundly criticised on all sides on the grounds that it was a plain open stretch of moorland which allowed the British army to make the fullest possible use of its artillery and cavalry.

This argument ignores O'Sullivan's undoubted point that the Highlanders also needed a clear run at their opponents – in effect they were not unlike cavalry in this regard. Moreover, both the earlier pitched battles fought during the campaign – Prestonpans and Falkirk – had taken place on ground which was just as featureless as that on which it was proposed that they should fight at Culloden.

Indeed, as O'Sullivan himself pointed out, at Prestonpans Sir John Cope drew up his army behind a ditch and an expanse of boggy ground. The rebels' initial reaction on discovering this was one of consternation, since there was no question of their being able to charge across such an obstacle. In the end, with the aid of a local guide, they found a way across under cover of darkness in order to face Cope's dragoons and artillery across a remarkably plain and open field.

Similarly the battle of Falkirk also affords some useful comparisons with Culloden. In the first place General Hawley had opened his battle with a cavalry charge launched against the rebel right wing. This was beaten off by the Highlanders in short order, suggesting that there was no reason why they should have been especially apprehensive of cavalry on the Culloden battlefield. Secondly, having defeated Hawley's cavalry the Highlanders then launched a general assault of their own upon the British infantry, and routed most of them. (Significantly, however, those British troops who did stand fast were posted behind a ravine.)

In neither battle had the rebels faced any artillery fire worthy of mention. At Prestonpans Cope's guns had been deserted by all but two men, while at Falkirk Hawley's had

Trooper, 15th Dragoons (ca. 1748), by David Morier. Raised as the Duke of Kingston's Light Horse in 1745, this regiment was a favourite of Cumberland's and was retained in service after Culloden when he became its Colonel-in-Chief. Much to his disappointment it was disbanded in 1748. The large green object sprouting from the trooper's hat is not an early plume but the sprig of green leaves employed as the Allied field sign. (The Royal Collection © 1994 Her Majesty The Queen)

never come into action at all. In both cases the speed of the rebel advance had been a significant factor in ensuring their ineffectiveness.

On the Jacobite army's past experience, therefore, there was nothing particularly amiss with Culloden as a battle-ground; indeed, providing they stuck to their usual tactics it offered significant advantages. In any case, for reasons shortly to be discussed, the battle was actually going to be fought on an area of Culloden Moor rather nearer to Inverness than the one picked by O'Sullivan and condemned by Murray as "an open muir ... not proper for Highlanders"; but that was still twenty-four eventful hours away.

CHAPTER SIX

Alarums and Excursions

Early the next morning, 15 April, all the Jacobite units then on hand were marched up from their bivouac areas around Culloden House to take up battle positions on the stretch of open moorland selected by O'Sullivan the previous day. It was naturally assumed that Cumberland intended to bring them to battle at once, and while the men waited in their ranks and files the Orders of the Day issued the night before will have been read out to them:

"It is His Royal Highness positive Orders that every person attach themselves to some Corps of the Armie and to remain with that Corps night and day till the Battle and persute be finally over. This regards the Foot as well as the Horse.

"The Order of Battle is to be given to every General officer and every Commander of Regiments or Squadrons.

"It is required and expected that each individual in the Armie as well officer as Souldier keep their posts that shall be alotted to them, and if any Man turn his back to run away the next behind such man is to shoot him.

"No body on pain of death to strip the Slain or plunder till the Battle be over.

"The Highlanders all to be in kilts and no body to throw away their Guns; by H.R.H. Command."

Morale was said to be high at the prospect of a battle; and the Prince, dressed in a tartan jacket and a buff waistcoat, proceeded to review his forces and deliver the usual inspirational speeches at the head of each regiment, "which they returned with loud huzzas". Just one element was lacking: the British army.

After a time, Lord Elcho was sent forward with a party of horse to reconnoitre towards Nairn and to give timely warning of Cumberland's anticipated approach. By about noon, however, it had become quite obvious to him that the British army had no intention of moving that day after all, so he left a small picquet and returned to report this to the Prince.

Meanwhile Lord George Murray and a number of the other Jacobite leaders had continued to press unsuccessfully for an immediate retreat to the high ground across the Water of Nairn. There was still every reason, they argued, to delay fighting Cumberland, even if it was for only another day or two. The Camerons had only arrived at Inverness the night before; two battalions of Frasers were at that moment on their way to rejoin the army, as were Cluny's McPhersons, Keppoch and his MacDonalds and some other reinforcements being gathered in Urquhart and Glenmoriston for Glengarry's Regiment, let alone the fairly substantial detachment still somewhere in the north with Cromartie. Even without Cromartie's men (who, unknown to the Jacobite leaders, were at that very moment being dispersed or captured by some of Loudon's Highland companies at Dunrobin), Murray forcefully argued that even a short postponement of the battle would see the army increased by

some 2,000 men. In the meantime Colonel Ker and Brigadier Stapleton were sent across the Nairn to reconnoitre yet another battle-site.

Now, however, Lord Elcho's astonishing news that Cumberland and his men were still encamped at Nairn appeared to put an entirely different complexion on the matter. When the Prince called a full council of war at Culloden House (the first since leaving Derby), Lord George Murray promptly changed his tune and instead urged a boldly aggressive scheme, proposing that the Jacobites should regain the initiative by going on to the offensive once again. Oddly enough, in his own suspiciously brief account of the conference Murray, far from admitting his own responsibility for proposing the desperate plan in the first place, merely records rather blandly:

"It was then proposed a night attack might be attempted. His Royal Highness and most others were for venturing it, amongst whom I was; for I thought we had a better chance by doing it than by fighting in so plain a field. . . ."

However, Elcho's recollection of the meeting was that Murray – finding that the Prince and his immediate advisors were still utterly opposed to any notion of retreating, or even temporarily uncovering Inverness – made a speech

". . . wherein he enlarged upon the advantages Highlanders have by Surprising their Enemy, and rather Attacking in the night time than in day Light, for as regular troops depend intirely upon their discipline, and on the Contrary the Highlanders having none, the Night was the time to putt them most upon an Equality, and he Concluded that his Opinion was that they Should march at dusk of ye Evening, So as that the Duke should not be aprised of it, that he Should march about the town of Nairn and attack them in their rear, with the right wing of the first line, while the Duke of Perth with ye left Should attack them in front, and the Prince Should support the Duke of Perths attack with the Second line."

Most of those then present at the council agreed to this plan; but although they might have thought that almost anything was better than simply waiting for Cumberland to come forward and meet them at his leisure, it was an extraordinary undertaking for an army in their present condition to even contemplate, far less to undertake. In the first place, perhaps more than any other episode in the campaign, this desperate proposal demonstrates that Lord George Murray's military abilities did not always match his conceit. Contrary to his airy assertion that the Highlanders' lack of "discipline" (which in the 18th century meant training) would stand them in better stead than the redcoats in the dark, all night operations, and particularly those carried out by large bodies of men, demand a very high standard of "discipline" from any troops engaged in them.

The only point which the plan might have been said to have in its favour was that, according to Elcho's report, the British cavalry was encamped out at Auldearn, and was therefore lying some two miles away from the main camp at Balblair just to the south-west of Nairn. Nevertheless, no one seems to have considered the likelihood that if a substantial part of the army was going to be expected to cross to that side of the river and march around Nairn in order to attack Cumberland's camp from the east or the south-east, they would run the risk of having the dragoons coming in on them from the rear while they were engaged with the infantry in the camp to their front.

Nor does anyone appear to have voiced serious concern at the probability of Cumberland's outlying picquets being able to give sufficient warning of the rebels' approach, darkness or no darkness. The Prince is often criticised for his apparently blind optimism, but all too many of the Jacobite leaders seem to have been infected by it that afternoon.

Whatever its chances of success, the venture was singularly badly timed in that the greater part of the army had not been fed since leaving Inverness the day before; and as the rebel troops had been unpaid for some time and were consequently unable to buy their own provisions, they were entirely dependent upon such rations of oatmeal or biscuit as might be served out from the army's magazines. Inasmuch as the greater part of the Scots population lived upon little besides oatmeal in the 18th century, this may in itself have been no great hardship to them; but unfortunately, since moving out of Inverness on the 14th no one had made any arrangements for the necessary supplies to be brought forward to the troops. This may have been because the battle was expected early on the 15th; it is more likely to have been simply the result of bad staff work.

O'Sullivan, as we have seen, had quite properly spent the previous morning reconnoitring the battle-site, but then in the afternoon found himself conducting a tense rearguard action as Cumberland's advancing forces bundled the Jacobites out of Nairn. In his unavoidable absence none of the more junior staff officers appear to have exerted themselves; and Cumberland's unexpected failure to oblige the Jacobites by accepting battle on the 15th meant that while the rebel generals wrangled amongst themselves over the next move, their soldiers had little to do all day but sit cold and hungry in the wet heather. By evening they were neither physically nor mentally prepared for the ordeal which lay ahead.

After the decision to counter-attack had been taken there was a somewhat cryptic exchange over the matter of the orders. Those issued on the night of the 14th, and read out on the morning of the 15th to the troops in anticipation of a battle that day, obviously needed to be updated. O'Sullivan, in his capacity as Adjutant General, was instructed to prepare fresh ones for the night attack; but at this point, according to his memoirs: "Lord George answered that there was no need of orders, yt everybody knew what he had to do."

Whether, as has been suggested, Murray was dropping a hint to the assembled officers that prisoners were not to be taken, or whether, as is more likely, he was merely giving vent to an impatience which had built up over the last few days, must remain a matter for conjecture.

By way of an elementary security precaution Murray had insisted that the army should delay moving off from Culloden until after dusk. When doubts were expressed in some quarters as to whether the army would then still be able to cover the eight miles or so to Nairn before daybreak, he confidently replied that he would "Answere for it". His concern for concealing the movement appeared to be vindicated

David, Lord Elcho (1721-1787), by Domenico Dupra. Commander of the Prince's Lifeguards, Elcho escaped from Culloden but had the misfortune to fall out with the Prince while remaining persona non grata *with the Government. (Earl of Wemyss)*

when the small squadron of naval vessels and transports accompanying the British army hove into view and dropped anchor just offshore at about six o'clock in the afternoon, but the delay fatally compromised the operation.

Opinions afterwards varied as to when the march actually began. As Captain Johnstone remembered it, the army was ordered to set off from Culloden at about eight o'clock in the evening, which was probably rather later than even Murray would have liked. This delay at least gave time for MacDonald of Keppoch to come up with his regiment. On the other hand, as soon as the army began assembling it was found that "a vast number of men had gone off on all hands to get and make ready provisions; and it was not possible to stop them. Then, indeed, almost everybody gave it up as a thing not to be ventured. His Royal Highness was extremely bent upon it, and said that, whenever we began the march, the men would be all hearty, and those that had gone off would return and follow."

This confidence was not shared by those officers who actually tried to round up the stragglers; and Lord Elcho reckoned that it was not until at about nine in the evening that the Jacobites finally marched off down the spine of the moor, leaving the heather set on fire behind them in the hope of giving the impression to the ships anchored offshore that the army was still encamped around Culloden.

Surviving accounts of the ensuing debacle are almost

Les Montagnards d'Ecosse en leur habits accûtumés avec un manteau pendant.

Berg-Schotten in gewöhnlichen Aufzug mit herab hangender Decke.

6
Un Montagnard d'Ecosse, qui prend son manteau sur les epaules, quäd il va pleuvoir. Ein seine Decke gegë de Rege, gleich eine Mantel über die Schultern schlagender Berg-Schott.

Iohan Christian Leopold excudit Augusta Vindelicor:

Three useful studies of Highlanders by a German artist, Johan Christian Leopold, providing good rear views of their short jackets. (NMS)

unanimous in depicting it as a sorry shambles from its confused beginning to its acrimonious end. The rebel army initially set off in what should have been three columns, following one behind the other: the first led by Lord George Murray, the second by Lord John Drummond and the third by the Duke of Perth. The composition of these columns presumably corresponded with that of the front-line divisions which each of them was to command in the battle next day; Lord George Murray's column certainly included his own Athollmen and Locheil's Camerons. Closely in the rear of Perth's column came the Prince himself with the cavalry, the remaining infantry regiments, and the French regulars.

Ahead of the army went a detachment of two officers and 30 men of the locally raised Lady MacIntosh's Regiment, to serve both as scouts and as guides for the main body, while more soldiers from the same regiment were posted with the other divisions to prevent straggling. Despite this sensible precaution, however, it soon proved impossible to prevent substantial gaps opening up between the columns and between the individual units within the columns.

The blame for this breakdown has frequently been thrown on the "heavily equipped French regulars", who are popularly visualised as toiling with difficulty in the rear; but they were in fact no more heavily encumbered than anybody else that night. The immediate problem, familiar to anyone who has ever undertaken a night march, was that obstacles such as walls and ditches invariably took far longer to cross in the dark than in daylight (the evening also appears to have been foggy, which cannot have helped matters); and that having successfully negotiated them, regiments would then naturally hurry onwards to make up for lost time, heedless of those still crossing behind them. Murray did his best to keep everything together, but although O'Sullivan mentions that officers were "posted all along the road yt the Colomn past by, to make every body follow, yt they may not mistake their way in the moor", their role and that of the men from Lady MacIntosh's Regiment seems to have been a passive one. Without proper policing of the long column, and supervision of the obstacles, the resultant gaps proved virtually impossible to close:

"As the highlanders had often marched more than two miles in an hour", wrote Murray, "it was hoped that they could have reached Nairn before two o'clock. But before Lord George had marched a mile, he received a message that half of the line was at a considerable distance, and orders to halt, or march slower, till the line should join. He received many messages by aides-de-camps and other officers, sent for the same purpose, by the time he reached six miles. Altho he did not halt, he marched always slower, hoping that would do: For he knew that a halt in the van occasions a greater one in the rear, when the march begins again; whereas by marching slow, the rear might have joined without that inconveniency."

Captain Johnstone had at one time commanded a company in the Duke of Perth's Regiment, but having fallen out with his Colonel, who ordered him to remain in Carlisle, he was now serving as a volunteer; in accordance with the "positive Orders that every person attach themselves to some Corps of the Armie" he joined Scotus's company of Glengarry's Regiment. He therefore found himself stumbling unhappily in the middle of Perth's column, and was afterwards able to recall the sorry experience of that night as an ordinary foot soldier rather than from the more rarified viewpoint of a staff officer. He describes the endless delays as being due not to the slowness of the French regulars in the rear, but to the predictable difficulties experienced by the Highlanders themselves as they floundered around in the darkness:

"This march across the country in a dark night which did not allow us to follow any track, had the inevitable fate of all night marches. It was extremely fatiguing and accompanied with confusion and disorder. The Highlanders, who could not keep together from the difficulty of the roads, were more or less dispersed and we had many stragglers. As there were a great many bad places to cross, it would have been impossible for the best disciplined troops to have preserved anything like order."

The plain fact is that despite Lord George Murray's earlier confident prediction a night march, and indeed any night operation, demands an extremely high level of training and practice. Not only was the Jacobite army simply not up to the task, but as the night wore on and the chances of their ever reaching the start line before daybreak became increasingly slim, relations between the officers also deteriorated markedly – this in its turn leading to yet further delays and confusion.

Murray's own column was supposed to cross the Water of Nairn two miles below Culraick, so that he could attack Cumberland's camp from the south-east, while Perth and his brother Lord John Drummond mounted a simultaneous frontal assault. It was now becoming increasingly obvious that this was no longer a practical proposition; and at last, with the army held up behind him by the park walls surrounding Culraick Wood, Lord George called a halt somewhere beyond Kilravock Castle to consider the deteriorating situation.

While Murray conferred with those officers immediately to hand Colonel Ker was, by his own showing, sent back down the line from front to rear with orders "to the respective officers to order their men to make the attack sword in hand, which was thought better, as it would not alarm the enemy so soon, and that firearms would be of use to them afterwards."

One of the officers who received this message remembered it in rather more detail; they were ordered not "to make any use of our firearms, but only of sword, dirk and bayonet, to cut the tent strings and pull down the poles, and where we observed a swelling or bulge in the fallen tent there to strike and push vigorously."

Given the timing indicated by Colonel Ker, this particular injunction certainly cannot be taken as evidence that the Jacobite leaders intended that no prisoners should be taken in the camp; but it does confirm that up until that moment at least, Murray was still hopeful of being able to mount some sort of assault on the Government camp.

He may well have been close enough to do it. Although Ker thought that the leading troops were just to the east of Kilravock, a local minister, George Innes, afterwards reckoned that they had actually reached Kildrummie, only two miles short of their objective; and a number of other officers afterwards claimed that they were near enough to hear the sentries calling out to each other.

Some of those waiting were certainly in an aggressive mood, offering various different lines of approach which might be taken to the camp, and generally agreeing that it "was better to make the attempt with four thousand men before daybreak, than with double the number after it was light."

This might very well have been so, but the trouble was going to be finding those 4,000 men. Murray thought that he had only the Atholl Brigade and Locheil's Camerons still with him at that juncture, making no more than 1,200 men in total; and there could be no question of going forward with them alone. Moreover, as he also pointed out to the assembled officers, in view of the time so far taken to march the six miles from Culloden it was going to be impossible for them to cover the remaining four miles (as he estimated it) before first light – and even then they would still need more time to set the army in order of battle before launching the assault.

At this inauspicious moment O'Sullivan turned up and "said he had just come from the Prince, who was very desirous the attack should be made; but as Lord George Murray had the van, and could judge the time, he left it to him whether to do it or not." O'Sullivan naturally remembered the conversation slightly differently, and in contrast to Murray's rather terse narrative his memoirs recount the exchange in vivid and at times unintentionally hilarious detail. According to him, he warmly pressed Murray to proceed with the attack, stressing the necessity of doing so:

" 'Gad Sr,' says Ld George, swearing, 'I desire no better, speak to those gents.' A Colonel of his Regimt swore & said if they were to be killed yt it wou'd be in plain day, & yt they wou'd see how their neighbours wou'd behave. (This is the Regimt yt must have the right of the first ligne). There was not an officer or soldier of them killed or wounded since the beginning of the Campagne. Another of the Regimt said, 'those yt are so much for fighting, why dont they come with us.' 'I dont know,' says Sullivan, 'to whom this discourse is adres'd, If it be to me, yu know yt it was not the first time yu saw me in the action, yu owned yr self & say'd it openly, yt yu saw no other General but the Prince & me at the battle of Falkirk. If Ld George will permit me, I offer to march in the first rank of his Vanguarde & will give him my head off my shoulders, wch is all I have to loose, if he does not succeed, if he follows, & if he follows, I am sure YU will, Gents.' "

What finally settled the matter was the arrival of Perth and his brother, who had gone back to report to the Prince and who now returned with the news that a particularly wide gap had opened up in the column which, even if the vanguard remained at Kilravock, could not be closed before daybreak. Nevertheless, the operation still could not be abandoned lightly, and in the best 18th century tradition Murray first set about obtaining the formal agreement of those officers who were present, presumably including O'Sullivan:

"It was agreed upon all hands that it must be sunrise before the army could reach Nairn and form, so as to make an attempt upon the enemy's camp; for one part was to have passed the water a mile above the town, to have fallen upon them towards the sea-side. The volunteers were all very keen to march. Some of them said that the red-coats would all be drunk, as they surely had solemnised the Duke of Cumberland's birthday. . . .

"But the officers were of different sentiments, as severals of them expressed. Locheil and his brother said they had been as much for the night attack as anybody could be, and it was not their fault that it had not been done; but blamed those in the rear that had marched so slow and retarded the rest of the army. Lord George Murray was of the same way of thinking, and said if they could have made the attack it was the best chance they had, especially if they could have surprised the

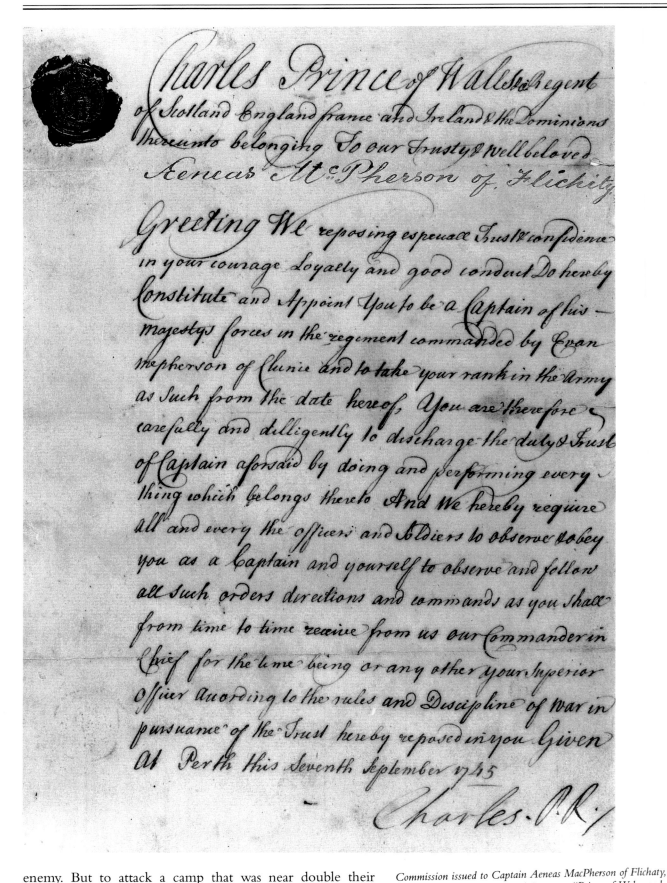

Charles Prince of Wales & Regent
of Scotland England France and Ireland & the Dominions
thereunto belonging To our Trusty & Wellbeloved
Aeneas McPherson of Flichity

Greeting We reposing especiall Trust & confidence
in your courage Loyaly and good conduct Do hereby
Constitute and Appoint you to be a Captain of his
Majestys forces in the regiment commanded by Evan
McPherson of Clunie and to take your rank in the Army
as Such from the date hereof, You are therefore
carefuly and dilligently to discharge the duty & Trust
of Captain aforsaid by doing and performing every
thing which belongs thereto And We hereby require
all and every the officers and Soldiers to observe & obey
you as a Captain and yourself to observe and follow
all such orders directions and commands as you shall
from time to time receive from us our Commander in
Chief for the time being or any other your Superior
Officer According to the rules and Discipline of War in
pursuance of the Trust hereby reposed in you Given
At Perth this Seventh September 1745

Charles. P.R.

enemy. But to attack a camp that was near double their number in day-light, when they would be prepared to receive them, would be perfect madness.

"By this time Mr John Hay [the Prince's secretary] came up and told the line was joined. He was told the resolution was taken to return. He began to argue the point, but nobody minded him.... It was about two o'clock in the

continued on page 75

Commission issued to Captain Aeneas MacPherson of Flichaty, and signed by Charles Edward Stuart as "Prince of Wales and Regent of Scotland England France and Ireland and the Dominions". An officer in Cluny's Regiment, Flichaty appears to have escaped prosecution after the rebellion. (NMS)

COLOUR PLATES A-D

Plate A1: Sergeant of Grenadiers, St. Clair's Royals

St. Clair's Royals, the 1st of Foot (known as the Royal Scots from early in the next century) justifiably prided themselves on being the oldest regiment in the British Army. Traditionally many of their officers and men were recruited in the Highlands at this time. The regiment was unusual in having two battalions, and both of them were represented in the campaign. The 1st Battalion was out in Flanders in 1745, but later served in the army group covering London. The 2nd Battalion was in Ireland when the rising began, but later served in the north, first under Hawley at Falkirk, and then under Cumberland in the first line at Culloden. Two "Additional" or recruiting companies were also in Scotland when the rebellion began, but were captured near Fort William.

This reconstruction is closely based upon one of the Swiss artist David Morier's series of grenadier paintings. These are often said to have been painted in about 1751 and to illustrate the revised dress regulations of that year; but the presence of Austrian soldiers in the background of at least one painting, and of soldiers in others wearing the Allied field-sign of a sprig of green leaves, may indicate that they were actually painted in about 1748, just two years after Culloden. Sergeants in all regiments wore plain white lace, but in the Royals, in recognition of their regiment's seniority, the corporals and privates also had plain lace – a privilege which they shared only with the three Footguards regiments. The embroidered "mitre" cap, and the by now purely decorative brass matchcase on the crossbelt, were distinctions of grenadiers; the sash which hides the waistbelt here, in crimson with a stripe of facing colour, that of a sergeant.

Plate A2: Officer of Grenadiers, 13th (Pulteney's) Foot

Although latterly they were to become the Somerset Light Infantry, Colonel Harry Pulteney's 13th Foot had in fact a long association with Scotland beginning in 1689 when, as Colonel Ferdinando Hastings' Regiment, they survived a Highland charge on the Braes o' Killiecrankie. In 1740 over a third of the officers then serving in the regiment were Scots, and this association was to continue long after the rebellion, with a prolonged period in Highland garrisons; even as late as 1761 at least one officer in six was Scottish and the Adjutant, Lieutenant William Bannatyne, came from Inverness-shire.

The regiment's facing colour was philemot yellow, a brownish shade supposedly resembling the colour of dead leaves, and the lace pattern of the rank and file was a yellow vandyked line on white. Interestingly they are clearly seen in a portrait by Morier depicting the Duke of Cumberland at Culloden. Unlike the grenadiers of Barrell's 4th Foot in Morier's later "Incident in the Rebellion" (ca. 1753), both officers and men are shown wearing long black gaiters rather than the somewhat impractical white ones in which 18th century soldiers are conventionally depicted. Culloden was of course fought on a cold day after a morning of squally showers, and this officer has dressed sensibly for the occasion by pulling a heavy greatcoat on over his expensive regimentals and replacing his elaborately embroidered mitre cap with an ordinary cocked hat. Battalion company officers normally carried espontoons or half-pikes, but grenadier officers traditionally had privately purchased fusils or light muskets, and these are depicted in both Morier's Culloden paintings.

Plate B1: Private, 21st (Campbell's) Royal North British Fuziliers

The form "North British" was used officially in an obvious attempt to emphasise the unitary nature of the state; in everyday speech "Scots" seems to have been as common. Although the Fuziliers (Fusiliers, Fuzileers – all spellings are found), like the Royals and Sempill's 25th, were permitted to beat up for recruits anywhere in the British Isles, they consciously and successfully strove to maintain their Scottish character, and well over two-thirds of the officers carried on the 1740 Army List were Scots. At Culloden the 21st stood in the front line, and earned considerable praise for their musketry. The fact that they afterwards returned only seven men wounded in the battle therefore reflects their success in keeping the clans at bay, rather than any reluctance to become more closely engaged.

In theory all ranks of this regiment ought to have worn mitre caps, but in practice these tended to be preserved for formal occasions and cheaper tricorne hats were worn in the field. In the 1742 Cloathing Book a fusilier was depicted as wearing a blue-fronted cap bearing a star on which was superimposed a red thistle on a green backing, surrounded by a yellow garter. Rather unusually the "little flap" was also blue, and bore a thistle in its natural colours rather than the white horse of Hanover. In ca. 1748, however, Morier painted a grenadier of the regiment wearing a cap very similar to that of the Royals, save for a blue and white tuft on the top, and the substitution of a thistle for the royal cypher within the garter. This may represent an alteration in style between 1742 and 1748, but it seems more likely that the caps worn by the grenadiers and battalion company men were slightly different.

Plate B2: Corporal, 25th (Sempill's) Foot

This regiment is proudly said to have been raised in just two short hours in Edinburgh on 19 March 1689 at the outset of the first Jacobite rising, hence their alternative title of "The Edinburgh Regiment". Like the 13th Foot they stood their ground at Killiecrankie; and it was appropriate, therefore, that having survived the first battle in the long series of Jacobite risings, both regiments should have fought in the last one at Culloden. Posted in the second line, they took part in the counter-attack to seal off the Jacobite penetration of the left wing; like Campbell's Fuziliers they were praised for the effectiveness of their musketry, though their losses were slightly heavier, with one man returned as killed and 13 wounded.

Also based on one of Morier's paintings, the soldier is identified as a corporal by the knot of white cord or tape hanging from behind his right shoulder. This badge of rank appears to have originated in the 17th century, and one theory holds that it recalls extra skeins of slowmatch carried looped round the shoulder by corporals in order to keep their files of matchlock musketeers supplied in battle. (It is equally possible that shoulder knots, and fringed epaulettes, are stylized survivals of the bunches of laces or "points" on the shoulders of the arming doublets once worn under plate armour. The appearance of shoulder knots and cords as part of the uniform of rank-and-file Dragoons, and as the distinction of aides-de-camp, perhaps tends to support this derivation, though their absence from the uniform of sergeants of Foot is puzzling. These are deep waters.) Marching equipment such as knapsacks, haversacks and canteens probably varied in materials and details of construction due to local manufacture. Unshaven cowhide knapsacks are shown by Morier; there were also simple canvas "duffle-bags" recalling the 17th century "snapsack".

As for the other infantry regiments at Culloden: Barrell's and Wolfe's had blue facings; Howard's, Prices's, Blakeney's and Ligonier's had buff; Bligh's, Cholmondley's, Monro's and Battereau's had yellow; and Fleming's had green facings.

Plate C1: Private, 64th (Loudon's) Highlanders

The unexpected outbreak of the rebellion in 1745 caught this newly raised Highland regiment scattered and still incomplete. Some elements were caught up in the debacle at Prestonpans; but other companies assembled at Inverness, and provided a useful stiffening for the 18 Highland Independent Companies and other loyalist troops raised for service in the north. The Argyllshire Militia were similarly reinforced at Culloden by Captain Colin Campbell of Ballimore's company of the 64th. After Culloden the regiment was reorganised, and eventually served in the Low Countries before being disbanded in 1748.

The Argyll Militia companies did not, so far as is known, wear any items of uniform at Culloden apart from red saltire badges in their bonnets; but Loudon's men wore red jackets with what appear to have been white facings – white was in fact a traditional facing colour for Scots regiments, and before the Union in 1707 coloured facings were almost unheard of. Unlike the better known Black Watch they had red plaids, and the tartan here, depicted in Allan Ramsay's portrait of Loudon himself, appears to be the sett now known as Stuart of Bute – an attribution which may arise from the portrait's being in the possession of that family in the 19th century when the Sobieski Stuart brothers forged their Vestiarium Scoticum, the fictitious source of many of the modern clan tartans. The buff shoulder belt is also taken from Loudon's portrait. Although this soldier, being a regular, would be fully equipped with firelock, bayonet and broadsword, the militiamen had only firelocks and bayonets.

Plate C2: Gunner, Royal Artillery

At least 20 out of the 106 NCOs and men serving in Captain-Lieutenant John Godwin's artillery detachment at Culloden can be identified as Scots, including Sergeant Edward Bristo, one of the six men afterwards returned as casualties (all six subsequently died of their wounds). No fewer than five out of the 15 officers and cadets standing on the moor were also Scotsmen, and one of them at least, Cadet Volunteer Simon Fraser, was evidently a Highlander.

This figure is taken from David Morier's magnificent panoramic view of the Royal Artillery in the camp at Roermond in Holland in April 1748, and chiefly differs from the rather earlier representation of a gunner in the 1742 Cloathing Book by the addition of a lavish quantity of yellow lace binding and button loops on the coat and waistcoat. Those gunners and matrosses who were not actually serving their guns were of course expected to defend them with firelock and bayonet, and the curious style of belly-box worn by this man is worthy of note. Morier's painting also shows what appears to be a uniformed artillery driver in a short light blue coat with white lace, buff breeches and black riding boots, but it is unlikely that any of Godwin's men would have worn such a uniform.

Plate D1: Trooper, 10th (Duke of Kingston's) Horse

This regiment was one of a number of volunteer units raised in Britain during the rebellion. The Duke of Cumberland for some reason took a fancy to them, and used the unit as his escort on a number of occasions. On their being disbanded after the rising he had them immediately re-enlisted on to the regular establishment as the short-lived 15th Dragoons. Although they were sometimes unofficially referred to as "hussars", since they were intended to serve in that role rather than as "heavy" dragoons, they should not be confused with the small detachment of Hanoverian hussars who formed Cumberland's permanent bodyguard and who are known to have been with him in Scotland. At Culloden, Kingston's Horse were initially formed on either flank of the third line under Brigadier Mordaunt, but before the battle began Cumberland moved both squadrons on to the right of the front line.

The green facings and yellow lace were derived from Kingston's own livery, but otherwise the regiment was rather unusual in being dressed in red coats. Most of the other volunteer units raised at this time (or at least those which had uniforms) appear to have worn blue in order to distinguish them from the regulars. Contemporary newspaper reports, for example, describe Oglethorpe's "Yorkshire Hunters", a cavalry unit which helped harry the rebels in the north of England, as wearing blue coats with scarlet facings, and gold-laced hats with – an unusual touch – green cockades.

Plate D2: Trooper, 10th (Cobham's) Dragoons

A weak squadron of Cobham's Regiment had been detached from the rest of General Hawley's command in order to scout to the northwards shortly before the battle, and there was at first some concern that they might miss it. They returned in time, however, and as a result elements of the regiment actually served on both flanks of the army. Consequently they later had the happy experience of being re-united in the centre of what had been the enemy position. Only a single man was returned as having been killed at Culloden and none claimed to have been wounded, although four horses were killed and five more wounded, probably in the fight with the Irish Picquets.

The uniform depicted here is again based upon one of Morier's paintings from ca.1748. Although the trooper's clothing is essentially unchanged from that depicted in the 1742 Cloathing Book, the saddle housings are now of a much more modern style and the earlier elaborate embroidery has been replaced with a smart braid trimming. Dragoons wore the right rear shoulder knot as a distinction of branch rather than rank.

The other regular dragoon regiment at Culloden, Kerr's 11th, wore a very similar uniform but with the white facings which indicated that it had originally been a Scottish regiment. Having led the crossing of the re-entrant between Culchunaig and Balvraid, they afterwards returned higher casualties: three men killed and three wounded, with four horses killed and no fewer than 15 wounded.

General arrangement drawings of the British infantry coat, after Morier, showing different styles of cuff and lace. The centre coat has the grenadier's "wings" – extra laced flaps sewn in at the shoulder. It is worth observing that while the 1742 Cloathing Book invariably shows the waistbelt worn over the coat, the Morier series shows two distinct styles: in one the lapels are buttoned across for warmth, and the belt is worn on top of the coat, as in the colour plates in this book; in the other, the lapels are displayed and the belt worn under the coat. The skirts were normally worn hooked together at the corners in "turnbacks" displaying the lining colour, to clear the legs when marching, but could be worn loose in bad weather. (Drawing: Gerry Embleton)

Plate A

A1: Grenadier Sergeant, St. Clair's Royals

A2: Grenadier Officer, 13th (Pulteney's) Foot

B1: Private, 21st (Campbell's) Royal North British Fuziliers

B2: Corporal, 25th (Sempill's) Foot

Plate C

C1: Private, 64th (Loudon's) Highlanders

C2: Gunner, Royal Artillery

Plate D

D1: Trooper, Duke of Kingston's Horse

D2: Trooper, 10th (Cobham's) Dragoons

E1: Highland soldier of Jacobite army

E2: Highland officer

F1: Lowland soldier, Stonywood's Battalion

F2: Fusilier, Régiment Royal Ecossois

G1: Trooper, Bagot's Hussars

G2: Trooper, Prince's Lifeguards

Plate H

H1: Fusilier, Régiment Berwick

H2: Trooper, Fitzjames's Horse

Plate E1: Highland soldier of the Jacobite army

The instructions issued by Lord Lewis Gordon to his officers on 6 December 1745 stressed that: "All men are to be well cloathed, with short cloathes, plaid, new shoes and three pair of hose and accoutered with shoulder ball gun, pistolls and sword." Although this was clearly regarded as the ideal, it appears rarely to have been achieved in practice, at least as far as the equipment was concerned. Although Highlanders are conventionally depicted carrying broadswords and targes, both contemporary accounts and the evidence of weapons recovered from Culloden Moor itself reveal that most of them were actually armed only with firelocks and bayonets – in this case, a French Modèle 1717 with an old-fashioned long branched bayonet. Ammunition for it is carried in a French gargoussier or belly-box, again of obsolete pattern.

Otherwise this soldier wears fairly typical Highland dress. Although there are indications that some tartan setts were traditional to certain areas, a system of "clan tartans" did not exist in the 18th century, and different setts were used entirely according to the wearer's fancy. To judge by contemporary paintings red or brownish-red setts were most popular. The amount of cloth required for the belted plaid largely depended on the individual, though it should be noted that plaiding was woven on a 27in. width, and consequently references to "double ells" actually signify double widths of material – the Scots ell was also comparatively short and at 37in. equated more readily with the English yard.

Plate E2: Highland officer (Colonel Francis Farquharson)

Although Highland dress in its various forms, together with a white cockade, was the nearest thing which most of the Jacobite army possessed to a formal uniform, even in the Highland regiments themselves not everyone could always be relied upon to wear it. When James Logie saw Farquharson of Monaltrie's Deeside men march into Aberdeen in February 1746 he noted that they "were dressed in highland clothes mostly" – so presumably some of them were actually wearing breeches. This figure is based upon various descriptions of Farquharson himself. After the Colonel was taken prisoner at Culloden, Logie laid a deposition to the effect that he had seen him in Aberdeen "with a white cockade and a broadsword – not in highland dress". However, another trial witness, Allan Stewart, a sometime sergeant in Ardshiel's Regiment, testified that although Farquharson was wearing a short coat and tartan trews while he was in Inverness, "some days before the battle of Culloden I remember to have seen said Colonel Francis Farquharson with a big blue coat on at the head of his regiment". This was presumably a large caped greatcoat of the kind depicted here. Most officers wore trews in preference to the kilt or plaid, since they were obviously much more comfortable for riding.

Basket-hilted broadswords and Scottish pistols seem to have been the obligatory equipment for all Jacobite officers and at least one of them, Captain James Johnstone, mentions carrying a blunderbuss as well at Culloden.

Plate F1: Lowland infantryman, James Moir of Stonywood's Battalion

Stonywood raised the second battalion of Lord Lewis Gordon's Regiment in the Aberdeen area; and although his Lordship sternly instructed him: "You'l advert what men you receive be sufficientlie furnished with plaids, short cloathes, hose, shoes and by all means swords with what other arms can be got", extant descriptions and trial evidence suggest that most men in this and other Lowland battalions simply wore their own everyday clothes. The reconstruction in this case is based upon items recovered from a corpse found in a peat bog at Quintfall Hill in Sutherland. Although coins found with the body dated it to the time of William and Mary, contemporary illustrations reveal that the styles of clothing worn by ordinary Scots were largely unchanged fifty years later.

The firelock is a Spanish weapon, part of a consignment landed at Peterhead, while the cartridge box or giberne is of an obsolete French pattern.

This particular regiment appears to have carried plain white colours. A white linen colour was certainly taken from Farquharson's battalion at Culloden, while a man named John Daunie, who left an account of the fight at Inverurie in December 1745, mentions a battalion with white colours which can be identified as Stonywood's. Unlike Farquharson's men, however, Stonywood brought their colours safely away from Culloden; and an officer in the regiment named John Martin afterwards told his interrogators that he had seen Stonywood tear his colours from the staff when the army was disbanded at Ruthven Barracks.

Plate F2: Fusilier, Régiment Royal Ecossois

This Scottish regiment in the French service initially stood in the second line at Culloden, and later some fought a desperate rearguard action against the British cavalry before being forced to surrender. Others, however, led by Major Hale, succeeded in escaping to Ruthven Barracks and did not surrender until 19 April. Originally it had comprised only a single battalion, but Lord John Drummond had been authorised to recruit a second, and appears to have picked up quite a number of recruits after landing in Scotland. Some of these recruits later had great difficulty in being accepted as prisoners of war rather than as rebels.

One of them was Lieutenant Charles Oliphant, a customs officer from Aberdeen, and this unusual uniform was described by one of the witnesses at his trial in 1747 (he was found guilty, but pardoned on condition of emigrating to America) : "Prisoner wore the uniform of Lord John Drummond's officers, viz; short blue coats, red vests laced with bonnets and white cockades." A drover named John Gray also described Drummond himself wearing the same uniform, although he helpfully added that the coat itself was also laced. This style was of course very Scottish, and the grenadier company even went so far as to wear kilts in place of the white breeches depicted here. By 1752, however, the battalion or fusilier companies were more conventionally dressed in full-skirted coats, and tricorne hats with white lace. The French infantry of the period seem to have worn white gaiters with all orders of dress; and we may presume that this regular unit may have been equipped with the Modèle 1728 musket.

Plate G1: Trooper, Bagot's Hussars

The Hussars, who had earned the respect of Cumberland's cavalry as a proficient reconnaisance unit, appear to have suffered quite heavy casualties at Culloden. When the battle began they were standing on the left wing, but a volunteer in the Lifeguards named John Daniel mentions that they were later moved into the centre and that he saw "many" dead bodies lying there. As they only numbered 26 troopers at the outset this could mean that they might have lost as much as half their strength. One of the casualties was the unit's commanding officer, Major John Bagot, a regular officer in the French service, who was badly wounded. Not surprisingly they soon moved from this exposed position, but whether they returned to the left, or joined the bulk of the Jacobite cavalry on the right is not clear.

A hostile witness to their progress through Kendal (who may have been James Ray) wrote: "They have several young Men clad in close Plaid Waistcoats, and huge Fur Caps, which they call their Hussars; but they have such scurvy Horses, that I have seen several of them exert all their Vigour to bring them to a Gallop; in Spite of which the poor Beasts immediately fell into a Pace more suitable to their Age and Infirmities." Another witness at Carlisle was rather more specific about the caps, describing them as "high rough red caps, Like Pioneers".

Plate G2: Trooper, Prince's Lifeguards

Tracing the movements of this unit at Culloden is complicated by the fact that while the greater number of them stood on the right under Lord Elcho, and helped defend that flank against Hawley's dragoons, another, smaller troop led by Lord Balmerino may have served on the left wing brigaded with what remained of Lord Strathallan's Horse; while yet another small detachment formed part of the Pretender's bodyguard under the command of Captain Shea, an officer in Fitzjames's Horse.

This reconstruction is principally based upon a contemporary print of Lord Balmerino as he appeared on the day of his execution wearing the regiment's uniform, and also upon a number of eyewitness descriptions all commenting on the blue coat turned up with red, the red waistcoat and the gold-laced hat. The coat itself appears to have been unlaced. At any rate Balmerino's coat appears to be quite plain, and a letter written from Leith shortly after Culloden mentions that: "The Pretender's Life Guards have suffered greatly. A person, this moment arrived, saw 26 of them in a heap, with the lace cut off their vests, and their tartan belts lying besides them." It seems unlikely that there would have been time to make up these uniforms while the rebel army was assembling at Edinburgh, and they were probably French cavalry coats.

Plate H1: Fusilier, Régiment Berwick

The Irish Picquets, a composite battalion formed of detachments from the French regiments Berwick, Dillon, Roth and Lally, stood on the left of the Jacobite second line at Culloden. According to Finlayson's map they initially moved forward in support of the Highland attack, but latterly they withdrew towards their original position and fought a gallant rearguard action against the British cavalry. In the process they are said to have suffered heavy losses, including their provisional commanding officer, Lieutenant Colonel Walter Stapleton of the Régiment Berwick. Some 46 men from this regiment were landed at Peterhead at the end of February 1746, although to judge by O'Sullivan's narrative they were considerably reduced in numbers by Culloden, and perhaps as few as 25 of them fought there in the ranks of the Picquets under Captains Nicholas Delahay and Patrick Clargue.

Both uniform and equipment are typically French in style, although the red coat worn by the Irish Brigade (among other foreign units) in French service recalls their British origin. The other Irish regiments with substantial contingents present at Culloden were similarly dressed. The famous Régiment Dillon had black facings on the coat cuffs, linings and lapels but wore red waistcoats and breeches. Roth (once the Royal Regiment of Ireland) had blue facings, waistcoats and breeches; and Lally, the junior regiment in the brigade, wore green cuffs and waistcoats but had white coat linings and breeches.

Plate H2: Trooper, Fitzjames's Horse

The bulk of this unit stood on the right of the Jacobite army at Culloden and participated in the blocking action against Hawley's dragoons; in the process they are said to have suffered quite heavy losses. A small detachment of 16 men led by Captain Shea formed part of the Prince's bodyguard, and although at one point they came under artillery fire they appear to have escaped unscathed, for all 16 of them (besides three officers) were reported to have ridden into Inverness to surrender the next day.

Like the Irish infantry regiments in French service they wore red coats, turned up in this case with blue. When they landed at Aberdeen in February 1746 they were reported to have brought "their horse-furniture, arms, breastplates and baggage" – indeed, they had no fewer than nine or ten cart-loads and 20 pack-loads of equipment. Although their men had only breastplates, worn under the coat, the officers of this regiment had complete cuirasses which they wore over it, and gold-laced hats. The Comte de Fitzjames, who was also the Colonel-Proprietor of the infantry regiment Berwick, took over the cavalry unit in 1733 and the green and white lace shown in the reconstruction is his livery. The sword-hilt is based on a surviving example, bearing the inscription FITZIAMES CAUALLERIE on the inside of the blade. The saddle housings were red, edged with Fitzjames's livery lace.

Suits of clothing recovered from bodies found in peat bogs at Barrock in Caithness, Arnish Moor on Lewis, and Gunnister in Shetland respectively. All now show varying shades of brown. Coin evidence suggests that all three men died in the early years of the 18th century, but contemporary illustrations show little or no alteration in style by the middle of the century. Many Jacobite soldiers would therefore have looked like these men, even those serving in the Highland regiments. (NMS)

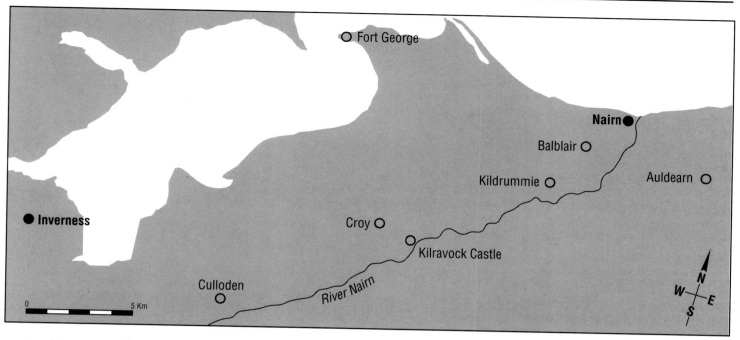

continued from page 62

morning (the halt not being above a quarter of an hour) when they went back in two columns, the rear facing about, and the van taking another way. At a little distance they had a view of the fires of the Duke of Cumberland's camp. . . . Daylight began to appear about an hour after. They got to Culloden pretty early, so that the men had three or four hours rest."

Murray's version of events suggests that the retreat was quite straightforward, and Andrew Lumisden explains the swifter progress in returning to Culloden by their marching back the shortest way "as we had not the same reason for shunning houses in returning as we had in advancing"; but in fact for most of the army the return journey was as wearying an ordeal as the outward march had been.

Although Murray's own division simply turned around to its left and followed him straight back to Culloden House by way of the church of Croy, the decision to follow a different but shorter route meant that the various bodies which had been marching behind them were at first unaware of the change of plan and blithely continued heading towards Nairn. Somehow O'Sullivan and the other officers sent back by Murray to acquaint them of the change of plan also managed to miss them in the darkness; and as John Daniel of the Lifeguards recalled, it was some time before the rear division actually realised that something was amiss:

"After we had marched till about three o'Clock in the morning, over double the ground that was necessary, we at last came pretty nigh the enemy's camp: and when we were supposing to surround them, and for that purpose in some measure drawing out; my Lord George Murray began to be missing; notwithstanding the Prince's Aides-de-Camp in riding from rank to rank, and asking, for God's sake! what has become of his Lordship, and telling that the Prince was in the utmost perplexity for want of him. In that situation did we remain a considerable time, till, day breaking fast in upon us, we heard that Lord George Murray was gone off with most of the Clans. . . . But O! for Madness! what can one think, or what can one say here!"

The Prince was equally unimpressed when Locheil eventually found him and reported that Lord George Murray and

the other officers had resolved to go back. "The Prince," said Elcho, who as the commander of his Lifeguard was presumably present during the exchange, "was not for going back, and said it was much better to march forward and attack, than march back and be attack'd afterwards, when the men would be all fatigued with their night's march. During the time of this Conversation the army, by what means I know not, began to move back. . . ."

Apparently the first intimation which the Prince received that the leading regiments had in fact turned back was when he encountered Perth's Regiment heading back towards Culloden. Not surprisingly, it was afterwards reported that he called out: "I am betrayed; what need I give orders, when my orders are disobeyed?"

Then Perth himself turned up at last with O'Sullivan, and confirmed that Lord George Murray had indeed ordered a retreat and was already well out of reach. At this the Prince put a brave face on things, and replied "T'is no matter then; we shall meet them, and behave like brave fellows."

After this, in Lord Elcho's words, he too turned around, "and in much Shorter time than they had march'd return'd to the parks of Culloden, where Every body seemed to think of nothing but Sleep. The men were prodigiously tired with hunger and fatigue, and vast numbers of them went to Inverness, and the villages about, both to Sleep and to pick up what little nourishment they Could gett."

The leaders too were so exhausted that on their arrival at Culloden they at once flung themselves down to sleep. The lucky ones, or rather the most senior, had beds, but most made do with tables, chairs and even the floor. O'Sullivan alone has a story of an encounter at the house in which the Prince "without the least anger" demanded to know what had gone wrong, whereupon Murray and Locheil proceeded to blame each other for the decision to turn back. It seems an unlikely exchange, particularly as the Prince seems to have convinced himself that the fault lay with Murray, and the truth of the matter was probably that no one had the energy at that moment for such recriminations.

Even so, they were not left undisturbed for long. A party of horse, probably the overworked Hussars, and some of Lady MacIntosh's men "yt knew the by roads", had been left behind near Culraick Wood to keep an eye on Cumberland's camp. Little more than two hours later they came in with the word that there was a party of cavalry (Kingston's Horse) within two miles and coming on fast, while the main body of the Government army was not far behind.

Their earlier disagreements temporarily forgotten, the Prince and his senior commanders all mounted their horses, ordered the drums to beat to arms, and sent word for the army to concentrate up on the moor. The Prince himself accompanied Locheil's Regiment to the top, doing his best to sound encouraging, but according to O'Sullivan he "in the bottom had no great hopes." If the Prince was indeed gripped by a fatalistic resignation, this might explain his passive role in the battle now about to be fought.

Earlier the Duke of Perth had persuaded him not to go back to Inverness to bring forward the desperately needed supplies, but to send Captain Robert Shea with Fitzjames's Horse instead. On reaching the burgh Shea apparently decided to let his men get some rest before escorting the provisions back to Culloden; but then came the news of Cumberland's approach, and the inevitable call to boot and saddle.

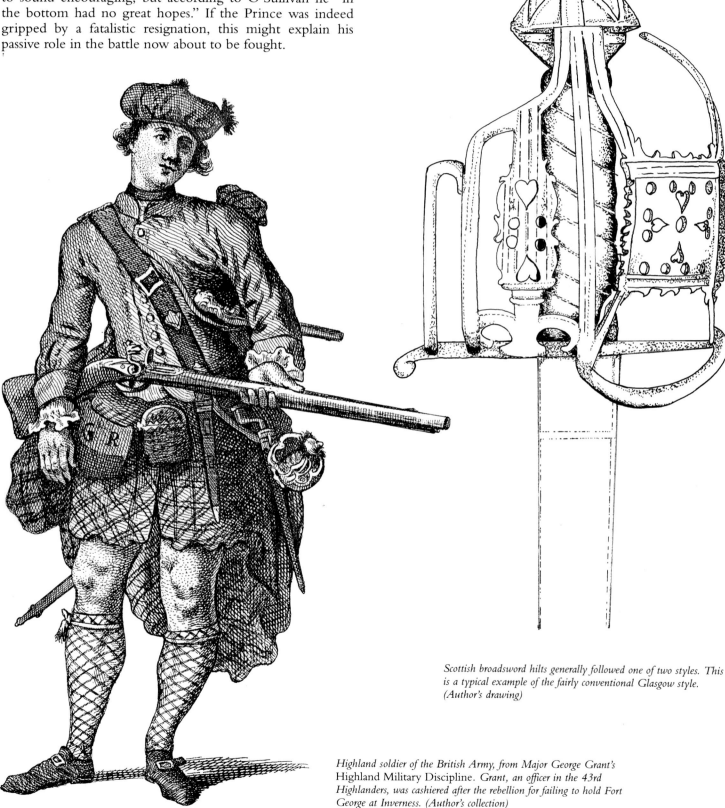

Scottish broadsword hilts generally followed one of two styles. This is a typical example of the fairly conventional Glasgow style. (Author's drawing)

Highland soldier of the British Army, from Major George Grant's Highland Military Discipline. *Grant, an officer in the 43rd Highlanders, was cashiered after the rebellion for failing to hold Fort George at Inverness. (Author's collection)*

One of those alerted by the trumpet call was Captain John-stone, who had earlier decided that he for one had done enough soldiering for one night:

"Exhausted with hunger and worn out with the excessive fatigue of the three last nights, as soon as we reached Cullo-den I turned off as fast as I could to Inverness, where, eager to recruit my strength by a little sleep, I tore off my clothes, half asleep all the while. But when I had already one leg in the bed and was on the point of stretching myself between the sheets, what was my surprise to hear the drum beat to arms and the trumpets of the picket of Fitzjames sounding the call to boot and saddle. I hurried on my clothes, my eyes half shut, and mounting a horse, instantly repaired to our army on the eminence on which we had remained for three days, and from which we now saw the English [sic] army at a distance of about two miles from us."

Undisturbed by all these alarums and excursions, the Duke of Cumberland's redcoats had toasted his twenty-fifth birth-

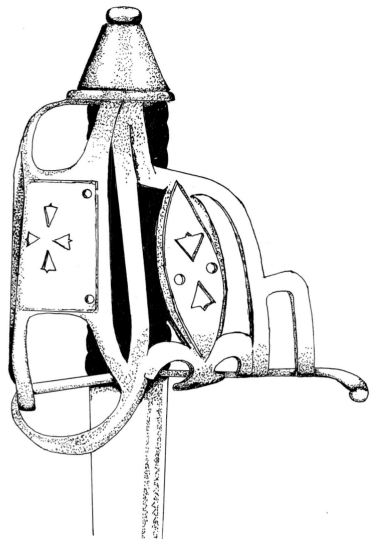

Crude Glasgow-style broadsword hilt as issued to NCOs and soldiers of regular Highland units. There was no regulation pattern for officers' swords. (Author's drawing)

A Stirling-style broadsword hilt – although the broad outlines are similar, Stirling hilts tend to be very much freer than those of the Glasgow type. (Author's drawing)

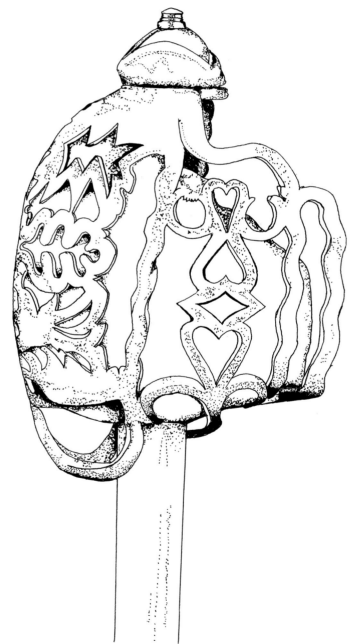

day with brandy and an extra ration of cheese before settling down to a good night's sleep. Reveille was sounded in Nairn at four o'clock on the morning of 16 April, and by a quarter past five the British army was on the march towards Inverness.

With both armies now committed to battle Cumberland saw no point in taking chances. His men halted frequently to dress their ranks and catch their breath, and marched with "arms secured and Bayonets fixed". Alexander Taylor, a private soldier in 2/Royals, considered this a very "uneasy" way of marching and no wonder: in the "Secure Arms" posi-tion a soldier carried his firelock tucked under his arm with the muzzle pointing downwards to keep it dry. With bayo-nets fixed, the men will constantly have been in danger of digging them into the rough ground as they marched.

By way of an advance guard Lieutenant Colonel John Campbell, younger of Mamore, commanding the Argyll Militia and a couple of companies of Loudon's 64th High-landers, was sent ahead with his own men and a troop of Kingston's Light Horse "to Examine the Roads and woods in the way." Not far beyond Kilravock they caught sight of the Jacobites, halted, and sent back word to Cumberland.

The thin mists of the previous night had given way to a cold, raw, gusting wind out of the north-east, bringing occa-sional "smart" showers of rain and sleet. When Cumberland

Donald Cameron of Locheil (1695-1748). His support at the outset of the rebellion was crucial in encouraging waverers to "come out" for the Prince. Despite being wounded at Culloden he at first attempted to keep his men in the field, but eventually fled to France. (Private Scottish collection)

heard from Mamore that the rebels were assembling up on top of the moor rather than in front of Culloden House he swung his army to the south in order to keep the wind at his back as he approached.

As the moor rose above them like a hill, Cumberland and his staff could see the rebels posted amongst some old walls and houses, and with no further need for them the units of the advance guard were recalled. Mamore was then ordered to divide his Highlanders between the right and left flanks

until the battle actually began, at which point he was to retire to guard the baggage. This was a sensible precaution, since only the regulars of the 64th Highlanders wore red jackets and the others might easily be mistaken for enemies in the confusion of battle. In the event, some of them were to see a good deal more fighting than they had bargained for.

When the army finally deployed at the foot of the moor Mamore, on the right, dutifully led his men back to the wagon lines, but on the left Major General Humphrey Bland ordered Captain Colin Campbell of Ballimore to stand fast with his half-battalion. Ahead of them lay the high dry-stone walls of the Culwhiniac enclosures, and if Bland's troopers were to get through them he was going to need infantry support.

CHAPTER SEVEN

Culloden Moor

Culloden Moor lies on the top of a broad ridge running roughly from east to west, some five miles to the east of Inverness. Although it might more properly be considered a part of the much larger Drummossie Moor, it has always been referred to as Culloden because it formed a part of that estate.

The ground was then, and to some extent still is, rather wet, being dotted about with a number of springs, and their attendant streams and boggy hollows. Generally speaking most of these springs are of no great military significance, although one of them, now known as the Well of the Dead – lying just behind the position occupied on 16 April by Barrell's Regiment – has earned a certain notoriety and usefully marks the site of the fiercest fighting.

Otherwise, save for some minor undulations, dips and hollows the ground, although rough, is fairly even in character, and falls down by some ten metres from the rebel right at Culchunaig, to Barrell's position just in front of Old Leanach. This slight declivity may have provided a little impetus to the Highland charge when it came; but there is also a much more noticeable fall of some 20 metres in a north-westerly direction from Culchunaig to the rebel left by the Culloden Park walls. From this point, across to the right flank of the Government line in front of the modern Hollybush Farm, the lie of the land is almost flat. Both the present condition of the ground and the testimony of survivors such as Captain James Johnstone indicate that in April 1746 this area was very wet indeed.

The ground to the north-west of the battlefield then falls away steadily down towards the shores of the Moray Firth. This open slope enabled the gentlemen of the Royal Navy to gain a reasonable view of the fight, but nothing of note occurred on it during the battle.

Towards the south-east, however, the alteration in height is quite marked. The ground on the immediate right of the rebel front line is reasonably flat out to a distance of about 300 metres; but then it plunges fairly steeply towards the gorge of the River Nairn, creating an area of dead ground, which was to be exploited during the battle by Hawley's dragoons.

According to the survey of the battlefield completed for Cumberland by Thomas Sandby on 23 April 1746, two large enclosures or parks ran down from the top of the ridge towards the river. Identified on his plan as "Culloden Parks", they are better referred here to as the Culwhiniac Parks, in order to distinguish them from the rather larger Culloden Parks stretching away from the rebel left down to the grounds of Culloden House itself.

Although most of the original six foot high dry-stone walls of the Culwhiniac Parks have now disappeared, the line of the field boundaries running from Culchunaig down to the River Nairn still coincides exactly with that shown by Sandby; while the wall separating the upper park from the lower seems from his plan to have lain along the line of the present B851 road. It is thus possible to fix their position with some precision.

It should be noted, however that the wire fence forming the present western boundary between the upper Culwhiniac Park and the moor proper actually lies some 130 metres further west than the wall did in 1746, and that the extreme western corner of the wall then lay just by the Culchunaig steading at GD 444739 (spot height 163 metres). Sandby shows no gates in the upper enclosure, but they must have existed, and in fact Finlayson shows one halfway along the western wall and another in the northern wall.

Although Government troops were able, as it turned out, to make their way through the enclosures during the battle without too much difficulty, the walls did provide some measure of protection for the Jacobite right wing. Unfortunately for them, Sandby's survey also shows another, smaller and probably ruinous partial enclosure with a roughy horse-shoe-shaped turf wall open to the north-east, lying between the two armies – or more precisely, lying between the top of the upper enclosure and the steading at Old Leanach. What appears to be a lane runs between the two enclosures, marking the boundary between the parishes of Croy and Daviot. Sticking out into the moor as prominently as it did, this Leanach enclosure was to have some interesting effects on the course of the battle.

Sandby also shows a number of "villages" or farm-touns in the vicinity of the battlefield. These small clusters of cottages and barns are chiefly useful as reference points for some of the incidents which took place during the fighting. The three most significant are Old Leanach, lying between Cumberland's first and second line on his left; Culchunaig, which marked the Jacobite right flank; and Balvraid, which is about 1000 metres to the south-west of Culchunaig and about twenty metres higher. A couple of bothies or small cottages also stood in the upper Culwhiniac Park, but neither played any part in the battle.

Much more significant was a stream which runs east from Balvraid to a point about 200 metres south of Culchunaig and there turns down, parallel with but up to 400 metres away from the Culwhiniac enclosure, to drain into the River Nairn. For much of its length this stream lies in a hollow way or re-entrant, which like the Leanach enclosure was to have a notable effect on events.

This particular "hollow way" should not be confused, however, with a shallow sunken road which wound around the Culchunaig steading and then ran close along the southern wall of the Culwhiniac enclosure down towards the river.

On the north-western side of the moor, the only notable feature shown on contemporary maps is the dry-stone wall surrounding the Culloden Parks, but this served only to define the battle-site on that side. Possibly of rather more significance was the Moor Road to Inverness from Nairn. This

Culchunaig Farm today. (Author's photograph)

This is the final, published version of Sandby's map. Note the relationship of the Jacobite front line to the enclosure walls, and the close proximity of the Leanach steading to the British army. (The Royal Collection © 1994 Her Majesty The Queen)

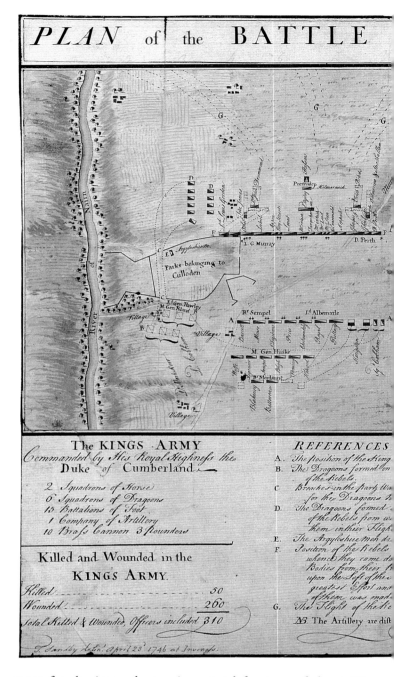

ran diagonally across the battlefield from Old Leanach to the present site of the King's Stables cottage, where it bisected the rebel front line some 400 metres from the south-east corner of the Culloden Parks. It then ran parallel to the wall of the latter at a distance of about 250 metres. The present B9006 substantially follows the line of this road, except for a recently constructed detour to the north while crossing that part of the moor now in the care of the National Trust for Scotland. The original road also appears to have swung briefly southwards around Old Leanach in order to avoid the steading and the Well of the Dead. Of itself, this unmetalled road was of no real military importance, but it does allow us to accurately pinpoint the position of Barrell's Regiment which, according to Sandby, drew up astride it; and it also appears to mark the boundary between the reasonably dry crown of the ridge and the much flatter boggy area to the north-west.

This, then, was the ground upon which, for better or for worse, the battle was to be fought. Before describing the dispositions of the opposing forces in any detail it may be helpful to first explain the simple calculation required to determine the extent of frontage occupied by each unit, and indeed the total length of the respective front lines.

The drill books of the day commonly laid down that 24in. should be allowed per file on the parade ground; but they also quite sensibly held that in the field, and particularly on rough ground such as the heather moorland of Culloden, a complete pace of 30in.(0.75 metres) should be allowed for each file.

Therefore, the first step in the calculation is to ascertain the number of bayonets in each battalion – that is, the number of privates and corporals, since officers, sergeants and drummers did not stand in the firing line itself. This figure is then divided by three – the number of ranks in which the firing line was drawn up – in order to arrive at the number of files. Multiplying this figure by 0.75 will then give the minimum frontage of the unit in metres.

However, in order to carry out the complicated platoon firing system properly it was necessary to leave a small gap between each platoon. A single pace was reckoned to be sufficient for each one; so an additional ten metres should be added to the total in order to allow for these intervals.

Thus, to take one example, Barrell's 4th Foot mustered 20 officers, 18 sergeants, 10 drummers and 325 rank and file on the morning of 16 April, drawn up in 108 files. At 0.75 metres per file this gives us a figure of 81 metres, plus ten

more for the intervals, to give a total frontage of about 90 metres for this particular battalion.

In calculating the full length of the firing lines it is also necessary to allow for rather larger intervals between the individual units. There are no hard and fast guidelines on this point, and the actual distances obviously depended to a considerable degree upon the particular tactical situation. Clear gaps are certainly shown on contemporary maps between each of Cumberland's battalions; and given that two guns were run forward through all but one of the gaps in the front line, the battalions must have been at least ten metres apart (equivalent, say, to four modern car-parking spaces), and were more than likely separated by about 20 metres.

The same set of calculations will obviously hold good for the Jacobite forces, with the possible proviso that contemporary French drill books called for units to be drawn up in four ranks rather than three while standing in line. Whether the Irish Picquets and the Royal Ecossois actually did so at Culloden is perhaps a moot point given that they were generally rather low in numbers. The Highland regiments in the

parison of Lord George Murray's obstreperous behaviour with his own serene air of confidence, but it does give something of a flavour of that frantic morning:

"Ld George comes up and tels Sullivan who had the honr to be near the Prince, yt he must change the order of battle, yt his Regimt had the right yesterday. 'But My Ld,' says Sullivan, 'there was no battle yesterday, besides it is no time to change the order of battle in the enemy's presence.' 'Laid up the men then, it's your businesse to set them in battle.' 'Yt I will My Ld,' says Sullivan 'if you'll be so good as to make them follow in their ranks, yt there may be more confusion, for there is nothing more dangerouse then to change Regimts from one ground to another in the presence of the enemy. The Prince carress'd Ld George, pray'd him to laid the men & yt he and Sullivan wou'd make them follow in their ranks. 'Gad Sr,' says Ld George swearing 'it is very hard yt my Regimt must have the right two days running' when it is he himself wou'd have it so absolutely, but 'Sr' says he again, 'the ground is not reconnoitred' 'I ask pardon,' says Sullivan 'here is as good a position as yu cou'd desir. Yu see yt Park before yu wch continues to the river with a wall six foot high, & them houses near it, wch you can fill with men, & pierce the walls, yt is on your right. Yu see this Park here is to be our left, & both in a direct ligne. If there be not ground enough, we'l mak use of the Parks & Il warrant yu My Ld' says Sullivan 'the horse wont come to yu there.' He [Murray] went off grumbling."

Although it may reasonably be doubted whether the Prince did indeed "caress" Murray after having earlier convinced himself that his Lieutenant General had betrayed him in aborting the night march, some other Jacobite officers, including John Daniel and Donald MacDonnell of Lochgarry, agreed with O'Sullivan's version of the question as to who should have the right, flatly contradicting Murray's professed reluctance to post his men there:

"The Mcdonnells had the left that day," said Lochgarry in a letter to his chief, "the Prince having agreed to give the right to Ld George and his Atholemen. Upon which Clanranald, Keppoch and I spoke to his RHs upon that subject, and begg'd he wou'd allow us our former right, but he intreated us for his sake we wou'd not dispute it, as he had already agreed to give it to Lord George and his Atholemen; and I heard HRHs say that he resented it much, and should never doe the like if he had occasion for it. Your Regt. that I had the honr to command at the battle was about 500 strong, and that same day your people of Glenmoriston were on the way to join us, on the other side of Lochness."

Whatever the truth of the matter, the Athollmen therefore took up a position close by the Culwhiniac enclosure wall. Most recent reconstructions of the battle have placed the Jacobite start line down in front of the now-vanished turf wall of the Leanach enclosure; but O'Sullivan's narrative, and the contemporary plans prepared by Lord Elcho, Thomas Sandby and John Finlayson are unanimously agreed in placing the right flank of the first line against the west corner of the upper Culwhiniac Park wall, at Culchunaig (GD444739), some 300 metres further back.

The "Park . . . to be our left, & both in a direct ligne" must therefore be the then extreme eastern corner of the Culloden Parks at GD452732, a point unequivocally confirmed by Sandby, who shows the front of the rebel army in a line with Culloden House itself, some 1600 metres further down the hill.

front line were certainly drawn up in three ranks, and the same may well have been true of those in the second.

As for the cavalry: once again, they were drawn up in three ranks, but in their case 1.5 metres should be allowed for each file – or 2.0 metres on rough ground – and an interval equivalent to the frontage of the unit was generally preserved between it and its next neighbour.

As the British army advanced to contact, the Jacobite deployment soon turned into an acrimonious muddle. It began badly enough with the uncomfortable realisation that insufficient men were actually present with their colours to draw up on the battlefield reconnoitred by O'Sullivan on the 14th. This must have been the flat area of moorland at GD4575, for Colonel Ker records that they "were drawn up a mile westward [of it], with a stone enclosure on the right of the first line, and the second at a proper distance behind; after having reconnoitred the inclosure, which ran down to the Water of Nairn on the right, so that no body of men could pass without throwing down the wall."

O'Sullivan's narrative is undoubtedly partisan in its com-

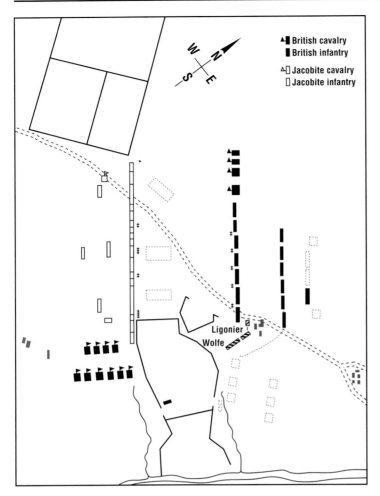

Ligonier
Wolfe
British cavalry
British infantry
Jacobite cavalry
Jacobite infantry

Culloden Moor: a composite plan based upon Sandby's preliminary sketches, which differ in certain respects from the eventual published version. Unit designations are omitted for clarity; but note the distribution of the Jacobite guns, and the redeployment of Wolfe's and Ligonier's Regiments – their second position being indicated by solid hatching. Also of considerable interest is the fact that Sandby shows Hawley's dragoons crossing a stream (barely visible on the published plan) before deploying to face the Jacobite right. The various units indicated only by broken lines are the original positions of the British cavalry, and the three Highland "attack columns" respectively.

Establishing the actual strength of the Jacobite army which drew up on Culloden Moor on the morning of 16 April is extremely difficult. In the first place, no morning states or other returns of the type available for the British army appear to have survived, although they certainly existed at one time. Consequently recourse has to be made to the figures quoted on Thomas Sandby's map, and in various Jacobite memoirs. The reliability of these figures is only to be guessed at, and even at best they tend to be expressed in round numbers. Nor is it immediately clear in most cases whether they include officers. However, since regular army returns commonly restrict their totals of effectives to private soldiers and corporals, it would not be unreasonable to suppose that the Jacobites did the same. Perhaps significantly, Thomas Sandby adds 1,674 officers and volunteers to his regimental totals, and this figure is sufficiently precise as to suggest that he may have been working from captured Jacobite documents.

Nevertheless, although Sandby's figures are probably the most accurate estimates of the nominal strength of each unit, there can be no guarantee that all of the men "carried on the books" were actually standing in the ranks when the battle began. All of the Jacobite accounts mention that large numbers of men fell out on the march back from the aborted night attack on Nairn and lay sleeping in odd corners. Some, like Captain Johnstone, even went all the way back to Inverness; and in all Lord George Murray reckoned that as many as 2,000 men were missing, though many, perhaps nearly all of them, had returned before the fighting actually began.

With that substantial proviso in mind, some kind of estimate can be made of the fighting strength of each regiment. On the right of the army stood Lord George Murray's Atholl Brigade: three battalions from Perthshire totalling, according to Sandby, some 500 men. Allowing for the necessary intervals between each battalion they should therefore have taken up a frontage of 140 metres. Next to the left came 650 Camerons under Donald Cameron of Locheil, taking up another 165 metres; then 150 men of the Appin battalion under Charles Stewart of Ardshiel; 500 Frasers, under Lieutenant Colonel Charles Fraser of Inverallochy; another 500 men in Lady McIntosh's Regiment; 150 Deeside men under Colonel Francis Farquharson of Monaltrie; 182 men of the combined battalion of MacLeans and MacLachlans; 100 Chisholms; 200 MacDonalds under Keppoch; another 200 in Clanranald's Regiment; and 500 in Glengarry's, led by Donald MacDonnell of Lochgarry – Sandby and Elcho both give a rather lower figure for the latter, but as Lochgarry actually commanded the battalion that day his account is presumably trustworthy.

All in all, there ought to have been something in the region of 3,832 rank and file in the front line, occupying, if we assume ten-metre gaps between each battalion, a total frontage of about 1000 metres. Since the distance between the west corner of the upper Culwhiniac Park and the then east corner of the Culloden Park wall is exactly 1100 metres, there was obviously ample room for them to do so. But then Lord George Murray decided that, come what may, he had to move his brigade.

The problem, of course, was the Leanach enclosure, which jutted out by 50 or 60 metres into the moor, forming an obvious barrier to his intended line of advance. He at first proposed to take his men forward and have it demolished, but on reflection he resolved, rather more practically, to simply advance a short distance down the moor, and to form his three battalions into column – six men deep instead of three – in order to be able to manoeuvre around the obstacle more easily when the time came. He may also have reasoned that since the turf walls masked his brigade from Cumberland's guns, it was quite safe to do so; but in fact this move resulted in a considerable dislocation of the rest of the front line.

As we have seen, the MacDonald Brigade on the far left was already unhappy at being denied the post of honour on the right, and although its officers had eventually been persuaded to accept the situation they were now in no mood to conform to Lord George Murray's advance. This was not simply a matter of pique. After all, if they were to move forward they would lose the protection of the park walls, and their left flank would be "in the air".

The Duke of Perth, commanding the left wing, tried his best to persuade them to move, but his efforts were unavailing, and in consequence the front line was thrown askew. Moreover it was now stretching itself along a rather longer frontage, and to his astonishment O'Sullivan heard a cry of "Close, close!". Upon investigation he found "intervals, yt he had not seen before."

While Murray rode across to the left wing to discuss this unexpected problem with Perth, and if possible to get the MacDonalds to move forward, O'Sullivan hurriedly turned to the second line "for there was no time to be lost, to fill up the vacansy yt was left (by Ld George's changement) . . .".

In fact there was no properly formed second line as such; there were far too few men standing in it for that. Instead there were simply three bodies, or brigades, standing behind the left, right and centre and formed in column in order to provide a mobile reserve for the front line units.

On the far left stood one of the two regular battalions, the Irish Picquets, while the other, the Royal Ecossois led by Lord Lewis Drummond, appears to have been over on the right. The Marquis D'Eguilles later put the strength of the two battalions at 302 and 350 rank and file respectively; but these figures may be a little too high, as 42 men of the Régiment Berwick are included in the envoy's total for the Picquets although O'Sullivan recorded in his memoir that he had only 25 men of that regiment with him on the 14th. On the other hand Captain James Hay, paymaster of the Royal Ecossois, later told his interrogators in Edinburgh Castle that the "French" contingent at Culloden had comprised 600-700 men; and by the very nature of his job he, if anyone, ought to have known. If the artillerymen and the 131 troopers of Fitzjames's Horse were not included in his estimate, he would appear to be broadly in agreement with D'Eguilles.

More or less behind the centre stood five more units under Colonel John Roy Stuart: the Duke of Perth's Regiment, John Gordon of Glenbucket's, John Roy Stuart's, Lord Kilmarnock's Footguards (probably commanded by James Crichton of Auchengoul), and Lord Ogilvy's two-battalion regiment. The latter apparently mustered some 500 men

between them, while Perth's had 300 men and the others about 200 apiece.

O'Sullivan afterwards recalled that he then brought forward Perth's and Strathallan's regiments to fill up the gaps in the front line, but he was evidently mistaken as to the latter corps, since it was a cavalry unit, and other accounts suggest that the second battalion brought forward was actually John Roy Stuart's.

Behind the far right wing were the two battalions of Lord Lewis Gordon's Regiment (he himself does not appear to have been present at Culloden): James Moir of Stonywood's 200 Aberdeen men, and 300 men from Strathbogie led by John Gordon of Avochie.

One last infantry unit which remains unaccounted for is Sir Alexander Bannerman's Regiment, a small corps of about 120 men from the Mearns. It might perhaps have been logical for them to have been brigaded with Lord Lewis Gordon's battalions, but there is no evidence of this, and

*Culloden battlefield, **Map 1**. This and the succeeding maps are based primarily upon the Ordnance Survey, Sandby's and Finlayson's plans, with additional details, particularly as to the movements of some of the smaller Jacobite units, taken from contemporary narratives. All units are shown to scale.*

Both armies are here arrayed in their initial positions. Artillery pieces are omitted from the map for the sake of clarity (see the composite of Sandby's sketches), but two cannon were placed just forward of the intervals between each of the battalions in the British front line. The eleven rebel guns were scattered rather more haphazardly across their front. The circular feature lying north of the road immediately behind Barrell's Regiment is the Well of the Dead. The Jacobite infantry units in the second line are deployed in column; and the small cavalry unit identified as "Shea" is the Prince's escort troop, commanded by Captain Shea of Fitzjames's Horse.

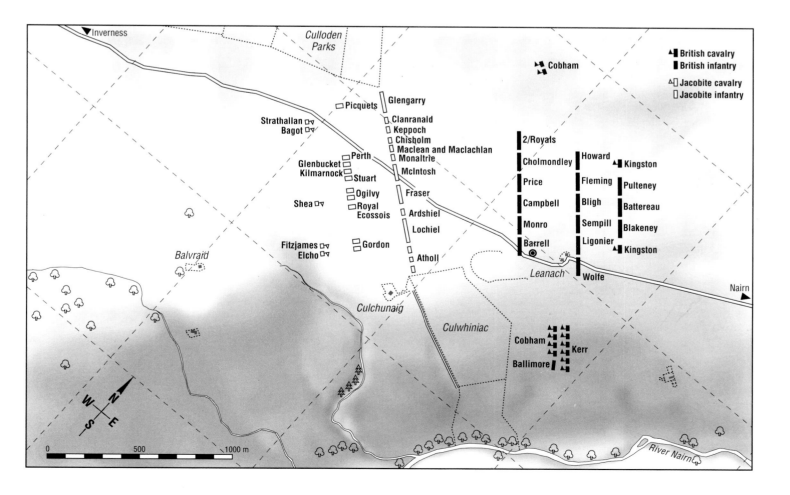

Old Leanach cottage viewed from the north. This is the only surviving building of a cluster depicted by Sandby lying between the first and second lines on the British left flank. In one of his plans Ligonier's Regiment is shown divided in two wings in order to clear it during "Daddy" Huske's counter-attack. (Author's photograph)

The same cottage viewed from the south. The deepest rebel penetration was halted at this point, about 80 metres short of it. (Author's photograph)

since a number of its survivors apparently made their way northwards after the battle it may reasonably be conjectured that the unit stood somewhere in the left rear of the army, as shown on Elcho's map.

Standing a short distance behind these reserve brigades were a scattering of small cavalry units. According to the plan in Lord Elcho's journal Bagot's Hussars were standing on the left and Lord Strathallan's Perthshire squadron was on the right; in fact both units seem to have been posted over on the left, although John Daniel mentions that the Hussars were temporarily moved into the centre during the battle – a point which is confirmed by Thomas Sandby, who also shows Lord Strathallan's men on the left.

Lord Elcho's own troop of Lifeguards and most of the mounted element of Fitzjames's Horse, led by Captains William Bagot and William Brennan, were brigaded together on the right, while a small troop of 16 men of the latter corps under Captain Robert Shea acted as an escort for Prince Charles Edward.

It is not clear, however, where what remained of Lord Balmerino's troop of Lifeguards was posted. Indeed, there is little evidence that they fought at Culloden as a distinct unit. John Daniel served with the troop and in fact carried its standard – "a curious fine standard with this motto 'Britons Strike Home' that was taken at Falkirk from Gardiner's Dragoons." He was for a time with the Prince's party, and states that 16 of Balmerino's troop acted as his escort. This would suggest that the escort was actually comprised of equal numbers of both Irish and Scottish troopers. Sandby's plan, however, shows Balmerino's to be brigaded with Lord Strathallan's men on the left.

In numbers, at least, the Jacobite cavalry were rather less than impressive. Sandby allows 70 troopers for the combined squadron formed by Balmerino and Strathallan, and another 70 for Fitzjames's Horse. If the 16 men riding escort for the Prince are added to this figure, then some 45 men of the regiment remain unaccounted for out of D'Eguilles' total of 131. Presumably they were serving on foot with the Irish Picquets. Lord Elcho's troop of Lifeguards mustered, by his own account, about 30 men; but Sandby's figure of 26 Hussars sounds rather more convincing than Elcho's 60, since the troop had mustered only 70 men when it was first raised in 1745.

As for the Jacobite guns, most published plans show 12 pieces of artillery grouped in either two or three batteries. No two sets of plans appear to agree on their distribution, but Sandby, who was undoubtedly in the best position to know, shows an irregular scatter of cannon spread most of the way along the rebel front line. Three are on the right, five planted more or less in the centre, and three more stand towards the left. This makes a total of eleven guns in all, and usefully corresponds with the report of eleven 3lb. cannon having been captured. A twelfth gun, shown by Sandby as emplaced on the extreme left of the rebel front line by the east corner of the Culloden Park at GD452732, was only brought up with some difficulty by French gunners after the battle had begun; it was probably one of the light "Swedish" 4lb. cannon.

*   *   *

On the other side of the moor, meanwhile, the British army's deployment was proceeding in a more professional manner.

They had marched from Nairn that morning in four columns. Three of the columns, each comprising five battalions ranked one behind the other, formed the main body while most of the cavalry formed a fourth column on the left, and the artillery and baggage marched behind the right hand column. The order of march was thus:

Horse	Monro	Price	Royals
	Barrell	Campbell	Cholmondley
	Ligonier	Bligh	Howard
	Wolfe	Sempill	Fleming
	Blakeney	Battereau	Pulteney

In order to deploy for action, the first, third and fifth battalions in each column stood fast, while the second and fourth battalions moved out and forward to fall in on the left of the first and third. By this means the army quickly and smoothly formed itself into two lines each with six battalions, and a reserve of three battalions in the third line.

This pre-planned deployment appears to have been practised as soon as they were formed up outside Nairn, and again on their first sighting the rebel army. As it was soon evident, however, that the Jacobites had no immediate intention of attacking, they formed their columns again and the advance was resumed until they reached the bottom of Culloden Moor.

There they eventually drew up with the left hand battalion of the front line – Barrell's 4th Foot – standing astride the moor road with their backs to the Well of the Dead, while the left of the second line – Wolfe's 8th – stood just south of the road and behind the steading at Old Leanach.

One squadron (two troops) of Cobham's 10th Dragoons was reconnoitring to the north; but the rest of the regiment, together with Kerr's 11th Dragoons, making ten troops in all, remained on the left wing and moved down towards the River Nairn with Ballimore's half-battalion of Highlanders. Kingston's Horse, being rather weaker, drew up in two squadrons one on either flank of the reserve battalions in the third infantry line.

At this point Lord George Murray began his "changement". This was wrongly interpreted by Cumberland and his staff as a general shifting towards the rebel right, an understandable error given that it was partially masked by the Leanach enclosure. Nevertheless, the apparent axis of any rebel advance certainly appeared to have shifted towards the army's right; and as that flank was already rather open, and liable to be outflanked by the rather longer rebel front line, Cumberland responded by prolonging his own first and second lines. This was accomplished by calling Kingston's Horse and two battalions – Pulteney's and Battereau's – forward from Brigadier Mordaunt's third line, leaving only Blakeney's 27th Foot standing in the rear. To the relief of all

Map 2. Only the necessary unit names are repeated here. Lord George Murray has taken the right wing forward and formed his Atholl Brigade in column in order to be able to clear the Leanach enclosure. This has dislocated the rest of the line, and three battalions – Perth's, Glenbucket's and John Roy Stuart's – are being brought forward from the second line to fill the gaps. As a result the axis of any rebel advance now appears to have shifted somewhat towards Cumberland's right, and he is beginning to respond to this apparent threat by ordering Kingston's Horse up from the reserve.

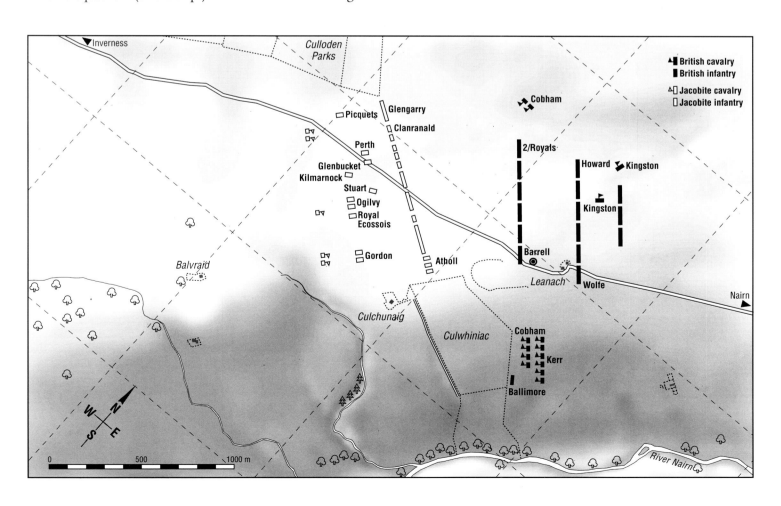

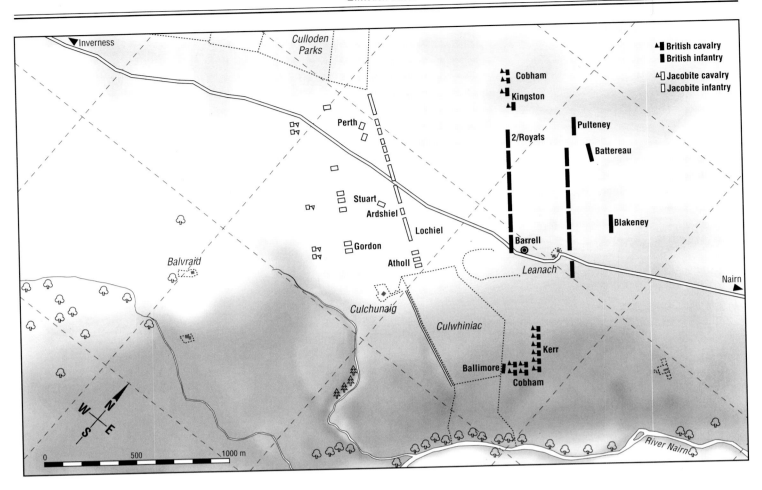

Map 3. *The re-adjustment of the initial dispositions continues on both sides, with Pulteney's and Battereau's regiments moving up from the reserve to prolong Cumberland's first and second lines respectively. On the British army's left, Ballimore's half-battalion of Highlanders and the two regular dragoon regiments are approaching the wall of the upper Culwhiniac enclosure.*

concerned, the missing squadron of Cobham's Dragoons also turned up at about the same time and formed with Kingston's on the right.

From left to right, therefore, the Government front line comprised: Barrell's 4th Foot, with 325 rank and file exclusive of officers, sergeants and drummers; Monro's 37th, with 426 rank and file; Campbell's 21st Royal North British Fusiliers, mustering 358; Price's 14th, with 304; Cholmondley's 34th, with 399; the 2/Royals, with 401; and Pulteney's 13th, with 410 men.

This gave Cumberland a total of 2,623 "bayonets" and 461 NCOs and officers in his front line, under the immediate command of Brigadier Lord Sempill. Allowing intervals of 20 metres between each battalion, it must therefore have occupied a total frontage of some 845 metres.

Kingston's Light Horse mustered 211 officers and men. It is not known precisely how many men belonged to Cobham's detachment, but as the whole regiment had 276 officers and men present at Culloden it would be reasonable to assign say 90 of them to this flank. Between them the cavalry will therefore have prolonged the front line by about another 200 metres.

The second line, commanded by Major General John Huske, comprised from left to right: Wolfe's 8th Foot, 324 rank and file; Ligonier's 59th, with 325; Sempill's 25th (Edin-

burgh), with 420; Bligh's 20th, with 412; Fleming's 36th, with 350; Howard's 3rd (Buffs), with 413; and Battereau's 62nd, with 354 – making 2,598 bayonets and 407 NCOs and officers in all, on a frontage of some 840 metres.

Mordaunt's remaining battalion, Blakeney's 27th (Inniskilling) standing in the rear, had 300 rank and file, 20 officers, 24 sergeants and 12 drummers.

Down by the river on the far left Generals Hawley and Bland had the other four troops of Cobham's Dragoons, a company of Loudon's 64th Highlanders and three companies of Argyllshire Militia in their front line, with all six troops of Kerr's Dragoons in support.

Assuming that there were 186 officers and men of Cobham's present on this flank, the 300 officers and men of Kerr's will have given Hawley something like 486 cavalry. As for the Highlanders, one British account quotes a figure of 140 men, but it is not at all clear whether this related to the Argyllshire men alone or also included Ballimore's regulars; there could have been as many as 200 in the ad hoc battalion. The remaining Highlanders stayed with the baggage which had been parked by the large flat stone, traditionally associated with Cumberland, near Leanach.

Cumberland's Commander Royal Artillery at Culloden was Lieutenant Colonel William Belford, who had under him Captain-Lieutenant John Godwin's detachment of the Royal Artillery manning ten 3lb. cannon – placed in pairs in the intervals between the original six battalions of the front line – and six Coehorn mortars placed in two batteries, one at each end of the second line. As for the gunners, examination of the surviving payrolls for Godwin's detachment shows that there were 106 NCOs, gunners and matrosses present, exclusive of ten officers and a number of volunteers.

CHAPTER EIGHT

Dragoons and Cannonades

Although the beginning of most battles is conventionally timed from the moment when the big guns open
fire, the battle of Culloden really started much earlier
than this – arguably, some time before the deployment of
both armies was fully completed. For the sake of clarity
over the developing movements on the extreme left of the
Government line it is perhaps best to abandon here strict
chronological sequence, and to follow these awhile independently of events in the centre of the battlefield.

As we have seen, despite Cumberland's orders that they
were to retire and guard the baggage during the action, a
half-battalion of Highlanders were scouting ahead of the two
dragoon regiments on the left wing. They comprised three
companies of the Argyllshire Militia, led by Captain John
Campbell of Achnaba, Captain Dugald Campbell of
Achrossan and a Captain Duncan Campbell, together with a
company of Loudon's 64th Highlanders led by Captain
Colin Campbell of Ballimore. As a regular officer Ballimore
had seniority, and therefore took command of the ad hoc
battalion.

Now they found themselves confronted by the six foot
high dry-stone walls of the Culwhiniac enclosures, running
all the way down from the top of the moor to the Water of
Nairn. There was no way around them.

"From this place," wrote Captain Duncan Campbell, who
led a company of militiamen from Glenorchy, "we sent to
acquaint General Bland that the Horse could go further. He
came up to the ground and ordered us to pull down the wall,
which was done so that the squadron could march abreast."

Hawley's aide de camp, Major James Wolfe, wrote the next
day that the two cavalry regiments had originally been posted
on the left simply because that was where the ground was
firmest. Peering over the wall, Humphrey Bland could now
see that the Culwhiniac enclosure appeared to be undefended, and thereupon sent to his immediate superior,
General Hawley, advising him that it appeared to be possible
to outflank the rebels by moving through it. By the time
Hawley and Wolfe came down to have a look for themselves
the wall had been successfully breached and Hawley
promptly took charge of the operation, ordering Ballimore's
Highlanders to break through the far wall as well.

According to a man named Lachlan Forbes, whose father
took on the tenancy of Culchunaig in the year after the
battle, the enclosure walls were broken some distance down
the hill below the steading, "quite as far or further down than
the park houses". Both Sandby and Finlayson show the
breaches cut in the upper enclosure walls a little above the
boundary with the lower enclosure – in other words, just a
few metres uphill of the present B851 road.

At this stage Hawley's prospects must have seemed quite
promising. If the rebel right flank could indeed be turned,
not only would their defeat be doubly assured, but there was
also every prospect that it would then be possible for him to
cut off any line of retreat across the Nairn to the hills beyond,
thus forcing them back on Inverness.

The imminent possibility that the Government army
might attempt something of this sort had not been overlooked by the Jacobite leaders, as John Cameron, later an
officer in Lord Ogilvy's French regiment, recalled:

"This made Locheil send to Lord George Murray, then on
the left with the Duke of Perth, to tell him of the danger.
Lord George Murray (whom I heard formerly say the park
would be of great service to prevent our being flanked) on
this took a narrower view of it and sent three gentlemen,
viz., Colonel Sullivan, John Roy Stewart, and Ker of Grydan
to view it down to the Water of Nairn. At their return they
said it was impossible for any horse to come by that way."

Nevertheless, Murray remained worried about it and
forcefully taxed O'Sullivan on the subject as the rebels took
up their positions on the moor. Notwithstanding the Irish-
man's inevitable and rather heavy-handed implication that he
had once again to calm down an over-excitable colleague,
O'Sullivan's account of the discussion is, as usual, instructive:

"The enemy appeared plainly in battle array, upon two
lignes, and in very good order, as they were near the river
side Ld George thought they were coming to take him in
flank 'Never fear yt My Ld' says Sullivan 'They cant come
between yu & the river, unless they break down the walls of
those two parks yt are between yu & them, but yu can
prevent them, but as I am sure they will not, & yt certainly
their left will be against this park where yr right is. My advise
wou'd be, as all their horse is at their left, yt we shou'd make
a breach in this wall, & set in this park Stonywood & the
other Regimt yt is in Colloum behind yu, who will take
their horse in flank, without fearing in the least yt they can
come upon him. If the horse is taken in flanck, with such a
wall as this between them, & those yt fires on 'em Il answer
they'd break. If they are once broak, the foot will not stand,
besides my Ld, if yu march to the enemy, as yu have no other
party to take, for I suppose yu don't pretend to measure yr
fire wth the English troops; in case yu are repulsed those
same troops yt you'l set in the park will protect yr retreat."

Despite O'Sullivan's tendency to condescension, his initial
reasoning was quite sound. The north wall was indeed
quickly breached by Ballimore's Highlanders thus allowing
both them and the dragoons to penetrate into the upper
enclosure; but as O'Sullivan's earlier reconnaisance had
shown, the banks of the river were sufficiently steep to
prevent the dragoons from making use of the dead ground in
the lower enclosure. Their advance was therefore made along
the bottom of the upper one, visible to the Jacobite right
wing and in particular in sight of those regiments which he
had posted to deal with the threat; James Moir of Stonywood's and John Gordon of Avochie's battalions of Lord
Lewis Gordon's Regiment.

Unfortunately neither of these battalions were actually

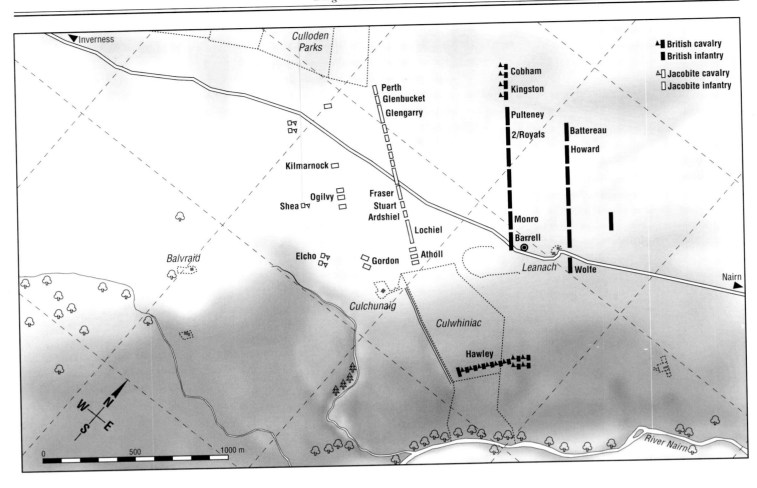

Map 4. *The rebel front line has completed its redeployment, with Perth's and Glenbucket's regiments now standing on the left flank, and John Roy Stuart's men standing on the left of Ardshiel's Stewarts. Realising that British cavalry have penetrated the upper Culwhiniac enclosure, O'Sullivan has ordered the two battalions of Lord Lewis Gordon's Regiment to take up a blocking position by the Culchunaig steading.*

posted inside the enclosure, as O'Sullivan had originally recommended. George Innes, a local Presbyterian minister (who appears to have been surprisingly well acquainted with more rebels than might be thought prudent for a man in his position), subsequently wrote that: "Some of Stoniewood's regiment assert, that Colonel Baggot had advised to post them along the outside of that park-dyke, which probably would have prevented a good deal of mischief these Campbells and dragoons afterwards did; but that Lord George Murray would not hear of it." Consequently O'Sullivan posted them instead in what he calls a "hollow way", advising Stonywood, "a very brave man", to keep a sentry posted on the top to warn of any approaching trouble.

Murray may well have feared that if Stonywood's and Avochie's battalions were actually posted inside the enclosure they might easily be cut off, or at least be unable to support the main battle on the moor. Whatever his reasoning, however, the predictable result was that Ballimore's Highlanders and the two regiments of dragoons following them were able to traverse the enclosure unmolested and then proceed to break through the south wall. Harry Ker of Graden rather sourly commented on the fact that they did so, "without receiving one shot from the two battalions that were placed to observe their motions"; but as the Aberdeenshire men were standing too far up the hill and on the wrong

side of the wall to intervene, this criticism is rather unfair. Whether Ballimore's men would still have been willing or able to break down the walls under fire from men posted inside the enclosure is questionable; but in any case the dragoons were soon to be adequately checked on the other side of the enclosure.

The scene of the eventual encounter is variously described as a "hollow way" or a "ditch", and is invariably identified in secondary sources as what the local historian Peter Anderson described in his useful, if now forgotten 1867 survey as the "hollow of some little depth bending around the Culchunaig farm steading on the east and north."

Although he made a brave attempt at it, however, Anderson, like many historians, was unfamiliar with the extent of frontage required by individual regiments and, as a consequence, of the true extent of the battlefield. By confining his study to the immediate area of the steadings at Culchunaig and Old Leanach he failed to appreciate that there are in fact two quite different "ditches".

The first is the sunken lane which he mistakenly identified as the site of the fighting. After looping around Culchunaig, this extends downwards from the steading towards the River Nairn, running contiguously for most of its length with the Culwhiniac enclosure wall itself. It would certainly appear to be the "hollow way" in which Stonywood's Aberdeen men were initially ordered by O'Sullivan to take cover; but there is also another, and very much more substantial cut lying rather further to the south-west.

Although most modern accounts of the battle place the ensuing action around the first of these, and more specifically in the area between the Culchunaig steading and the Culwhiniac enclosure walls, the gap between the two features is only a hundred metres wide, allowing barely sufficient room for the deployment of the two troops making up a single squadron of dragoons.

Given the obvious impossibility of squeezing no fewer than ten troops of dragoons into such a confined space, let alone the four infantry battalions and the two troops of cavalry opposing them, the fighting must actually have taken place not around Culchunaig itself; but instead across the prominent re-entrant running roughly from east to west at GD4407354-7, more or less on a line stretching between Culchunaig and the much larger steading at Balvraid, about 500 metres to the south-west. This re-entrant is formed by a stream which later turns south to run more or less parallel with the Culwhiniac enclosure wall, at a distance varying from about 400 to 500 metres. Lord Elcho, who himself took part in this particular action, simply refers to it as "a ditch which Cover'd the right wing" – a description which clearly fits this substantial re-entrant rather better than the shallow stretch of sunken road over by Culchunaig.

Captain Duncan Campbell of the Argyll Militia stated that: "The Dragoons went out and formed at a distance, facing the rebels"; Finlayson's map also shows them swinging very wide of the Culwhiniac enclosure; while Thomas Sandby appears to clinch the matter by depicting the dragoons taking up their battle positions on the far side of the stream.

Had General Hawley been obliging enough to simply come storming up the hillside within the enclosure, Stonywood's and Avochie's battalions, securely lining the outside of the wall, ought to have been quite sufficient to stop him; but once the dragoons instead broke through the south wall and passed out on to the open slopes beyond, the threat to the Jacobite right wing and rear assumed a much greater significance.

The two Aberdeenshire battalions were swung around to face downhill, and Lord George Murray responded to the threat by ordering Lord Ogilvy's two battalions to march across from the reserve behind the centre of the first line; "and to Lord Ogilvie said, he hoped and doubted not but he would acquit himself as usual."

Meanwhile Hawley, having breached the south wall and as yet unable to see the full strength of the defensive line being thrown together against him, was making what turned out to be a serious blunder. Instead of keeping Ballimore's Highlanders with him, he now ordered them to remain within the

The remains of the Culwhiniac wall at about the point where Ballimore's half-battalion broke through, below Culchunaig. It was of course rather higher in 1746. (Author's photograph)

Culwhiniac enclosure. Why he did this is not entirely clear. Unable to see properly over the crest, he may simply have wished to secure his own flank; or perhaps he considered it safer to leave them mewed up in the enclosure where, lacking uniforms, they were less likely to be mistaken for rebels than on the open moor. Whether he also ordered them to harass the rebel right wing, or whether Ballimore decided to do so on his own initiative is also unclear; Duncan Campbell specifically states that "we were ordered to attack them", but it would anyway have made sense for them to properly secure the enclosure. Whatever Hawley's reasoning, however, it was a decision he soon had cause to regret. (One is tempted to wonder whether there was any exchange of opinions on the point between the bad-tempered commander and his immediate subordinate; Humphrey Bland was, after all, one of the most influential theoreticians in the Army.)

There is similarly some doubt as to where Ballimore's Highlanders eventually came into action, but the evidence points to their remaining within the relative safety of the Culwhiniac enclosure. A scatter of graves lying just inside the former Leanach enclosure wall are traditionally identified as being those of some of the Campbells who broke the park walls; but only six men of Ballimore's company of the 64th (besides himself), and none of the militiamen, were returned as killed. (One of the graves was subsequently found to contain the skeleton of a tall man who had been shot through the head, but while it is tempting to speculate that it might have been Ballimore himself, he is in fact recorded as having been buried in Inverness.)

Moreover, for the Highland companies to have ended up in the Leanach enclosure they must either have retraced their steps back through the breaches, or else passed through the gate in the upper part of the enclosure and crossed the lane separating the two. This is certainly not impossible, but Duncan Campbell makes no mention of it, and both Sandby's and Finlayson's maps show them to have remained within the Culwhiniac enclosure.

Campbell of Airds' account clearly relates that: "Ballimore & his command were ordered to break down them Dykes & make way for the Horse which they Executed, & taking advantage of the Second Dyke as a Breast Work fire Closs on a strong party of the Rebels that then formed the Right, Composed of Lord John Drummond's men being part of the Enemy's second line."

Although Airds watched the battle from the comparative safety of the baggage train (and by the sound of it must have obtained a good view from the top of a wagon), he evidently got the details of this particular struggle from those of his comrades who were there. Just as importantly, the fact that they engaged Drummond's Royal Ecossois rather than the Highlanders in the rebel front line also points to their having stayed within the Culwhiniac enclosure.

This, however, is to anticipate matters a little. Having thus rather short-sightedly dispensed with their infantry support, Generals Hawley and Bland crossed the stream and swung northwards. Deploying into two lines, the dragoons then found their path blocked by the Jacobite regiments hastily establishing themselves along the line of the re-entrant between Culchunaig and Balvraid. Included amongst these now were two small cavalry units; and James Maxwell of Kirkconnel, Major of Elcho's Lifeguards, recorded that:

"Lord George ordered the Guards and Fitzjames's horse quite to the right flank, and made them form opposite to the

Trooper, 10th (Cobham's) Dragoons, 1742. Red coat; light yellow facings, waistcoat and breeches. Saddle housings are yellow, with mixed red, green and black embroidery. The cloak is red lined yellow, rolled with the red outermost. The housings had almost certainly changed by 1746 to those shown on Colour Plate D. (NMS)

dragoons, upon the brink of a hollow way; the ascent was somewhat steep on both sides, so that neither could pass safely in presence of the other."

Lord Elcho's own narrative suggests that only his own Lifeguards and 70 troopers of Fitzjames's Horse, supported by John Gordon of Avochie's Regiment, stood between the dragoons and the moor. Had this been so it is unlikely that General Hawley's two dragoon regiments would have been held up for so long, and in fact three other Jacobite infantry units can be firmly identified as having taken part in the action.

Since Elcho is at least gracious enough to acknowledge the assistance of Avochie's men it may safely be assumed that they eventually stood next to the cavalry, while James Moir of Stonywood, with the second (Aberdeen) battalion of Lord Lewis Gordon's Regiment, stood on Avochie's left. Lord Ogilvy's two battalions appear from contemporary maps to have ended up on the right of the cavalry (see Maps 7 to 12 in the following chapters).

This was something more formidable than either Hawley or Bland had bargained for. In order to force their way across such an obstacle they would almost certainly require some kind of infantry support. Ballimore's men might have been able to provide it, had they not been left behind in the enclosure and probably by now beyond recall.

This predicament was presumably what James Wolfe was obliquely referring to when he wrote to his father, General Edward Wolfe, in October 1751: "I have surveyed the field of Culloden with great exactness, and find room for a military criticism. . . . The actors shine in the world too high and bright to be eclipsed; but it is plain they don't borrow much of their glory from their performance on that occasion. . . . You would not have left those ruffians the only possible means of conquest, nor suffer multitudes to go off unhurt with the power to destroy."

As Wolfe was serving on General Hawley's staff at Culloden he must have taken part in this particular action; and writing the next day to a friend, Major Henry Delabene, he noted that once in position, Hawley halted the brigade and made no attempt to get across the re-entrant until the sound of firing begin to slacken over on the moor.

It is to that central confrontation that we must now return, and to the first exchange of fire.

*　　　*　　　*

Afterwards there was considerable disagreement amongst the participants as to what time that firing actually began. Some, such as Edward Linn of the Royal Scots Fusiliers put it as early as "a little past 12 of the clock", as did a volunteer named Michael Hughes who was standing in the ranks of Bligh's 20th Foot. Andrew Lumisden, one of the Prince's ser-

The "hollow way" or sunken lane running parallel with and outside the southern wall of the Culwhiniac enclosure; Culchunaig is in the background. Stonywood's regiment and the Lifeguards sheltered here early in the battle, but it evidently provided no obstacle to Hawley's dragoons. (Author's photograph)

vants, put it as late as two o'clock; and Private Alexander Taylor of the 2/Royals reckoned that it began half an hour later still.

Wolfe himself thought that it was "about one in the afternoon", as did Captain Alexander Stewart of Kerr's Dragoons, and the volunteer James Ray, who was also waiting with Cobham's to cross the re-entrant. Both of them, of course may simply have heard Wolfe call out the time – he was given to such gestures – but at least two other officers anonymously quoted in contemporary newspapers put it at "about a quarter after one" and "about five past one" respectively. On the Jacobite side, Sir Robert Strange also thought that the cannonading began at about one o'clock.

On balance, therefore, it seems to have begun at around about one o'clock; and there is at any rate complete agreement that it was the rebels who fired the first shot, and almost certainly fired it in response to one of the Duke of Cumberland's aides, Lord Bury, being sent forward to reconnoitre what looked like a battery half hidden by the projecting Leanach enclosure.

It was indeed a battery; and from it John Finlayson, a cartographer and mathematic instrument maker from Edin-

Map 5. *British cavalry are about to break through the second enclosure wall. Realising that Lord Lewis Gordon's Regiment may not be able to hold them off, Lord George Murray has now ordered the two battalions of Lord Ogilvy's Regiment over to the right as well. Fitzjames's Horse and Elcho's troop of Lifeguards are also moving to meet the threat. On the moor itself the bombardment has probably begun.*

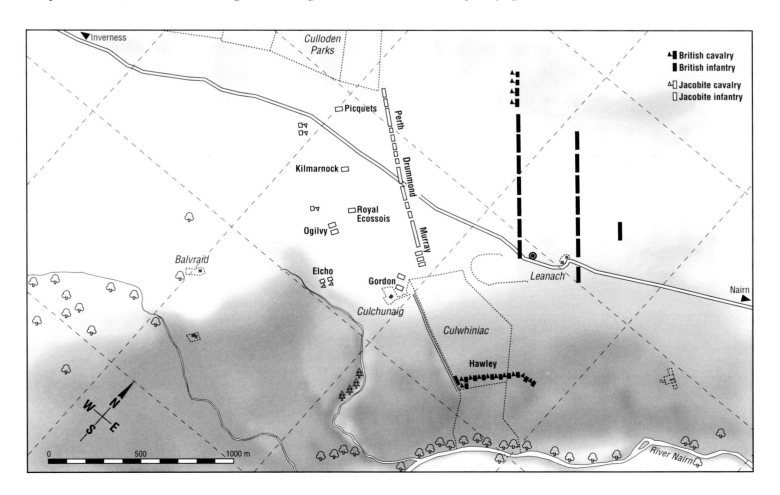

burgh, proceeded to demonstrate the fact to the young officer in the clearest possible manner.

It is commonplace to dismiss the effect of the Jacobite bombardment as being wholly insignificant, and some secondary sources refer to only a couple or so men being killed by it. There is no doubt that the exchange was somewhat uneven, but the rebel guns were not wholly ineffective. It is in fact possible to arrive at a reasonably accurate picture of the damage which was done by the Jacobite artillery. Battereau's 62nd Foot had an officer, Captain Carter, and two men wounded; Howard's 3rd (Buffs) had one man killed and two others wounded, one of whom must subsequently have died as only Private Charles Appleton, disabled in the right hand, survived to claim a pension. Fleming's 36th had six men wounded. All three regiments stood in the second line and were not subsequently engaged by Jacobite infantry, so all of these casualties can confidently be attributed to artillery fire.

Another unit standing in the second line – Bligh's 20th Foot – suffered more casualties than any other except Barrell's and Monro's. It lost four men killed outright, and Lieutenant Trapaud and 16 men wounded, of whom only five (Corporal George Fowkes, and Privates John Byram, Robert Spence, Archibald Smith and Joseph Simmers) actually appear to have survived. It is likely, however, that most of these casualties were sustained during General Huske's counter-attack against the Jacobite right wing, for not all of the injuries recorded were artillery related.

Other British units in the middle of the front line suffered a similar level of casualties, but it is impossible to distinguish between those who might have hit by artillery shot and those men who were killed or wounded during the later infantry battle. Price's 14th Foot, for example, returned Captain Alexander Grossett killed and Captain Andrew Simpson and eight men wounded. Grossett was in fact murdered by a Jacobite prisoner while serving on the staff and was not standing with his regiment at the time; but apart from Captain Simpson, only two of the men returned as wounded appear to have survived the experience – Richard Dennison, who lost his left leg, and John Ross, wounded in the right ankle. The 21st (Fusiliers) similarly returned seven men as wounded, of whom only one, Fusilier Mark Whitehead, afterwards claimed a pension on the strength of a wound in the right thigh.

It is very much more difficult to assess the scale of the casualties inflicted on the Jacobites by the British guns. Captain Godwin began firing a few moments after Finlayson – the Reverend George Innes's account says that the Jacobite guns fired twice in a ripple across their front before Godwin replied – but just as few witnesses were afterwards able to agree as to just when the firing began, there is similar disagreement over the duration of that firing.

Still-current stories that the clansmen were subjected to a hail of cannon-shot for upwards of 30 minutes seem to have originated in second hand reports from Edinburgh, and were subsequently inflated by Home's classic but flawed *History*, for none of those who actually stood on Culloden Moor record that it lasted any great time at all.

James Wolfe, who as a staff officer was supposed to take especial note of such things, reckoned afterwards that: "The cannon in particular made them very uneasy, and after firing a quarter of an hour obliged them to change their situation and move forward . . ."

Some witnesses thought that even less time elapsed before the commencement of the rebel assault. Joseph Yorke, one of the Duke of Cumberland's aides, wrote that: "When our cannon had fired about two rounds, I could plainly perceive that the rebels fluctuated extremely, and could not remain long in the position they were then in without running away or coming down upon us; and according as I thought, in two or three minutes they broke from the centre in three large bodies. . . ."

There is in fact a general consensus on the part of British officers that the attack was made within a very short time of Godwin's opening fire. Perhaps the most precise estimate came from Campbell of Airds, safely back with the baggage and therefore able to view the exchange with a certain degree of detachment, who opined that "The Cannonading Continued about nine minutes". To have quoted a time so precise as nine minutes Airds must have been consulting his watch. Wolfe was presumably doing the same, but he was listening to rather than watching the battle on the moor when he claimed that the guns were firing for upwards of fifteen minutes. Possibly, therefore, Airds may have been referring only to the time which elapsed between the first shot being fired and beginning of the infantry attack – or even, as we shall see, to the firing during that attack.

Nevertheless, if a period of some 15 minutes of uninterrupted bombardment by the British guns is accepted – which might allow for some of those rounds actually fired into the rebels as they advanced – it is then possible to arrive at a rough estimate of the likely number of casualties which might have been suffered by the Jacobites during this early phase of the battle.

In the first place, although Captain Godwin's men were obviously better trained than their rebel counterparts, their target was at best over 500 metres away, and perhaps as much as 700 metres on the right of the field – ranges which approached the effective limits of the little 3lb. cannon. Theoretically each of these guns could be loaded and fired twice

Royal Artillery at Roermond, 1748, by David Morier. The mounted officer pointing to his right is thought to be Lieutenant Colonel William Belford, Cumberland's commander of artillery at Culloden. (The Royal Collection © 1994 Her Majesty The Queen)

Map 6. *The British cavalry are now clear of the Culwhiniac enclosure but are still moving south-west in a column, in order to avoid the defended Culchunaig steading. Ballimore's Highlanders are moving up through the enclosure. The remaining regiments of the Jacobite second line have been consolidated ready for the assault.*

a minute with ball, and if each round struck home on the rebel front line it could have killed or maimed three or even six men in its passage through the ranks.

It can safely be assumed, however, that for so long as the rebels remained standing at the top of the moor Godwin will have prudently opted for a slower but steadier rhythm of fire, maintaining a rate more like one round per minute from each of his ten guns. If the cannonade was maintained for between nine and 15 minutes, then between 90 and 150 roundshot will have been fired in that time.

Statistical analysis of the hits recorded as having been achieved by similar artillery pieces at around this range in contemporary tests, and of the casualties inflicted during some other 18th century battles, suggests that in ideal conditions some 40% of these rounds might have struck their target, which is assumed in this case to be the rebel front line. Unfortunately for the British gunners, the conditions at Culloden were far from ideal.

A cannonball was not expected to impact directly upon the target, but was aimed in such a way as to strike the ground somewhere in front of it, and then to skip or bounce towards and through the body of men chosen to receive it. Naturally the cannonball performed best if the ground was firm and level; but at Culloden the moorland was soft and far from flat – balls might very easily bury themselves on impact or be deflected from their course. Attempting to drop them nearer to the intended target might be more effective, but would involve a greater risk of simply plunging the ball straight into the earth due to the consequently steeper trajectory. Again, Godwin's crews were firing uphill, which made it even more difficult to judge the required trajectory. Finally, a tendency for the recoil to dig the gun trails into the soft

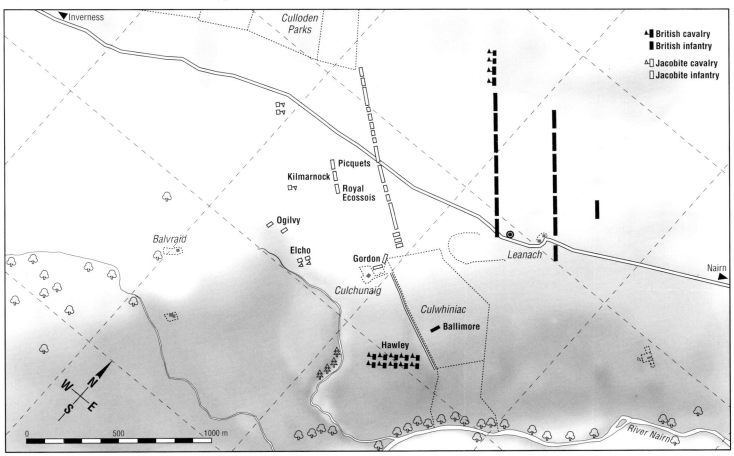

ground with each discharge will also have hampered consistent shooting, especially on the British army's right wing — which was in any case furthest away from the enemy.

There was also the problem of the resultant powder-smoke. It is commonly held to be disadvantageous to fire black-powder weapons directly into the wind, since the thick white smoke will then be blown back into the firers' faces. Such discomfort, although real (especially for infantrymen), is actually quite transient. The real problem arises when the wind is blowing from behind, as it was for Godwin's gunners: while the smoke is blown clear of the guns and their crews, it is blown away towards the target, thus obscuring it and making it almost impossible for the gunners to watch and correct the fall of their shot.

There is certainly ample testimony on the Jacobite side that a fair proportion of the rounds being fired at them were in fact going over the heads of the clansmen standing in the front line; George Innes, for one, wrote unequivocally that "many of the balls went quite over the Highland lines".

To their considerable dismay, some of them landed around the Prince and his party. He himself afterwards claimed to have had a horse shot from under him (it survived), and a groom named Thomas Ca was killed while leading a sumpter horse just a few yards away. Sir Robert Strange, a volunteer in the Lifeguards, witnessed the result of another of these "overs"; he also implies that only a short time elapsed before the clans went forward:

"One Austin, a very worthy, pleasant fellow, stood on my left; he rode a fine mare which he was accustomed to call his lady. He perceived her give a sudden shriek, and, on looking around him called out, 'Alas, I have lost my lady!' One of her hind legs was shot and hanging by the skin. He had instantly dismounted and, endeavouring to push her out of the ranks, she came to the ground. He took his gun and pistols out of the holsters, stepped forward, joined the Foot but was never more heard of. The Prince, observing this disagreeable position, and without answering any end whatever, ordered us down to a covered way, which was a little towards our right, and where we were less annoyed by the Duke's cannon; he himself with his aides-de-camp, rode along the line towards the right, animating the soldiers. The guards had scarce been a minute or two in this position, when the small arms began from the Duke's army, and kept up a constant fire; that instant, as it were, one of the aides-de-camp returned, and desired us to join the Prince."

The "covered way" in question was presumably the sunken lane over by Culchunaig, rather than the re-entrant defended against Hawley's dragoons, since no mention is made of them. John Daniel, who was carrying the troop's standard, was fated not to reach it, for: "We had not proceeded far, when I was ordered back, lest the sight of my standard going off, might induce others to follow . . . coming to the place I was on before, and seeing it covered with the dead bodies of many of the Hussars who at the time of our leaving had occupied it. . . ."

In view of the frequency with which rounds were evidently flying over the heads of the front-line units, therefore, Captain Godwin will have been doing pretty well to average just one casualty amongst the front line regiments for each round fired. In other words, over the period of between nine and 15 minutes during which the bombardment probably lasted, his men are unlikely to have inflicted more than between 90 and 150 casualties of all kinds on the rebels.

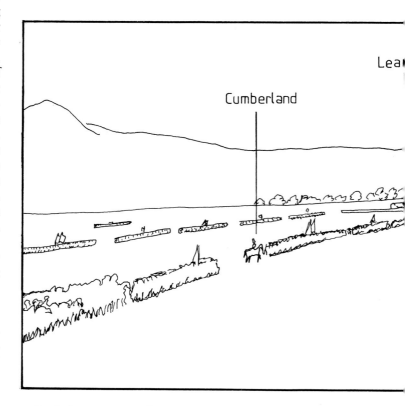

Such losses were of course serious enough in themselves; but although a detached statistical view can hardly have been expected of those men actually maimed or killed by the incoming rounds, they hardly represent the bloody massacre so often pictured by later writers. There is certainly no question, as at least one has suggested, of as many as a third of the men in some regiments being killed or incapacitated at this time. In any case, the location and the distribution of the

The battle as seen by an eyewitness, Thomas Sandby. The three figures in the foreground have presumably been added for dramatic effect. (The Royal Collection © 1994 Her Majesty The Queen)

Key to Sandby's sketch. The cavalry unit on the extreme left is identified by Sandby as Kingston's Horse. (Author)

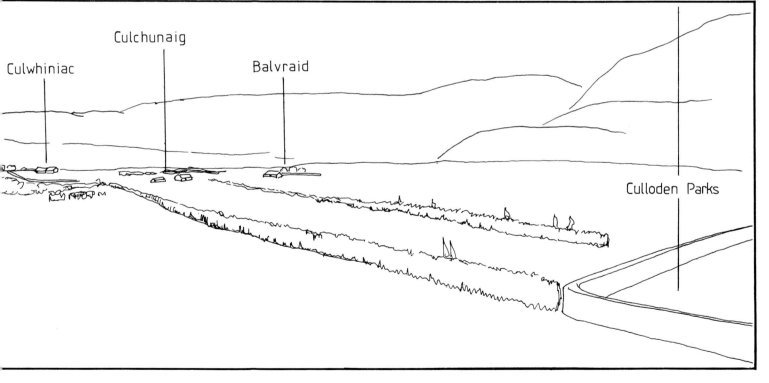

Culwhiniac

Culchunaig

Balvraid

Culloden Parks

known mass graves clearly points to most of the rebel casualties having been suffered after the charge began rather than while they were still standing at the top of the moor.

Nevertheless, if the physical effects of the Royal Artillery's bombardment have largely been overestimated by earlier historians, there is no doubting its psychological effects on the Jacobites.

Although the experience was always extremely unpleasant, regular troops could, to a certain degree, be "hardened" to artillery fire, and indeed veteran units might even take a kind of perverse pride in their ability to soak up relatively heavy casualties. The various units in the Jacobite front line, however, had never been exposed to artillery fire like this before, and their reaction to the bombardment was out of all proportion to the casualties actually being suffered. Soon they were loudly clamouring to be led forward.

CHAPTER NINE

Like Hungry Wolves

Whilst the bombardment which the Jacobites now faced while standing on top of the moor was therefore neither unduly prolonged, nor as destructive as most secondary sources tend to suggest, it was undoubtedly a new and unsettling experience for the clansmen. Realising that they could not be expected to stand it for much longer, Lord George Murray urgently sent back to the Prince for formal permission to launch the attack.

Charles Edward had in fact given the necessary orders twice already. On the first occasion, while the armies were still deploying, Murray had refused to move on the understandable grounds that insufficient men had been assembled at that time – McNab of Inishewan thought there were only 1,700 men in the front line; and a second, later injunction to advance had been lost when the messenger, Captain Lachlan MacLachlan of Inishconel, was decapitated by a cannon-ball. Although Murray had not acted upon the first order for perfectly good reasons, it seems strange that he did not interpret it as carte-blanche to advance as soon as he did feel able to do so. Why he felt it necessary to expose his men to the British artillery fire until once more receiving express instructions to attack must remain a mystery. At any rate, in time Ker of Graden duly received the required permission, and as "the right was further advanced than the left, Colonel Ker went to the left, and ordered the Duke of Perth, who commanded there, to begin the attack, and rode along the line till he came to the right, where Lord George Murray was, who attacked, at the head of the Atholl men."

The Highland charge had begun; but within a few short minutes a number of factors saw it begin to degenerate into a bloody shambles.

On past experience the Jacobite line might have been expected to advance at a fairly steady pace until within musket-shot of the Government front line – say to a distance of about 50 metres – before firing a single volley, and then quickly rushing in under the smoke. As it was, finding themselves on the receiving end of sustained artillery fire bred such an impatience amongst the Highlanders that when the order was given they immediately surged forward at a run. Many of the front rank men simply broke ranks, threw down their firelocks without discharging them, and drew their swords at once – something which is, interestingly enough, depicted by both Sandby in his watercolour, and by Morier in his painting of Cumberland at Culloden.

To Joseph Yorke and some of the other eyewitnesses in the Government ranks the rebels certainly appeared to be coming down upon them in a disorderly manner: "They broke from the centre in three large bodies, like wedges, and moved forward. At first they made a feint, as if they would come down upon our right, but seeing that wing so well covered, and imagining that they might surround the left because they saw no cavalry to cover it, two of these wedges bore down immediately upon Barrell's and Monroes regiments, which formed the left of the first line; and after firing very irregularly at a considerable distance, they rushed furiously in upon them, thinking to carry all before them, as they had done on former occasions."

Sandby too, in one of the preliminary sketches for his published map, depicts three deep columns: but Finlayson, perhaps rather more convincingly, shows the front line units retaining something of their formation until they were about halfway down the moor. It seems unlikely that the rebels would have begun to coalesce into columns or wedges (through a process more akin to fluid dynamics than to any evolution found in drill-books) until after they had delivered their fire.

Whether they succeeded in maintaining their formation or not, the Highlanders probably looked sufficiently intimidating to the waiting regulars; but then both the guns of the Royal Artillery, and the terrain itself, took a hand. Once the rebels came down within 300 metres of the British front line Captain Godwin's men stopped firing roundshot and loaded with canister (or grapeshot, as it was popularly known).

The effect was devastating. A running man encumbered with all his clothing, equipment and weapons can reasonably be expected to cover some 300 metres of fairly level ground in just 90 seconds. During that time, however, an artilleryman could also fire off about four rounds of canister, or perhaps even five if he was lucky and had a crack guncrew; and a single round of 3lb. canister would probably succeed in knocking over an average of eight to ten men. In the words of Michael Hughes, a volunteer who was standing in the ranks of Bligh's Regiment: "Their lines were formed so thick and deep that the grapeshot made open lanes quite through them, the men dropping down by wholesale."

Thus, allowing for the likelihood of the four guns positioned in the gaps between 2/Royals, Cholmondley's and Price's regiments being aimed rather towards the rebel left, the six guns firing on the Jacobite centre and right divisions were now, very suddenly, killing or wounding something in the region of 40 to 60 men every 25 seconds. Moreover, given that the Atholl Brigade under Lord George Murray was at first partially sheltered by the turf wall of the Leanach enclosure, it is probable that all six guns were in fact firing on Locheil's Camerons and part of the centre division, commanded by Lord John Drummond.

The storm of canister fire had two immediate effects. The rebel officers were accustomed to leading from the front, and therefore suffered disproportionately high casualties – amongst them Locheil himself, who went down with both ankles shattered. Secondly, Lady MacIntosh's men in the centre then appear to have shied away from the guns, inclining towards their right instead of coming straight on. It has also been plausibly suggested that this swerve was in large part caused by the simultaneous discovery that an expanse of wet, boggy ground lay between the moor road and the

British front line. Then again, blinded by the thick white powder-smoke blown into their faces, they may simply have followed the road itself. Be that as it may, most of the Highlanders in the centre certainly appear to have finished up following the line of the road. In so doing they not only lost contact with the units on their immediate left which, for reasons which will shortly be examined, were already hanging back; but they also came into violent collision with Murray's right hand division, which was simultaneously moving out to its left in order to clear the protruding Leanach enclosure wall.

What followed is as easily imagined as described; and all the time Godwin's artillerymen continued firing into the tightly packed and now disordered mass of men. The immediate result was that by the time the Highlanders eventually reached the British line they may well have received five or even six discharges of canister, and consequently will presumably have suffered anything up to about 300 casualties without inflicting a single one in turn.

Moreover, once they came within about 50 metres of the Government front line this particular body of clansmen were also fired into by at least three infantry battalions: Barrell's, Monro's, and Campbell's Scots Fusiliers. Between them these regiments mustered some 1,100 bayonets; and an unnamed Corporal in Monro's related that they had time to fire one round apiece as the Highlanders came in, and then gave them another in their teeth:

"... they began to play their Cannon very briskly upon us; but as soon as we saw them pointed, we stoop'd down, and the Balls flew over our Heads. Two Pieces of our Cannon play'd from our Left to their Right, which kill'd many of them, and made their whole body determine to come down

Culloden Moor today, looking towards the position of the Jacobite front line. Barrell's Regiment was posted slightly forward of the small pond and it may have contributed to their splitting in two as they fell back. (Author)

Map 7. *On the moor the Jacobite infantry have commenced their attack – divisional commanders are identified. Perth's regiments on the left are lagging behind in boggy ground, while the second line units are drifting over to the right. Behind the Jacobite right the British cavalry under Hawley are crossing the stream and beginning to climb up towards the moor.*

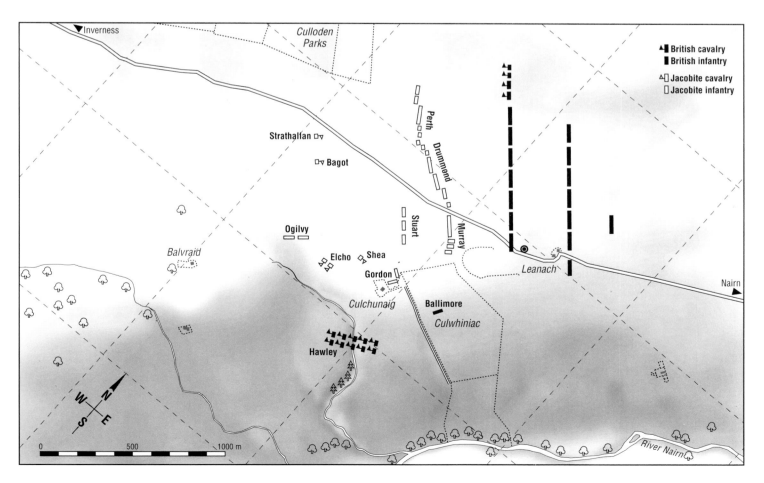

upon our Left, compos'd of Barrel's, Monro's, and the Scots Fusiliers. When we saw them coming towards us in great Haste and Fury, we fired at about 50 Yards Distance, which made hundreds Fall; notwithstanding which, they were so numerous, that they still advanced, and were almost upon us before we had loaden again. We immediately gave them another full fire. . . ."

He may not have been exaggerating, for even allowing for as little as one round in every ten fired at point blank range actually finding its billet (as contemporary tests would suggest), the initial ripple of platoon volleys alone will have dropped about a hundred of the oncoming Jacobites. Notwithstanding these terrible losses the Highlanders – those on the right and in the centre at least – pressed forwards, running across the front of Campbell's and Monro's to fall

upon the 325 rank and file of Barrell's Regiment standing on the extreme left of the British front line.

In the past such an onslaught might have been expected to send the redcoats streaming to the rear in panic-stricken flight; but there was general agreement amongst most correspondents afterwards that Barrell's at first bravely stood their ground. Once again, there were a number of reasons for this. There appears to have been a general feeling amongst the ranks of the British army that they had to get a grip of themselves and stand up to the "terrible boasting highlanders"; and Barrell's, one of the few regiments to see off their attackers at Falkirk, were able to face the present onslaught with more confidence than most. Another factor which cannot be ignored is that the sight of their would-be attackers blundering into and tripping over each other under a storm of fire

Although now enclosed within the expanded Culwhiniac park, the flat ground viewed here from the site of the Leanach enclosure was part of the moor in 1746; the Jacobite right wing advanced across it towards camera, before veering into the centre to avoid the Leanach wall. (Author's photograph)

Map 8. *The rebel charge on the moor is already running into trouble as the right wing tries to clear the Leanach enclosure. The left wing continues to make slow progress. The British guns are now firing canister. On the southern edge of the moor the British cavalry begin to deploy into line, with Cobham's Dragoons in front and Kerr's in support; the Jacobites in turn begin to form a defensive line against them.*

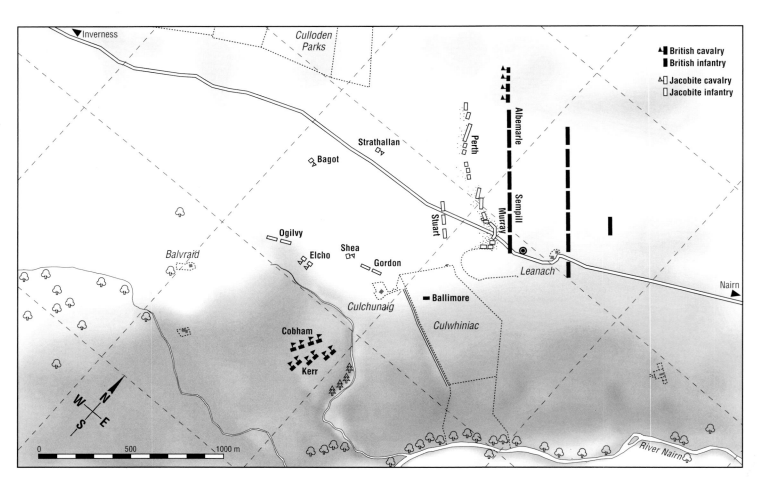

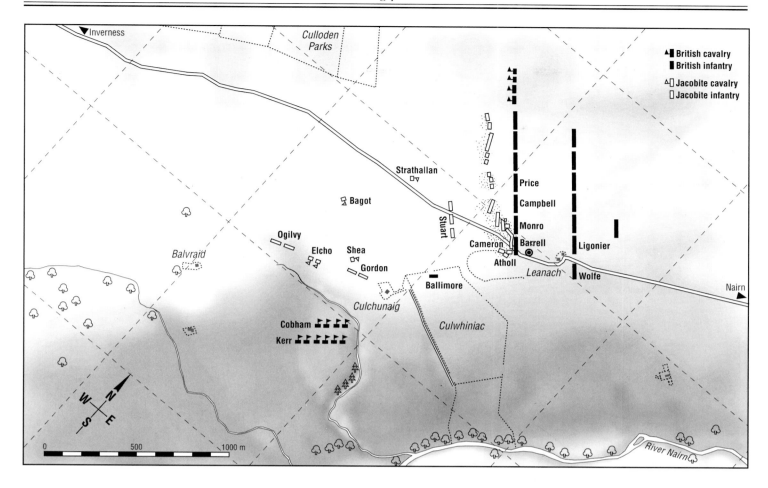

would have helped the redcoats to suppress any incipient panic.

Cumberland's own official account of the battle pays tribute to the way in which Barrell's and Monro's "fairly beat them with their bayonets: There was scarce a soldier or officer of Barrel's and that part of Monroe's which engaged, who did not kill one or two men each with their bayonets and spontoons." Another letter related "That general Barrell's regiment gained the greatest reputation imaginable in the late engagement; the best of the clans having made their strongest efforts to break them, but without effect, for the old Tangier-ines bravely repulsed those boasters, with a dreadful slaughter, and convinced them that the broad sword and target is unequal to the musket and bayonet, when in the hands of veterans, who are determined to use them – After the battle there was not a bayonet in this regiment but was either bloody or bent."

This gallant stand was more than paid for in blood; and although another correspondent paid particular tribute to the variation in their bayonet drill, he ended on a less happy note:

"The alteration was mightily little, but of the last consequence. Before this, the bayonet man attacked the sword man right fronting him: now the left hand bayonet attacked the sword fronting his next right hand man. He was then covered by the enemy's shield where open on his left, and the enemy's right open to him. This manner made an essential difference, staggered the enemy, who were not prepared to alter their way of fighting, and destroyed them in a manner rather to be conceived than told. When the rebels made some impression on Barrel's regiment its giving ground proved fatal to Lord Robert Ker; who not observing his men's giving back,

Map 9. *On the moor the Camerons have struck Barrell's Regiment and other units are following them; however, the rebel front line is now completely fragmented. To the south, with Jacobite cavalry and infantry forming on the other side of the deep re-entrant, General Hawley has slowed the advance of the British cavalry. Ballimore's Highlanders have almost reached the west wall of the Culwhiniac enclosure without encountering any opposition.*

remained a few yards forward alone. He had struck his pike into the body of a highland officer; but before he could disengage himself, was surrounded, and cut to pieces."

He was not the only one. Afterwards Barrell's returned 16 men killed outright, besides Ker, together with a further five officers and 103 men wounded. Amongst those injured was their commanding officer, Lieutenant Colonel Robert Rich, who went down with a hand sliced off and half a dozen cuts on his skull as he tried to save one of his regiment's colours. Defending the same colour, Ensign Brown was trampled underfoot and badly knocked about, but nevertheless he still managed to cling on to it. Captain John Romer, Lieutenant James Edmonds and Ensign Campbell were also wounded, though not as seriously.

The names of many of the casualties amongst the ordinary soldiers of Barrell's have also survived. We read of 37-year-old Isaac Midgely from Halifax, awarded a Chelsea pension on the strength of his being disabled in the left hand, besides receiving 14 other wounds; Ralph Jackson, a 24-year-old from Oldham, was similarly disabled in the left hand – the hand most advanced along the stock of the musket during bayonet fighting, and terribly vulnerable to a sword-cut. Samuel Hunt, an agricultural labourer from Leicestershire, was wounded in the head and right hand; David Lofty was shot through the right arm; Corporal John Griffith lost the

King's colour, Barrell's Regiment (4th Foot). Lieutenant Colonel Rich and Ensign Brown were both badly wounded while defending this colour. It shows obvious signs of damage. (On loan from the Stewart Society to the NMS)

use of his left leg, and George Webb was shot through the left arm. Most of Barrell's were Englishmen, but there were Scots among their wounded too, including John Telford from Dumfries, and John Low, a baker from Alford, who eventually got his Chelsea pension as a result of being shot through the left leg and thigh at Culloden. Again, the number of wounds to the left side of the body remind us of the redcoat's stance in hand-to-hand fighting.

Against all the Highlanders' expectations, then, Barrell's at first refused to run; but almost at once the rebels lapped around their flanks, overrunning Sergeant Edward Bristo's two guns and fatally wounding the Sergeant and five of his men:

"Making a dreadful huzza, and even crying 'Run, ye dogs!', they broke in between the grenadiers of Barrel and Monro; but these had given their fire according to the general direction, and then parried them with their screwed bayonets. The two cannon on that division were so well served, that when within two yards of them they received a full discharge of cartridge shot, which made a dreadful havoc; and those who crowded into the opening received a full fire from the centre of Bligh's regiment, which still increased the number of the slain. However, such as survived possessed themselves of the cannon, and attacked the regiments sword in hand. . . ."

It has been suggested that Barrell's men retreated into the intervals between the second line battalions, and this was no doubt what they ought to have done; but in the circumstances it seems likelier that as they jostled backwards they split into two halves in order to avoid the Well of the Dead, and thus moved outwards rather than straight back.

As they fell back, the weight of the rebel attack now fell largely upon Monro's Regiment to their immediate right; but as the anonymous Corporal records, this battalion managed rather more successfully to hold its ground: "the Front Rank charged their Bayonets Breast high, and the Center and Rear Ranks kept a continual Firing . . . the Rebels designing to break or flank us; but our fire was so hot, most of us having discharged nine Shot each, that they were disappointed."

It was one of the officers of Monro's (possibly the Adjutant, or so it may be inferred from his duty to compile the casualty list) who left what is perhaps the most spirited and vivid account of the battle in a letter written to a brother officer stationed in Newcastle Upon Tyne. Although the edited highlights as printed in the *Scots Magazine* have been quoted many times, the full text as it originally appeared in the *Newcastle Journal* is worth reproducing here:

"The Hurry I am in going to collect the number of killed and wounded, scarce allows me time to tell you, that Yesterday we had the bloodiest Battle with the Rebels that ever was fought in the Memory of Man. The same Morning we march'd from Nairn, and met the Gentry about Noon near Culloden, the Lord President's House, three Miles from hence, where we cannonaded each other for some Time; at last the Rebels advanc'd against the Left of our Line where was Barrel's Regiment, and the late Sir Robert Monro's, now Col. De Jean's. Barrel's behaved very well, but was obliged to give Way to their Torrent that bore down upon them; Their whole Force then fell upon the Left of ours where I had the Honour to command the Grenadier platoon; our Lads fought more like Devils than Men. In short we laid (to the best of my Judgement) about 1600 dead on the Spot, and finished the Affair without the Help of any other Regiment. You may judge of the Work, for I had 18 men killed and wounded in my Platoon. I thank God I escaped free, but my Coat had six balls thro' it. I must now tell you, that in the Midst of the Action the Officer that led on the Camerons call'd to me to take Quarters; which I refus'd, and bid the Rebel Scoundrel advance, he did, and fir'd at me; but providentially miss'd his Mark: I then shot him dead, and took his Pistol and Dirk, which are extreamly neat.

"The French have all surrendered Prisoners of War: We have taken their Cannon and Baggage; Lords Kilmarnock and Cromarty are among the Prisoners of Distinction. Our Regiment had ample Revenge for the Loss of our late Colonel, Sir Robert, and the rest of our Officers, whom the Scoundrels murdered in cold blood, but (as I told Lord Kilmarnock) we had ample Revenge in hors. For I can with great Truth asure you, not one that attack'd us escaped alive, for we gave no Quarters nor would accept of any. Our Reg-

Regimental colour, Barrell's Regiment (4th Foot). This all-blue colour is unusual in not having the Union flag in the canton. (On loan from the Stewart Society to the NMS)

Culloden, by Laurie and Whittle – probably the best of a plethora of engravings purporting to depict the battle. Cumberland's position is dictated by dramatic effect rather than historical accuracy; he was actually with the right of the line. Why Barrell's men (right foreground) are thrusting their bayonets with their left hands is not explained, unless it was simply done in order to depict them face on. Just visible in a bank of powder-smoke, a Highlander is shown with his hand on one of Barrell's colours. (NMS)

iment took three Stand of colours. Our Wounded are Capt. Kinnier and Lieuts.Lort and King, and Ensign Dally kill'd. I now give you Joy of the Day; and be assur'd never was a more compleat Victory gained – Our Gaols are full of them and they are brought in by Hundreds."

The exaggerations in this account are perhaps pardonable in the circumstances; but in those first few moments of the Highland attack Monro's men were falling quickly. Besides the officers, 14 men were returned as killed (just two less than in Barrell's), and 63 wounded (including John Tovey, 55 years of age and "born in the army", who had his jaw shot away).

Left to their own devices for very much longer Monro's too would have been swept aside like Barrell's; but the stubborn stand by both regiments gave "Daddy" Huske time to prepare a counter-attack. Even as Barrell's began to give way under the pressure, he swung Wolfe's and Ligonier's regiments around to the left, and brought up Sempill's and Bligh's as well to seal off the penetration.

Modern accounts of the battle, all faithfully following the version in Home's *History of the Rebellion in the Year 1745* published in 1802, state that Wolfe's Regiment was positioned just by the Leanach enclosure, slightly forward of the rest of the front line and at a right angle to it, some time before the rebel assault began. They would thus, improbably, have presented an open flank to the oncoming Highlanders; obviously worried by this, some historians have instead positioned them inside the enclosure. In point of fact every writer in the British ranks who refers to the crucial part played by Wolfe's tells how they only marched up into a flanking position *after* Barrell's were hit.

One such writer, James Wolfe, was of course on the other side of the Culwhiniac enclosures by this time with General Hawley and his dragoons; but he held a Captain's commission in Barrell's, and naturally took a great interest in what happened both to that regiment and to his father's, which was commanded that day by Lieutenant Colonel Edmund Martin:

"The Regiment [Barrell's] behaved with uncommon resolution ... they were however surrounded by superiority, and would have all been destroyed had not Col.Martin with his Regiment (the left of the 2nd line of Foot) mov'd forward to their assistance, prevented mischief, and by a well-timed fire destroyed a great number of them. ..."

Indeed, one of Sandby's preliminary sketch maps even shows Wolfe's wheeling in on the extreme left, while Ligonier's men are at the same time dividing themselves into two wings in order to be able to clear the Leanach steading to their immediate front. The matter is in any case conclusively settled by a letter from Captain-Lieutenant Thomas Ashe Lee of Wolfe's Regiment:

"Poor Barrell's regiment were sorely pressed by those desperadoes and outflanked. One stand of their colours was taken; Collonel Riches hand cutt off in their defence. ...We marched up to the enemy, and our left, outflanking them, wheeled in upon them; the whole then gave them 5 or 6 fires with vast execution, while their front had nothing left to oppose us, but their pistolls and broadswords; and fire from their center and rear, (as, by this time, they were 20 or 30 deep,) was vastly more fatal to themselves, than us."

Indeed it was. Ensign Bruce was the only casualty subsequently returned by Wolfe's Regiment, and Ligonier's had none at all, probably because the clansmen were by this time halted on the other side of the Well of the Dead. Sempill's (Edinburgh) Regiment lost one man dead and 13 more wounded, but at least some of these may have been the result

"An Incident in the Rebellion of 1745". Although the Highlanders in Morier's famous picture of Barrell's Regiment in close engagement during the battle are popularly said to have been modelled by Jacobite prisoners some time in 1746, examination of the lace pattern on the grenadiers' coats, which differs from that shown in 1742 and ca.1748, shows that it was actually painted at a rather later date. Examination of the regiment's movements would suggest a date of around 1753, which would also be consistent with the style of shoulder wings worn on the grenadiers' coats. The "Highlanders" were therefore probably simply modelled by men from the other half of the grenadier company, with costume painted in from another source. If Morier did produce a Culloden painting in 1746 it was presumably his portrait of Cumberland at the battle.

Although the rank and file, the sergeant (identified by his halberd and waist sash) and the drummers wear grenadier caps, the two officers wear hats; one carries a fusil, the other a spontoon. The front rank appear to be in the drill posture "Charge your bayonets breast high". (The Royal Collection © 1994 Her Majesty The Queen)

of artillery fire, since it is otherwise difficult to account for the bruise which was apparently so severe as to render Private John MacDonald unfit for any further service.

Bligh's, coming up on the right of Sempill's to plug the gap between them and Monro's, suffered more heavily than any other regiment in the second line, with four men killed and 16 wounded besides Lieutenant Trapaud. Once again, some of these casualties might be attributed to artillery fire but others were certainly suffered at this time; Joseph Simmers, for example, was wounded in the head, and Archibald Smith had the misfortune to be "shot in the mouth and wounded in the side."

The losses being suffered by the British regiments on the left were as nothing, however, by comparison with the terrible casualties which they were inflicting upon the clansmen facing them. Some Jacobite accounts, including Lord George Murray's, claim that having broken through Barrell's the Highlanders were fired upon by a previously unseen battery on the extreme left of the British line. No such battery existed (apart from the irrelevant Coehorn mortars); but the infantry firepower now being brought to bear on the rebels was certainly heavy enough to account for this impression.

If Barrell's, with 17 men killed and 108 wounded out of 325, are discounted as being temporarily out of action, the Jacobite column was now partially surrounded by no fewer than 1,900 men of Wolfe's, Ligonier's, Sempill's, Bligh's and Monro's regiments. Even though the front rank stood fast with charged bayonets – as described both by the Corporal of Monro's and by an officer in Wolfe's, who declared that they "plied them with continual fire from our rear and fixt bayonets in front" – that still left something like 1,200 soldiers firing into the Highlanders at point blank range.

The Corporal of Monro's reckoned that he and his comrades fired off about nine rounds apiece in the course of the battle, including the two volleys with which they saluted the rebels as they approached. In the second line, Captain Lee of Wolfe's reckoned that five or perhaps six volleys were fired by his regiment before the enemy broke. Once again, even at the most conservative estimate of one round in ten taking effect, in just two terrible minutes as many as 700 clansmen must have been killed or seriously wounded (for a solid

point-blank hit from a .75in. soft lead ball anywhere in the body or limbs would be, at least, disabling).

The true figure might well have been higher still; and it is no coincidence that the macabre outline of this great Jacobite column can still be traced today in the long slew of mass graves running westwards from the Well of the Dead.

But what of the rest of the Jacobite front line? Their inclination to their right ought to have resulted in Lady MacIntosh's Regiment and the Frasers attacking Campbell's Scots Fusiliers; but once again they shied away from the regular platoon volleys, as Private Edward Linn recorded:

"They came up very boldly & very fast all in a Cloud together, Sword in hand; they fired their pieces & flung them away, but we gave them so Warm a Reception that we kept a Continuall Closs ffireing upon them with our Small Arms; besides, 2 or 3 of our Cannon gave them a Closs with grape shott which galled them very much. . . ."

As a result the clansmen continued their slide to the right, following the Camerons and the Stewarts into the great hole

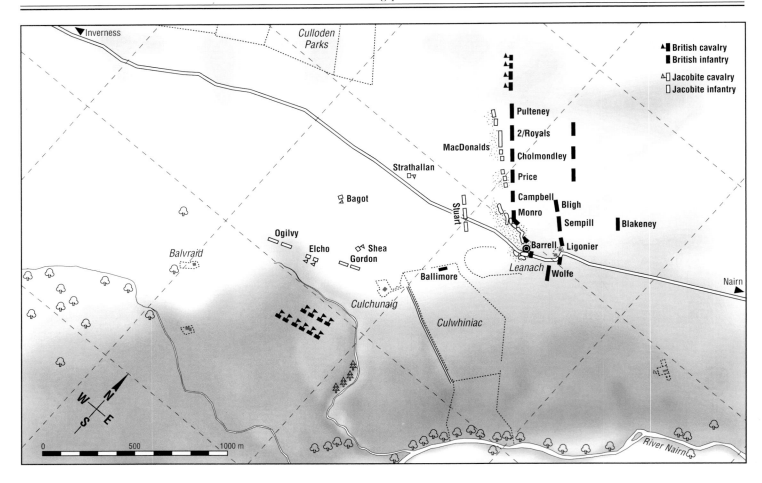

Map 10. *As Barrell's Regiment is broken in two and pushed back by the oncoming Jacobites, General Huske orders up four regiments from the second line – Bligh's, Sempill's, Ligonier's and Wolfe's. Ligonier's Regiment has to divide into two wings in order to get past the Old Leanach steading. Ballimore's Highlanders are now lining the Culwhiniac enclosure walls.*

torn in the British front line. At least one of them, Major Gillies McBean of Lady MacIntosh's Regiment, was later seen lying dead some distance beyond Sergeant Bristo's guns; but as they fought their way past Campbell's and Monro's they continued to suffer terrible casualties, and both regiments lost their commanding officers – Lieutenant Colonels Alexander McGillivray of Dunmaglas and Charles Fraser of Inverallochy. The Frasers also lost their colours, for "A blew silk colours with the Lovat arms, Sine Sanguine Victor" must have been one of the three trophies afterwards claimed by Monro's. Another was presumably the "white silk colours with the Stewart's Arms, God Save King", lost by John Roy Stuart's men; but the third remains unidentified, since those carried by both Lady MacIntosh's and the Appin Regiment are known to have been saved.

Further towards the Jacobite left it was a different story. As we have already seen, the MacDonalds were unhappy about their position on the left. On the face of it this had been a dispute over ancient precedents, though it soon became clear that they were principally concerned by the fact that this flank would be wide open if they advanced beyond the Culloden Park walls. The immediate result was that when Lord George Murray moved the right wing forward to its new jumping-off point, the front line was not only thrown askew, but large gaps opened up in it.

O'Sullivan, who whatever his faults was doing rather more

to run the army that day than Murray, partially remedied this by bringing up two regiments from the second line – Perth's and Glenbucket's – and positioning them on the extreme left of the front line, where they are depicted by Sandby. As O'Sullivan notes: "The MccDonels by this had no more the left, they were almost in the Center." They may still not have achieved the desired, if quite impractical result of being transferred to the right wing, but at least they were now no longer "demoted" to the left – and rather more importantly, Perth's and Glenbucket's regiments were now covering their flank.

Nevertheless, despite Ker of Graden's sensible precaution of passing on the order to attack to the left wing first, their subsequent advance was slow and hesitant. This was largely due to the nature of the ground which they had to cross. Captain Johnstone, who was with Glengarry's men, went so far as to say that the ground was not only marshy, but "covered with water which reached halfway up the leg." Indeed, unlike many writers both then and afterwards, he thought the bog "well chosen to protect us from the cavalry of the enemy." But despite this "advantage", and their success against Hawley's dragoons at Falkirk, the MacDonalds still appear to have been very wary of the cavalry. Thus, while the Jacobite units in the centre and on the right wing advanced at a run the MacDonalds and some of the units on their immediate right advanced much more slowly, and eventually halted altogether once they came under fire from the Government front line.

"Sullivan was at the left, with the Duke of Perth & Ld John where they had only foot over against, & of consequence most of the fire. Our left flinches, the Duke of Perth runs to Clenronald's Regimt takes their Collors & tells them from that day forth he'l call himself MccDonel if they gain

the day. Lord John & Sullivan brings up the left again."

But still they would not close. "They came running on in their wild manner," wrote Cumberland, "& upon the Right where I had placed Myself, imagining the greatest Push would be there, they came down three several Times within a Hundred Yards of our Men, firing their pistols and brandishing their Swords, but the Royals and Pulteneys hardly took their Firelocks from their shoulders. . . ."

One of those standing in the ranks of the Royals was an Ayrshire man named Alexander Taylor. Like Edward Linn of the Scots Fusiliers, he afterwards wrote to his wife, telling her of the battle and of how the Highlanders "came running upon our front line like troops of hungry wolves, and fought with intrepidity. But the thunder of our fire, and the continuation of it, began to slacken their fury. . . ."

It was the marshy ground which doomed their assault. They advanced no less bravely than their comrades on their right, and encountered the same remorseless platoon fire rippling up and down the red-coated battalions; but while Lord George Murray's men were carried forward through it by the

Captain Lord Robert Kerr, Barrell's Regiment. Yet another Scottish officer serving in a notionally English regiment, Kerr was killed while commanding the grenadier company of Barrell's at Culloden. (NMS)

Map 11. *General Huske's counter-attack is now properly under way; his regiments are coming into action and stabilising the situation on the left wing of the British army. The penetration is being sealed off. On the Jacobite left the MacDonald regiments are unable to close with the British units facing them, and the attack is beginning to falter. Realising the strength of the enemy position in front of him, Hawley has pushed his stronger regiment, Kerr's Dragoons, forward of Cobham's.*

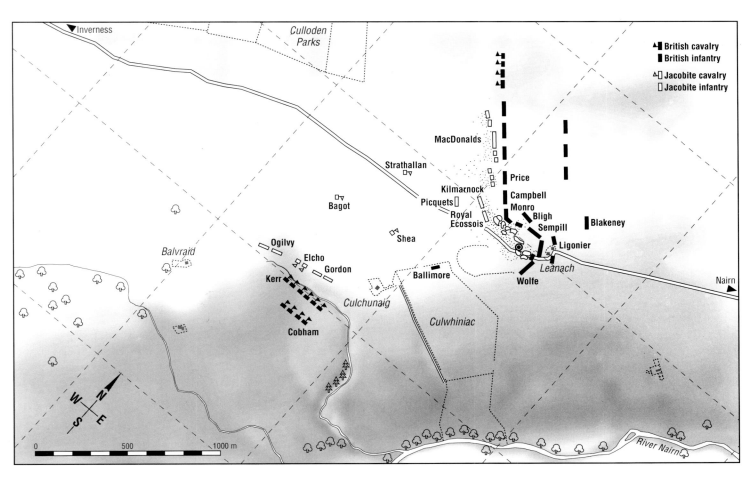

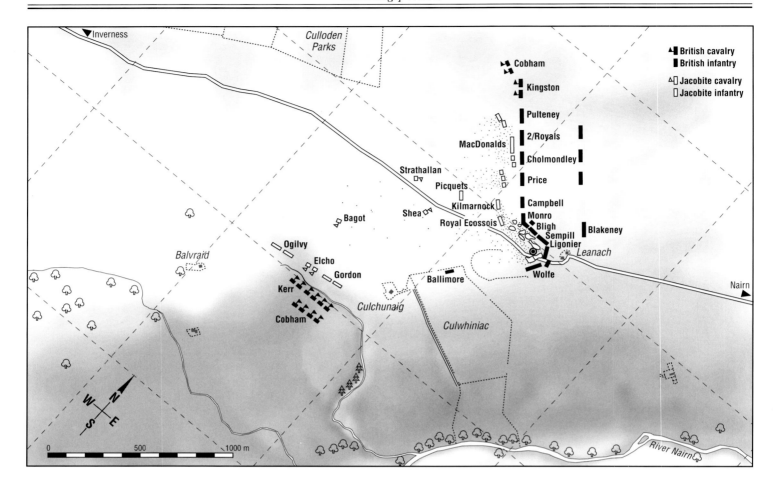

Map 12. *The Jacobite right wing is now a stationary mass, flayed by close range musketry. Where they are standing is the area in which the mass graves will be dug after the battle. Elsewhere rebel units are beginning to give way, despite Lord George Murray's bringing forward Lord Kilmarnock's men and the Royal Ecossois. At the re-entrant Hawley's dragoons are beginning to press forward; and on Cumberland's direct orders the two troops of Cobham's Dragoons on the extreme right of the British army are also beginning to move.*

sheer impetus of their charge, the Jacobite left wing was literally bogged down, and shot to pieces without ever making contact.

This is starkly evident from the casualty lists of the four regiments facing them: Pulteney's suffered no casualties at all, Cholmondley's had one man killed and two wounded, Price's had Captain Andrew Simpson and eight men wounded, while the Royals returned a mere four men wounded. (Two of them, Alexander Buchannan and John Reynolds, were both wounded in the left leg, but how John Ross came to be disabled by a rupture at Culloden must remain a minor mystery.)

Once again, by contrast, the Jacobite losses appear to have been very much higher, and the officers, leading from the front, took more than their fair share. Perth's and Glenbucket's regiments must have hung back, for few officers from either battalion are known to have been hit, although Major Robert Stewart of the former had his horse shot from under him and was pinned to the ground underneath it. Colonel Lachlan MacLachlan was slain by a cannon-ball, and all the officers in the little independent company formed by the Chisholms of Strathglas were killed or wounded; their white linen colours with the motto "Terrores Furio" were

later pulled from underneath a pile of bodies. The Farquharsons paid an even higher price, with at least 13 officers killed, and they too lost their white linen colours.

With only two cannon playing directly upon them the MacDonalds may not have been quite so badly hit, but even so Keppoch was shot down and Clanranald received an ugly head wound. Although the third commanding officer, Lochgarry, escaped unscathed many of the other MacDonald officers were killed or wounded including Captain Alexander MacDonnell of Scotus. Johnstone was standing beside him when he fell, just twenty paces short of their objective and still believing that they could yet win the battle, when to his dismay he realised that the right wing was giving way.

Lord George Murray meanwhile was trying desperately to retrieve the situation over there:

"Our men broke in upon some regiments on the enemy's left; but others came quickly up to their relief. Upon a fire from these last, and some cannon charged with cartouch shot, that they had, I think, at their second line, (for we had passed two that were on their front,) my horse plunged and reared so much, that I thought he was wounded; so quitted my stirrups, and was thrown."

Running back through the smoke he found only three battalions close enough to be of any assistance; these must have been the Royal Ecossois, Lord Kilmarnock's Footguards, and the Irish Picquets, for the other units in the second line had all been either called away to defend the threatened right flank, or else already brought forward to join the first line.

"I brought up two regiments from our second line, after this, who gave their fire; but nothing could be done – all was lost."

CHAPTER TEN

This Most Glorious Victory

The Jacobite collapse came very suddenly. The Highland right wing, still jammed tightly together in a solid, almost stationary mass, was by now almost surrounded by British infantry on three sides, and still caught in that terrible crossfire at point-blank range. They stood a few moments longer, some of them even throwing stones in their frustrated rage. Then they broke; and as they ran back their panic and despair spread rapidly along the line from right to left. All at once it seemed that the whole rebel army was in full flight – "which by the way," said Campbell of Airds, "was the pleasantest sight I ever beheld."

Meanwhile, no doubt encouraged by the evident inability or unwillingness of the Duke of Perth's division to close with the British front line, the two troops of Cobham's Dragoons on the extreme right of that line had begun, probably on their own initiative, to edge forward. Recognising that his moment had come, Cumberland at once galloped across to them and, in the words of an eyewitness, "clapping some of them on the Shoulders, [he] call'd out, 'One Brush, my Lads, for the Honour of Old Cobham'; upon which, rather like Devils than Men they broke through the Enemy's Flank, and a total Rout followed."

Both Glenbucket's and the Duke of Perth's regiments, which were supposed to be providing left flank protection for the MacDonald brigade, appear to have been hanging too far back. They were making no attempt to close with the British front line, and were thus in no position to properly screen the MacDonalds. O'Sullivan, still striving with Perth and his brother Lord John Drummond to hold the left wing together, quickly realised that the battle was lost. Contrary to what is sometimes said, Prince Charles Edward was not at that moment standing far in the rear but was actually somewhere in the centre, vainly trying to stem the swelling flow of fugitives, and O'Sullivan's chief concern now became the safety of his master:

"About this time Lord George goes off with the most part of the right, Sullivan seeing this runs to (Captain) Shea yt commanded fitz James's Squadron & tels him, 'yu see all is going to pot. Yu can be of no great succor, so before a general deroute wch will soon be, Sieze upon the Prince & take him off.' The Prince was at this time rallying the right ... the Prince wont retire notwithstanding all yt can be told him. Sullivan seeing a Regimt of horse yt was all the day upon a hight at a great distance but in a ligne wth the right of the enemy, where it was thought Cumberland was, seeing this Regimt marching towards our left, as if they were to cut our retrait runs to the Prince, and tels him yt he has no time to lose yt he'l be surrounded imediately if he does not retir 'Well,' says the Prince, 'they wont take me alive' Sullivan prays him to look behind him, & yt he'd see the whole moor cover'd wth men yt were going off & yt half the Army was away. The Prince looks, sees it is true, everybody presses him, in short he retirs but does not go far, comes back again, sees

this Regimt of horse very near on our left wch was the MccDonels, yt were quite uncovered, sees it is time & retirs."

He got clean away, probably escorted for at least a part of the way by Perth's and Glenbucket's regiments, for both got away more or less intact, and was pursued only by a variety of extremely unkind rumours as to the state of his health (the most lurid of them being that one of his buttocks had been shot away by a cannonball). Nevertheless, although both the Prince and the men belonging to his Highland regiments were now intent simply on escaping from the field, the battle was still not quite over. Despite the fact that the day was plainly lost, some Jacobite units were still fighting, and fighting hard; but they were quickly isolated in the sea of fugitives, and steadily picked off one by one.

As the Jacobite front line crumbled under the relentless volley-firing the Irish Picquets began drawing off, back

One of the melancholy cluster of grave markers on Culloden Moor; this particular one is said to identify a trench filled with the bodies of men from a mixture of clans. It was here, at the left of the British line, that the Jacobite advance was brought to a halt, virtually surrounded in Huske's counter-attack, and where the greatest casualties were suffered. Afterwards the dead were buried where they lay, regiment by regiment. (Author's photograph)

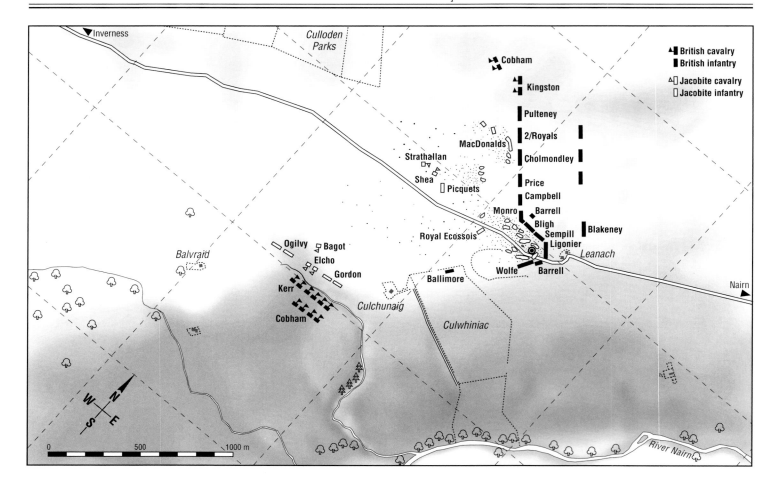

Map 13. *A general collapse of the Jacobite front line is now imminent. Many units are breaking up, especially on the right, and the supporting units, including the Irish Picquets, are beginning to withdraw. As yet the British cavalry have not crossed the re-entrant.*

towards their original position somewhere in the vicinity of the cottage now known as "The King's Stables". They never reached it. Halfway across the moor they were intercepted either by Kingston's Horse, or more probably by the two troops of Cobham's Dragoons from the Government right wing.

"Stapleton makes an evolution or two, fires at the Dragoons & obliges them to retire ..." said O'Sullivan; and this may well have been the moment when Captain Ranald MacDonald of Bellfinlay, who was then lying on the moor in the agony of two broken legs, had a volley fired over his head by some "French" troops. At much the same time a French engineer officer named Du Saussay providentially turned up to assist them with a gun (probably one of the light, iron-barrelled "Swedish" 4lb. pieces) and a properly trained crew for it. Having thus given Cobham's men due notice, the Picquets tried to resume their orderly withdrawal.

Exactly what happened next is unclear; but by the end of the battle Stapleton was fatally wounded, and Captain Hay of the Royal Ecossois opined that about a hundred of the Picquets were also killed or wounded – nearly half their strength at Culloden. O'Sullivan, who may just possibly have been a witness to their fate, simply relates that after firing a volley at the dragoons "the Picquets throws themselfs into the Park yt was on our left, continues there fire where Stapleton was wounded, & are at last obliged to give themselfs up as prisoners of War."

While there is no reason to doubt that the Picquets did

indeed finally take cover within the walls of the Culloden Parks and employed them as a breastwork, their retreat to those walls must have been precipitate, for there is a wide discrepancy between their estimated hundred-odd casualties and those few reported by the victorious dragoons.

In fact Kingston's Light Horse returned only one man as wounded at Culloden and lost three horses in all, while Cobham's Dragoons had a single man killed and nine horses killed or wounded – including one ridden by a cheerfully philosophical trooper named Enoch Bradshaw:

"... we lost but one man," he wrote to his brother some time afterwards, "tho I fear I shall lose my horse, he having at this moment of writing a ball in his left buttock. 'Twas pritty near Enoch that time, but, thank God, a miss is as good as a mile, as we say in Gloucestershire."

Given this disparity it seems that Cobham's, far from retiring when they were fired upon by the Picquets, may merely have regrouped before launching a proper charge and riding right over the Irish battalion, pursuing the survivors into the park. Once they had thrown themselves inside the walls the Irish were safe for the moment, and the cavalrymen left them alone, pushing on down the Inverness road in search of easier prey.

On the southern side of the moor it was a very similar story. Lord Kilmarnock's Footguards and the blue-bonneted regulars of the Royal Ecossois had been brought up from the second line by Lord George Murray to reinforce the faltering attack, and were engaged in a long range firefight, probably with Campbell's Scots Fusiliers, when the rout began. Contemporary French tactical doctrines laid little stress on prolonged exchanges of fire, and with the world visibly collapsing about them they may have fired no more than a single volley; then Kilmarnock's men broke and fled while, with their honour satisfied, the Royal Ecossois executed an equally hasty withdrawal under artillery-fire.

Kilmarnock subsequently related that instead of pulling straight back with the bulk of the fugitives, both regiments struck off to the Jacobite right in order to gain some shelter beyond the projecting walls of the Leanach enclosure:

"... when the second Line, where I was, broke, I was next to Lord John Drummond's Regiment, and went with them and the other Low Country Foot along the Wall to the South of the Field of Battle which covered us from the Cannon shot of the Duke's Army."

They were not out of danger yet, however, for as soon as they came level with the Culwhiniac enclosure the Royal Ecossois were fired upon by Ballimore's Highlanders.

As we have seen, once the Culwhiniac walls were breached General Hawley had ordered Ballimore's four companies to remain within the enclosures, and as he moved off towards Balvraid they climbed to the top of the slope, where they found themselves looking at the right flank of the Jacobite army. At first they had fired at long range and to little effect on some of Lord Lewis Gordon's men; but then the Royal Ecossois appeared. Small though his little battalion might be, Ballimore was determined to get into the battle, and after firing a volley at the retreating Jacobites he promptly led his men out through the west gate.

It proved to be a fatal decision, for although they were falling back the Royal Ecossois still had plenty of fight left in them and, as Campbell of Airds sadly reported: "It was in passing a slap [opening] in the second Dyke that Ballimore was Shot Dead, and that Achnaba received his wound of which he Dyed next day."

Not surprisingly, with their leaders so peremptorily shot down, the rest of the Highlanders decided to stay under cover after all. Captain Dugald Campbell of Achrossan, who was also a regular officer in the 43rd Highlanders, presumably took over the half-battalion, and ordered his shaken command to return the fire. Ballimore's company afterwards reported only two men wounded in the battle, but had no fewer than six men killed (besides the gallant Captain). This is a reverse of the usual proportions of killed and wounded, and perhaps indicates that the bulk of the casualties were shot through the head while they were still sheltering behind the Culwhiniac wall.

One of the Campbell officers afterwards reported that his men had only fired four rounds apiece, and even with the aid of the wall to steady their firelocks the Highlanders cannot have hit very many of the French regulars. Nevertheless the firing was sufficiently dangerous to drive the Royal Ecossois away from the shelter of the wall, back out on to the moor — and straight into the path of the advancing dragoons.

General Hawley's cavalry brigade had finally got into action. The rebels facing them appear to have been forming their fighting line not too far from the 170 metre contour, and notwithstanding his somewhat diabolical reputation Henry Hawley was unable to see through solid hillsides. As it was he could still see no fewer than four infantry battalions as

Map 14. *The rout has begun; all the units in the Jacobite front line are now pulling back in disorder. The Royal Ecossois and Lord Kilmarnock's Footguards are moving along the Culwhiniac wall in order to gain some shelter from the artillery fire. Only those units lining the re-entrant are standing firm, and Lord Lewis Gordon's two battalions are engaged in a long range firefight with Kerr's Dragoons.*

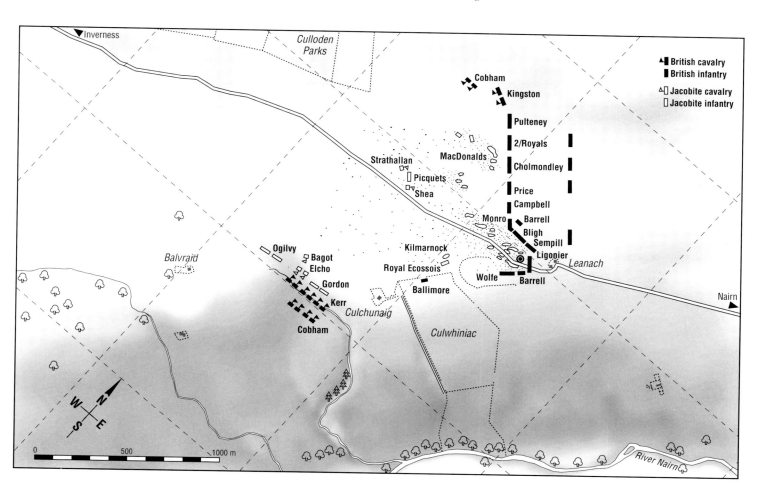

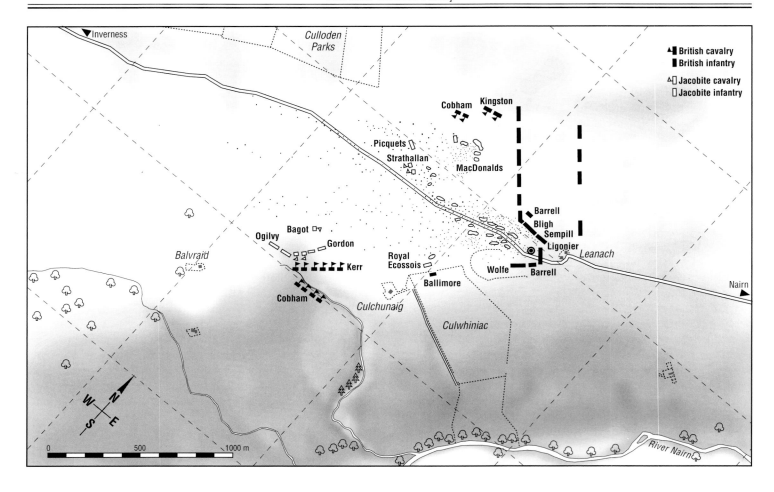

Map 15. *Most of the Jacobite army is now in flight. The British army's front-line units have checked firing and, alerted by this, General Hawley has pushed Kerr's across the stream, causing Lord Lewis Gordon's battalions to fall back. On the British right wing Kingston's Horse have followed the lead given by Cobham's and are driving towards the fleeing enemy. Ballimore's Highland companies have engaged the Royal Ecossois and the other fugitives from the Jacobite right wing.*

well as some horse facing him, and for all that he knew there might be others waiting behind the crest. As James Wolfe noted, he elected to wait until a slackening in the sound of musketry from the moor indicated that the rebels were on the point of breaking.

Initially his advance had been led by four troops of Cobham's Dragoons, but now he must have prepared for the assault by passing the six troops of Kerr's through the intervals in Cobham's four troops to take their place in the forefront of the advance. Although this alteration is nowhere mentioned by any of the participants, the evidence for it having taken place is quite compelling.

Lord Elcho is just as reticent about this episode as he is about all the other "acts of rebellion" in which he was personally involved, and regrettably he devotes only a couple of non-committal lines to it in his narrative. Nevertheless he does categorically identify the leading dragoon regiment on his sketch map of the battlefield as Kerr's. James Wolfe, who as Hawley's Brigade Major ought to have known which regiment led the advance, at first appears to confuse the two of them in his letter to Major Delabene by stating that Kerr's had only two squadrons on this flank and Cobham's three, but in the end he too is positive that it was Kerr's who led the actual assault over the re-entrant.

Lastly, there is the unequivocal evidence of the casualties: in contrast to Cobham's reported loss of one man killed and nine horses killed or wounded (and on balance these are most likely to have been shot on the other side of the battlefield by the Irish Picquets), Kerr's Dragoons had three men killed and three wounded. One of the troop commanders, Captain Alexander Stuart, wryly wrote to his brother that he had "received no hurt, though pretty nigh being demolisht." The regiment also reported the loss of no fewer than 19 horses killed and wounded. In the ordinary run of things these casualties might still be regarded as rather light, but since they lost twice as many horses and men as the other two regiments together, Kerr's men must obviously have faced rather tougher opposition in the battle than either Cobham's or Kingston's.

The rebels evidently got the worst of the affair. Since the re-entrant naturally prevented either force from actually launching a conventional cavalry charge, both sides used their carbines and pistols rather than swords. One correspondent in Leith afterwards reported that: "The Pretender's Life Guards have suffered greatly. A person, this moment arrived, saw 26 of them in a heap. . . ." There was a popular tendency to identify all rebel horsemen either as Lifeguards or Hussars, but if this report was true it indicates that over half of the Lifeguards who fought at Culloden were killed or wounded there, either by artillery fire or by Kerr's Dragoons.

Fitzjames's Horse may have been equally hard hit. The 16 troopers providing escort for the Prince came through the battle unscathed, and Captain Shea rode into Inverness with them to surrender on 17 April. The main body of the regiment, however, which had been with Elcho on the right, must have retreated with the rest of that wing to Ruthven

Barracks; for they did not surrender until the morning of Saturday the 19th, when 30 troopers and five officers turned up at Inverness. This might suggest that about 20 of them were killed or wounded at Culloden.

At all events, according to Wolfe, Hawley "was (when the fire of the Foot began) posted with his Dragoons opposite to the extremity of the enemy's right wing, and as soon as the Rebels began to give way and the fire of the Foot slacken'd, he ordered Genl Bland to charge the rest of them with three squadrons, and Cobham to support him with two. It was done with wonderful spirit and completed the victory with great slaughter."

As the dragoons crossed the re-entrant and came up over the crest the surviving Jacobite cavalry and the two battalions of Lord Lewis Gordon's Regiment were already falling back, while Lord Ogilvy's two well-disciplined Forfarshire battalions formed themselves into a square formation. All of them then retired in fairly good order towards Balvraid, shepherded at a respectful distance by Kerr's men. They halted there for a time to let the stragglers from the front line units come up; then retired southwards, crossing the Water of Nairn by the ford at Faillie and making their way to Ruthven Barracks.

Meanwhile, with their path now cleared, Cobham's Dragoons also rode up the slope and out on to the moor just in time to intercept the Royal Ecossois. Had Ogilvy's and Gordon's men been able to hold the ridge for just a few moments longer the Ecossois might perhaps have been able to join them, but instead they found themselves cut off by the excited horsemen.

Most accounts of the battle blandly imply that all the French troops, led by the dying Stapleton, surrendered at Inverness some time later that same afternoon; but the burgh lay five miles from the battlefield along a road choked with fugitives and marauding dragoons, and it is most unlikely that the majority of the Royal Ecossois ever got so far.

Captain James Hay reckoned that his regiment lost about 50 men at Culloden, only half the number of casualties which he said were suffered by the Picquets. Like the Picquets, though, they too numbered their commanding officer, Lord Lewis Drummond, amongst them; luckier than Stapleton, he only lost a leg. A proportion of the Royal Ecossois may have been killed or wounded by artillery fire, and others must surely have fallen in the brief exchange of musketry with Ballimore's Highlanders over by the Culwhiniac enclosure. The fact that Cobham's Dragoons came through the battle virtually unscathed rather argues against the Royal Ecossois having made much resistance to the cavalry, and with their retreat cut off a fair number of them must have bowed to the inevitable and laid down their arms on the spot.

Writing the next day, however, Wolfe reckoned that only a part of the regiment were amongst the prisoners, and certainly only eight officers of the Ecossois signed their paroles on 17 April, as against no fewer than 24 officers of the Picquets. Another letter from Inverness, dated 19 April, also confirms this with a report that 30 of Lord John Drummond's Regiment (the Royal Ecossois) had just surrendered that morning, along with the last of Fitzjames's Horse. Obviously, therefore, a part of the regiment must in the end have managed to get away with the rest of the right wing to Ruthven Barracks, still carrying their distinctive colours – a St.Andrew's cross emblazoned with a huge thistle, and dusted with gold fleurs-de-lis.

The surrender of at least a substantial part of the Royal Ecossois effectively marked the end of organised resistance; and for a while the cavalry from the British right and left wings roamed at will amongst the last of the fugitives still scattering over the moor.

James Johnstone, for one, was extremely lucky to get away: "I remained for a time motionless, and lost in astonishment; then, in a rage, I discharged my blunderbuss and pistols at the enemy and immediately endeavoured to save myself like the rest. But having charged on foot and in boots I was so overcome by the marshy ground, the water on which reached to the middle of the leg, that instead of running I could scarcely walk. I had left my servant, Robertson, with my horses, on the eminence about six hundred yards behind us where the Prince remained during the battle, that I might easily know where to find my horses in case of need. My first object on retreating was to turn my eyes towards the eminence to discover Robertson; but it was to no purpose. I neither saw the Prince, nor his servants, nor anyone on horseback. They had all gone off and were already out of sight. I saw nothing but the most horrible of all spectacles; the field of battle, from the right to the left of our army covered with Highlanders dispersed and flying as fast as they could to save themselves."

Most of the Jacobite army's senior officers escaped, though there is little evidence to support claims that Lord George Murray was one of the last to leave the field. His fellow Lieutenant General, the Duke of Perth, also got away (though not before he had for some inexplicable reason stopped to change his clothes on the battlefield – the subsequent discovery of his breeches occasioned some amusement in the British ranks).

Others were less lucky. Lord Kilmarnock had ridden away from the Royal Ecossois when they were ambushed by Ballimore's Highlanders, and headed towards some red-coated cavalrymen whom he is said to have mistaken for Fitzjames's Horse. Realising his mistake just in time, he turned away from them only to be captured by Kerr's Dragoons.

Another Jacobite leader caught by the dragoons was Lord Strathallan. The circumstances of his death are not entirely clear, but he seems to have had his horse shot from under him, and by the time he mounted another he was surrounded by dragoons. Unlike Kilmarnock, who was saved at the intercession of Lord Ancrum, he was run through by Lieutenant Colonel George Howard after refusing to surrender – though what Howard was doing there in the first place is not explained, since his proper station was with his regiment, the Buffs, in the second line.

Strathallan's men and some other rebel cavalrymen, having abandoned their commander to his fate, got away in a body estimated by John Daniel to be about 40 strong. Wounded in the arm, but still carrying his troop's standard, Daniel had been joined by Lord John Drummond just after the Royal Ecossois were surrounded; at the head of this little group of horsemen they got away to the hills, and there dispersed.

As the battlefield rapidly emptied Hawley organised a proper pursuit. Some of Cobham's men were already chasing the fleeing Jacobites down the Inverness road; now General Bland and Lord Ancrum were ordered to follow after them with the rest of the cavalry. Their task was two-fold. In the first place they were to harry the fugitives unmercifully and prevent any possibility of their rallying again – the traditional and bloody employment of victorious cavalry throughout history. Ordinarily they might perhaps have been better

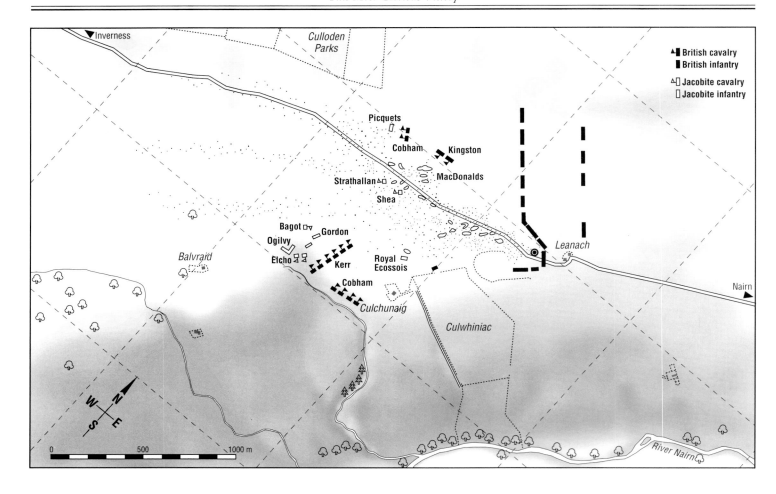

Map 16. *To the north of Balvraid, Lord Ogilvy's Regiment is beginning to form a defensive square as Lord Lewis Gordon's Regiment and two small cavalry units fall back before Kerr's Dragoons. Covered by Kerr's, Cobhams's Dragoons are climbing out of the re-entrant and will soon be in a position to get in amongst the fugitives. In front of the British right, Kingston's Horse are moving to cut the Inverness road while the two troops of Cobham's attack the retreating Irish Picquets.*

The re-entrant looking east. The rebels were drawn up along the crest to the right of the photograph. The slope itself does not appear to be much of an obstacle, but the stream is very marshy. (Author's photograph)

employed in destroying the rebel rearguard which was now regrouping around Balvraid, but they had good reason for taking the Inverness road: the tolbooth and a church in the burgh were full of British prisoners, chiefly men from Guise's and Loudon's regiments, and it was feared that the defeated rebels might be in the mood for reprisals.

A sense of urgency was therefore added to the normal bloodthirsty excitement of the chase, and as one correspondent (probably an officer in Cobham's) remarked: "the dragoons and Light Horse pursued, calling out 'Cut hard, pay

em home.'" All are agreed that a "prodigious slaughter" ensued. James Wolfe, who may have been riding down the road himself, remarked to his friend Major Delabene: "The Rebels, besides their natural inclinations, had orders not to give quarter to our men. We had an opportunity of avenging ourselves for that and many other things, and indeed we did not neglect it, as few Highlanders were made prisoners as possible."

Cumberland wrote: "Major General Bland had also made great Slaughter, & gave Quarter to None but about Fifty French Officers and Soldiers He picked up in his Pursuit" – obviously the remains of the Irish Picquets and Du Saussay's gunners.

Inverness, not surprisingly, was in a state of bedlam. As the Prince left the field he ordered Captain Felix O'Neill of Lally's Regiment to ride to the burgh and warn his adherents to make their escape. It is likely, however, that he was preceded by the first of the fugitives; and amongst them was the Master of Lovat.

Whether or not the Master actually fought at Culloden is by no means certain. Lord George Murray twice categorically stated that he did, but there is otherwise general agreement that he and his battalion of Frasers were still marching up towards the moor when he met the rest of the army fleeing towards him. At this point, according to a popular report, he briskly faced them about and retraced his steps with barely a pause, keeping his colours still flying and the piper still playing. He is also said to have talked loudly for a time of holding the narrow bridge over the River Ness; but by the time the dragoons arrived he and his men had probably decamped.

The cavalrymen clattering excitedly into the burgh met no resistance, although Captain Johnstone, who had eventually found himself a horse, claimed to have heard a brief but intense burst of firing as he rode past. Despite Captain O'Neill's warning there were still plenty of bewildered Jacobite non-combatants milling about in the streets: "There were vast numbers of them, some crying, some mourning. Some stood astonished and did not know whither to turn themselves."

One report in the newspapers did rather darkly assert that some of the defeated rebels had been "asking" about the British prisoners held in the church, but all of them were released unharmed after the Army formally took possession of the burgh. The honours were done at about four o'clock by Captain James Campbell of Ardkinglas at the head of the grenadier company of Sempill's 25th (Edinburgh) Regiment. Cumberland himself followed close behind, after pausing on the road to accept the formal surrender of Stapleton and his men, so setting the seal on what had clearly been a decisive victory.

By a fairly broad consensus the battle is unlikely to have lasted more than about 40 minutes; and by the end of it Cumberland was able to report that his triumph had cost only 50 officers and men killed, 259 wounded and one missing – although as we have seen in passing, a fair number of the wounded were soon to succumb to their injuries.

Just how many men the rebels lost must remain a matter for conjecture. By the Well of the Dead, where they had been hemmed in by Huske's counter-attack and then shot down by repeated volleys at close range, the clansmen were in some places lying four deep. George Innes, the Jacobite-leaning Presbyterian minister, asserted that one of Cumber-

Trooper, 11th (Kerr's) Dragoons, 1742. Red coat and breeches; white cuffs, collar patches and waistcoat; light buff turnbacks. Light yellowish saddle-housings with mixed red, green and black embroidery. Red cloak, lined yellow (light buff?), rolled with lining outwards. These housings had probably been changed to the style shown on Colour Plate D by 1746.

William Kerr, Earl of Ancrum (1710-1775) was a Scottish officer first commissioned in 1735. Lieutenant Colonel of the 11th Dragoons and an aide-de-camp to Cumberland at Culloden, he was later Colonel of the 24th Foot before succeeding his brother Lord Mark Kerr as Colonel of the 11th Dragoons in 1752. Most of the regiment's officers were Scots, and several of them were Kerrs. (NMS)

land's regimental surgeons had very carefully counted some 750 bodies lying on the moor, besides those cut down on the fringes or on the Inverness road. Conservative estimates allow around 1,500 fatalities in total, though the final figure may well have been much higher.

Jacobite sympathisers were quick to point to the numbers of "innocent civilians" who were also cut down on the road; but since very few of the rebels wore anything which could be recognised as a military uniform this was probably inevitable. Michael Hughes, coming down the road a little later with Bligh's Regiment, remarked that it was "covered with dead bodies, and many of the inhabitants, not doubting of success, who came out of curiousity to see the action, or perhaps to get plunder, never went home to tell the story, for being mixt with their own people we could not know one from the other." Many of the unfortunate fugitives were no doubt unarmed, having flung away their weapons in their haste to escape. But if the British cavalry are to stand indicted for killing unarmed fugitives, then some of those self-same fugitives must themselves stand indicted for their equally ruthless slaughter of fleeing soldiers at Prestonpans and

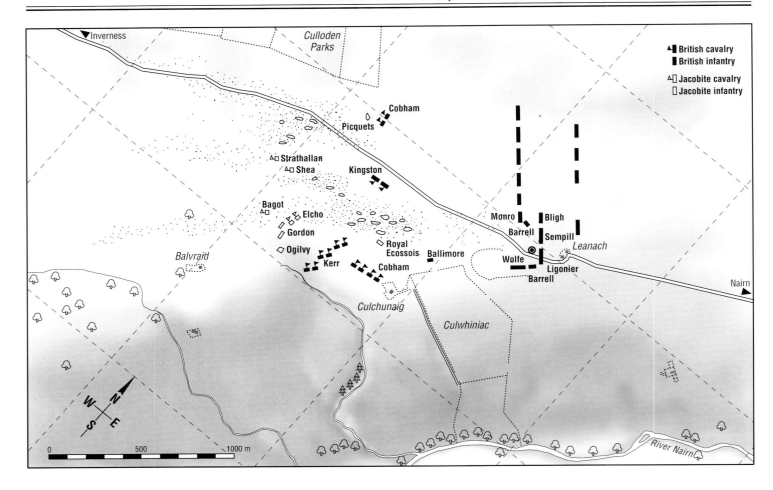

The re-entrant looking northwards to Culchunaig (behind the trees on the right) and the battlefield. This is Hawley's viewpoint; from here he was quite unable to see what was happening on the moor, or what lay behind the crest. It is not surprising that his advance was rather cautious. (Author's photograph)

Falkirk. From the dawn of history and up to the present day, armies have always suffered the greatest losses when beaten and running; and the defeated have always found it perilously difficult to get their immediate surrender accepted.

This is, indeed, a consistent theme in the many letters written by British soldiers who were present at Culloden. They hated and feared the Highlanders' broadswords and the savage, tearing injuries which they caused. Moreover, unlike the impersonal and in some ways dispassionate exchange of volley fire to which they were accustomed on continental battlefields, the infliction of those terrible face-to-face injuries by the Highlanders seems to have been regarded as in some special sense deliberate, and even vindictive – an illogical view, perhaps, but certainly one sincerely held by the soldiers of the day. This attitude was particularly coloured by stories of the dreadful slaughter at Prestonpans and by their own more direct experience at Falkirk.

Consequently there was a desperate atmosphere of "kill or be killed" during the battle itself, and of justified vengeance during its immediate aftermath. All the correspondents were quite open about this, and freely admitted that – with the rather pointed exception of the French regulars, whose status was clearly felt to be more legitimate than that of the rebels – little mercy was shown to the defeated Jacobites during the battle and the subsequent pursuit. The officer of Monro's whose letter is extensively quoted in the previous chapter certainly had no hesitation in stating that he and his men gave no quarter; but he also explicitly linked this ruthless approach to the supposed cold-blooded murder of several of the regiment's officers at Falkirk.

In short, the British army's attitude during the battle and in the hours immediately following it can perhaps best be summarised in the robust language of their descendants today: "Big boys' games – big boys' rules. . . ."

This is not to say, however, that once the heat of the battle cooled they still refused to take any prisoners. Accusations that the British army ran amuck after their victory and ruthlessly bayoneted every wounded rebel they could lay their hands on are disproved by the very large number of prisoners taken, and by the ample testimony that a high proportion of those prisoners were in fact wounded. One officer noted that over 200 prisoners had been taken, "most of whom are terri-

bly wounded". An officer of Wolfe's wrote that at the height of the battle his regiment was ordered to take the rebels in flank, and "soon made the place too hot for them, retook the Cannon, and took a great Number of Prisoners; more than we should have done, had we known their Orders, which was, to spare neither Man, Woman, nor Child."

The number of captives was in fact quite impressive; in his official dispatch, written on the 18th, Cumberland announced that 326 rebel and 222 French prisoners (in the latter case at least, exclusive of officers) were then in custody – and these figures were to rise steadily over the next few days.

The other trophies with which victories are customarily graced were equally numerous. The eleven brass 3lb. guns and Du Saussay's iron four-pounder were abandoned on the moor; and in Inverness another ten pieces of field artillery and eight small swivel guns were found, together with 22 ammunition carts, 37 barrels of powder and 1,019 roundshot of various calibres. There were also 2,320 firelocks, 1,500 cartridges, five hundredweight of musket balls, and just 190 broadswords and blades.

A respectable number of the rebels' colours were also taken, and these, Cumberland decided, should be handed over to the civil authorities for appropriate disposal. The receipt given for them by Major Hu Wentworth a month after the battle interestingly provides a description of each:

Map 18. *For all practical purposes the battle is now over. Ignoring Ogilvy's and Gordon's still formed units, which are retreating towards Balvraid, Kerr's Dragoons and Kingston's Horse are harrying the fugitives. The greater part of the Royal Ecossois are being attacked by Cobham's.*

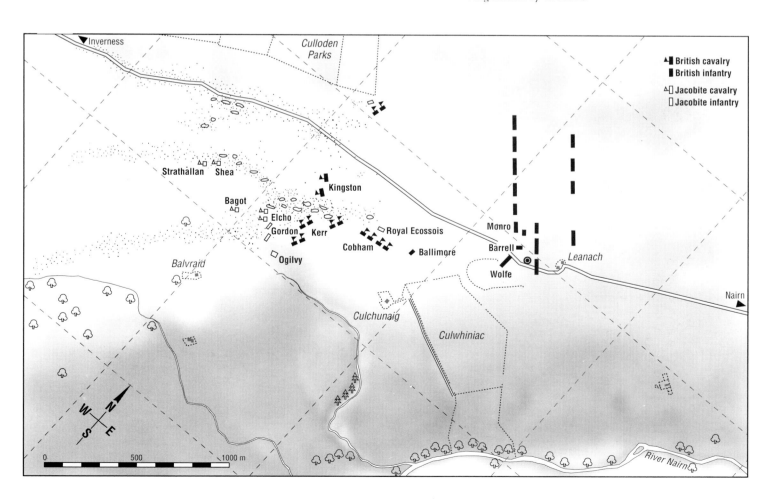

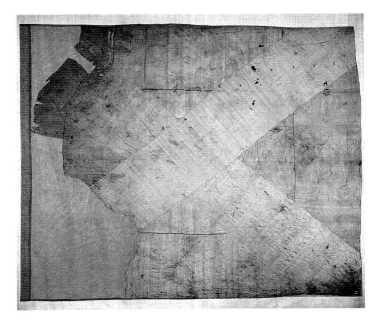

Appin banner, a yellow saltire on blue, originally carried at Culloden by one Dugald Stewart and after his death by several others, until stripped from the staff and carried from the field by a man named Donald Livingston. The staff may have been one of the three trophies claimed by Monro's Regiment. (On loan from the Stewart Society to the NMS)

Ardshiel's colour, another yellow saltire on blue carried by the same regiment at Culloden. (NMS)

"Received from Lieutenant Colonel Napier the following Rebel colours, viz:-

1. On a staff a white linen colours belonging to the Farquharsons.
2. On a staff a white linen colours, motto 'Terrores Furio', Chisolmes.
3. On a staff a large plain white colours, said to be the standard.
4. On a staff a blue silk colours, 'Sursum Tendo'
5. A staff the colours tore off.
6. Do.
7. On a staff a white silk colours with the Stewarts Arms 'God Save King'
8. On a staff a white silk colours, in the canton St.Andrew's cross.
9. On a staff a white silk with a red saltire.
10. A blew silk colours with the Lovat arms 'Sine Sanguine Victor'
11. A white silk with a blue saltire.
12. Piece of blue silk with a St.Andrew saltire 'Commit the Work to God'
13. A white linen jaik with a red saltire.
14. One of Lord Lovat's camp colours

Which colours I am to deliver to the Lord Justice Clerk at Edinburgh.

Hu Wentworth
Inverness May 11th 1746"

On 4 June 1746 they were burnt with due ceremony before a large crowd in the Grassmarket by the common hangman. There was no mistaking the message: the rebellion was over.

CHAPTER ELEVEN

Afterwards

The question of what happened to the Jacobite wounded after the battle is one which has never properly been addressed. Indeed, we do not even know how many wounded were left lying on the field in the first place, for there is certainly evidence on both sides that a fair number of them were carried from the field by their retreating regiments. A courier delivering a despatch to the post at Taymouth two weeks after the battle reckoned to have seen "near 500 of the rebels, most of them wounded and many dying in huts on the way." Judging by the numbers of prisoners afterwards recorded as being in custody at Inverness, however, hundreds more were perforce abandoned on the moor to the mercy of Cumberland's army.

Contemporary British accounts openly admitted that no prisoners were taken at the height of the action and few in the pursuit; but it has also become an article of faith amongst generations of writers that in the days which followed those wounded men left lying out on the moor were systematically murdered.

There is no doubting that the Government soldiers believed that they had ample justification for treating the defeated rebels harshly. In the pocket of one of the Jacobite officers captured on the 16th a copy of their orders had been found, containing the ominous line: "It is His Royal Highness positive Orders that every person attach themselves to some Corps of the Armie and to remain with that Corps night and day till the Battle and persute be finally over; and to give no quarters to the Elector's troops on any account whatsoever."

Other versions of the orders in question do not include the injunction to take no prisoners, and this particular copy has been vigorously denounced as a crude forgery got up in order to justify the killings which took place after the battle. Yet this is far from self-evident. The document in question is written in an unknown hand upon a much-folded sheet of paper which also contains the text of a declaration issued by Lord John Drummond in December 1745. It is clearly not one of the copies originated by Lord George Murray's aides; but if anything this tends to support its authenticity. Although senior officers and regimental commanders were accustomed to receiving such orders signed by the General's hand, their juniors had to scribble their own copies or summaries on any scrap of paper which came to hand, and in so doing they frequently recorded verbal instructions and emphases not always written down in the original.

In this case the orders were actually issued for the expected battle on 15 April. When this did not take place O'Sullivan proposed that fresh orders should be drawn up for the abortive night attack, but as we have seen Lord George Murray brusquely "answered that there was no need of orders, yt everybody knew what he had to do."

It has even been suggested that this was a rather unfortunate phrase which might have been understood, intentionally or otherwise, to mean that no prisoners were to be taken. His words might perhaps bear this interpretation in our own day; but in their true context there seems little reason to seek behind their obvious meaning. That said, given the desperate nature of the rebels' enterprise it would at least have been understandable if such a hint had been given verbally to the senior officers then present, and had later found its way into writing at company level.

Be that as it may, the question of the Jacobite order's authenticity is largely irrelevant, since the evidence actually suggests that although few prisoners were taken during the battle on the 16th the British army did not, as is popularly supposed, respond to the news of the order's discovery by going out and bayoneting the enemy wounded out of hand.

Much of the hostile evidence concerning the alleged killings was amassed in the years after the battle by a minister named Robert Forbes, and collected together in several manuscript volumes of notes and letters which he entitled *The Lyon in Mourning*. Forbes was a far from disinterested party, who had been arrested in July 1745 while on his way to join the Prince and imprisoned in Edinburgh Castle until the rising was over.

Although some of the many incidents which he records, particularly the summary execution of some wounded men at Culloden House by a detachment from 2/Royals, are backed up by independent testimony, others are more suspect. A well-known case is that of Captain Ranald MacDonald of Bellfinlay, last encountered lying helplessly on the moor with both legs broken by canister and the Irish Picquets firing over his head. Despite this ordeal Bellfinlay survived to become a frequent correspondent of Forbes, supplying many details to him on demand (not all of them entirely consistent); but it is his initial testimony which is most interesting:

"He remained likewise in the field all that night after he was stript of all his cloaths, his very shirt and breeches being taken from him. But as he was young and of a robust constitution he lived till next morning, when he saw that cruel command coming to execute their bloody orders, and saw many of his unhappy companions putt to death in cold blood. They were just presenting their firelocks to his own breast when he was saved through the clemency of Lieutenant [James] Hamilton who, if he remembers, belonged to Cholmondley's regiment, and who took him to a neighbouring country house. Next day he was brought along with wounded redcoats to Inverness, they cursing and abusing him all the way for a damn'd rebellious rascal."

While this statement is clear enough in claiming that the wounded men lying on the moor were being shot all around him, he does not explain why he alone of them was spared by Hamilton. What is more, his recollection of being brought in from the moor on the second day after the battle, the 18th, is corroborated by a letter written on that date by a sergeant in

Highland soldier and corporal copied from Van Gucht for Grose's
Military Antiquities. *The plaids are drawn fairly reliably, and the*
corporal, identified by his right shoulder knot, has his hair brushed
up under his bonnet in accordance with the prevailing regulations.
(Author's collection)

Howard's Buffs, who inter alia remarked that "our Army
killed between 2 and 3000 of the Rebels, besides Numbers
coming in Wounded." Obviously, Bellfinlay was not the only
wounded rebel to be carried into Inverness that day.

There is certainly ample testimony on all sides that a high
proportion of the hundreds of prisoners held there were
wounded men, who quite patently had not been bayoneted

where they lay. Indeed, the names of 92 of the prisoners
known to have been in custody immediately after the battle
simply vanish from the records within a matter of days, presumably because they had already succumbed to their
wounds.

The survivors, having been taken in arms against the forces
of the Crown, were all theoretically liable to stand trial for
their lives on a charge of treason; but for a particular category
of prisoners retribution was to come more swiftly.

On the 17th, which was evidently a busy day for all concerned, the Sergeant-Majors of each regular battalion were
ordered to visit all the prisoners, "taking the names of those

Dr. Archibald Cameron (1707-1753), Locheil's brother, and Lieutenant Colonel of his regiment. Like Locheil he escaped to France, and is later known to have been a captain in Ogilvy's Regiment, but was arrested and executed after returning to Scotland in 1753. (NGS)

The fate of the rest is obscure. The chances are that a fair number of them were wounded and subsequently died of their injuries, but others may simply have been discharged to their units. Eleven men, all from Guise's Regiment, were certainly released and returned to duty at the intercession of an Inverness minister named Alexander McBean. His name might suggest kinship with some of the rebel officers of Lady McIntosh's Regiment, but in fact his son Forbes McBean was an officer in the Royal Artillery (he would later command a battery at Minden), and although his son was not serving in Godwin's detachment this connection presumably gave him the ear of Major Belford and, through him, the Duke himself.

In the case of Guise's men, McBean must have urged that there were grounds for compassion. Unlike the other deserters found in the rebel ranks they had been captured at Fort Augustus only a short time before Culloden, and then held in appalling conditions: "Our men really have been pretty severe," wrote one officer, "and gave little Quarter, being exasperated at the Treatment our Prisoners met with, they being found in dark Dungeons at Inverness, almost naked and eat-up with Vermin."

Some corroboration of this even came from within the Jacobite ranks. Lord George Murray wrote how: "An officer of our army had got a new corps raised, and they were very ill-clothed. What possessed him, I cannot tell; but a complaint was brought me, that he and his men were stripping the prisoners in the church of their coats, to clothe his own men. ... This was a week before the battle of Culloden." Murray reckoned that he got the coats returned, but whether, in view of the officer's testimony, he was as successful as he claimed is open to conjecture. George Innes, the Presbyterian minister turned Jacobite sympathiser, also spoke of the deserters' plight: "they were busy at Inverness hanging up the poor men, whom they called deserters, many of whom had been obliged to list in the Highland army for mere subsistence, the government never vouchsafing to send any relief to such of their men as were taken."

Not surprisingly, having released those of their men still held in Inverness after the battle, the army then took some satisfaction in thrusting the captured rebels into those self-same "dark Dungeons".

In any army the dirty jobs are always handed out to penal detachments and other low status second-line troops. It would be natural to suppose, therefore, that the task of clearing the battlefield at Culloden was allocated to the despised "Vestry men" rather than to the regulars; and the presence there of these undisciplined thugs may well account for those atrocities on the fringes of the battlefield which can be verified as having taken place. The surviving returns reveal that the Vestry men were certainly allocated the equally unpopular job of prisoner-handling. It would be hard to imagine a more brutal set of jailers than this sorry collection of petty criminals, and this should be borne in mind when considering the subsequent complaints of bad treatment by the prisoners.

Apart from a natural desire to shift such tasks on to somebody else, there was good reason for employing the Vestry men in this way and thus keeping the trained regulars in the ranks of their regiments. The Jacobite army might have been decisively beaten, but the rebellion was not yet over.

who had been in any of the Regiments in our Service"; and again on the 19th, after the last of the Royal Ecossois and Fitzjames's Horse surrendered, Sergeants were again ordered to comb them for deserters. Whether any were found amongst the latter does not appear, and in the circumstances it would be surprising if they had been; but according to the return annexed to Cumberland's official despatch those prisoners examined on the 17th included "Eighty-nine deserters from different regiments of the King's troops. . . ."

Desertion alone could of course be punishable by death, and taking service with the rebels or the French naturally compounded the offence. Actually, as a group they fared rather better than might have been expected, probably because they were something of an embarrassment to the Army. Although the *Scots Magazine* duly reported their capture, and the *Newcastle Journal* printed a list of the names of 49 English deserters taken there (the overwhelming majority of them from Guise's 6th Foot), other journals such as the *Gentleman's Magazine* tactfully censored all references to their existence. The Orderly Books record that only 30 deserters in total were condemned by drum-head courts-martial and executed in the weeks following the battle.

*   *   *

Ruthven Barracks. After falling to the rebels the barracks are said to have been burnt down; nevertheless some Jacobite soldiers are known to have been quartered here, and a large part of the army assembled at Ruthven after Culloden. During the subsequent counter-insurgency operations a company of the 43rd Highlanders was also stationed here. (Author's photograph)

Having fled the field, most of the clansmen understandably dispersed to their homes; but the Lowland regiments which had formed the rearguard at Balvraid held together and spent the night of the battle at Corrybrough, some four miles south-east of Loch Moy. From there they made their way to a rendezvous at Ruthven Barracks. Some 1,500 men assembled there; about half of these were from the four battalions which formed the rearguard at Balvraid, but elements of the Royal Ecossois under Major Hale, the Duke of Perth's Regiment, and most of the surviving Jacobite cavalry are also known to have been present, along with Cluny's Regiment, which had not taken part in the battle.

Prince Charles Edward, however, was not present. During the retreat he had paused by the ford at Faillie for a brief conference with some of his surviving officers. Not surprisingly this soon became acrimonious, and even more so when the Prince declined to accompany the remnants of his army southwards to Ruthven. He was bound for France. Lord Elcho, the hot-headed commander of his Lifeguard, was so disgusted that he took his leave with the memorable retort: "There goes a damned Italian coward!"

Nevertheless, there was at first some brave talk at Ruthven of continuing the fight; but then orders arrived from the Prince, directing them to "shift for themselves". Destitute of food, ammunition, money, and now the will to fight, they dispersed on 18 April.

"At first we had great hopes of rallying again", said John Daniel; "but they soon vanished, orders coming for every one to make the best of his way he could. So some went one way, some another: and those who had French Commissions surrendered; and their example was followed by my Colonel,

Lord Balmerino, tho' he had none. Many went for the mountains, all being uncertain what to do or whither to go."

Those officers and men belonging to the Royal Ecossois and Fitzjames's Horse who were confident of being treated as prisoners of war gave themselves up at Inverness on the 19th, while the others, presumably deserters or other recruits picked up since their regiments came to Scotland, attempted to escape individually. Not all of them made it. Major Hale, for example, was killed in the fight at Loch nan Uamh (see below); Captain James Hay gave himself up in Edinburgh on the 29th; and a trooper of Fitzjames's named Lawrence Nicol turned up in Aberdeen as late as 5 May.

In a final flourish, Lord Ogilvy's Regiment marched off home in a body by way of Braemar, where Mr.Garden, the minister of Birse, saw them pass through "some with Arms, many without, some wounded and all in the greatest Confusion". They eventually disbanded at Clova on the 21st. The two Aberdeenshire battalions appear to have been disbanded at the barracks, for Ensign John Martin of Stonywood's subsequently confessed that "he was at Ruthven after the Battle, where there were several hundreds of the Rebels, and that Stonnywood his Commander came and told his People that orders were given that they should all disperse and shift for themselves, and that he saw Stonnywood tear the Collours from the staff."

Had the rebellion ended at Ruthven Barracks on 18 April the story of the next few months might have been less bitter. Having decisively beaten the rebels, Cumberland had no wish to see his army become bogged down in an open-ended counter-insurgency campaign in the hills. His regiments were urgently needed in Flanders where the French were about to open their summer campaign. Consequently he re-issued an earlier proclamation, "requiring all common and ordinary People who have borne Arms, and been concern'd in the rebellion, to bring in their Arms to the Magistrate or Minister where the Notice shall reach them, and give in their Name and Place of Abode, and submit themselves to the King's Mercy."

Those who did so were in fact treated very leniently. Unless criminal charges were also outstanding they were generally left alone or, if brought to trial, were acquitted if they could prove that they had surrendered in accordance with the terms of the proclamation. These terms were not of course extended to the rebel officers; but now Cumberland also took the bold step of putting out secret feelers, offering an amnesty even to the leaders if they too would submit promptly.

Surprising though this offer might seem in view of what followed, it is confirmed both by Drummond of Balhaldy (admittedly not the most reliable of sources), and by Lord John Drummond; the latter stated, in a memorandum presented to King Louis XV in April 1747, that after Culloden an offer of an amnesty was indeed made by Cumberland to Locheil, and that Locheil had rejected it since he was confident that the Prince would return, as he had apparently promised, with French help.

The promise of French aid had been a recurrent theme throughout the rising and, apart from Drummond's Royal Ecossois and the Irish Picquets, it had invariably proved illusory. Now, however, when it was far too late, two French frigates, the *Mars* and the *Bellona*, nosed into Loch nan Uamh on 30 April.

On 2 May they were gallantly but unsuccessfully attacked by three Royal Navy sloops, the *Greyhound*, *Baltimore* and *Terror*. After a six-hour battle in the narrow confines of the loch the little sloops drew off to lick their wounds, and the Frenchmen hastily set sail before they could return with reinforcements. On board they carried a number of prominent Jacobite leaders, including the Duke of Perth (who died on the way back to France), his brother Lord John Drummond, and Lord Elcho; but behind them on the beach, packed in six casks, they left £35,000 in gold.

Before the arrival of the frigates Locheil and the other chiefs might well have been disposed to respond positively to Cumberland's offer of an amnesty; but now, with their pockets full of French gold, they took the fatal decision to fight on. At a meeting of the remaining Jacobite leaders at Murlaggan, near the head of Loch Arkaig, Locheil, Lochgarry, Clanranald and Barisdale agreed to raise their men once more, to bring them to a rendezvous a week later at Invermallie, and then to join with Keppoch's and Cluny's men in order to resume the campaign. Significantly, in the meantime, Locheil sent a desperate appeal to Cluny begging for a supply of meal with which to feed his men.

There is a certain vagueness about when this gathering took place, but it must have been some time towards the end of May; and, perhaps predictably, it was something of a fiasco. Locheil was reported to have brought in about 300 men, but none of Clanranald's people turned up, while Lochgarry and Barisdale raised only about 150 men apiece. Many of Lochgarry's, particularly those from Glen Urquhart and Glenmoriston, had already surrendered, and as soon as he had got their arrears of pay he moved off again in search of food, with a vague promise to return in a few days. Barisdale too judged it prudent to make his excuses, and left Locheil at Achnacarry. What he may or may not have known was that Fort Augustus had been re-occupied on 17 May by three regular battalions – Howard's, Cholmondley's and Price's – and eight Highland companies.

Next morning, a body of Highlanders appeared on a nearby hill. Locheil at first supposed them to be Barisdale's

Sir Stuart Thriepland of Fingask (1716-1805); detail of a portrait by William Delacour. Belonging to an established Jacobite family, Fingask served throughout the campaign in a medical capacity. Treating the wounded Locheil after Culloden, he subsequently escaped to France but was not attainted, returned to Scotland, and eventually became President of the Royal College of Physicians in Edinburgh. (Private Scottish collection)

men returning as he had promised; "but he was soon undeceived by some out-scouts he had placed at proper distances who told him these men were certainly Loudon's, for they saw the red crosses in their bonnets."

At this unwelcome news Locheil at last recognised that the dream was over, and dispersed his followers without offering resistance. Unfortunately the damage was done; the offer of an amnesty had been rejected, and Cumberland himself followed with the greater part of his army a week later, intent on stamping out the last desperate embers of rebellion.

In the weeks which followed the clans of the Great Glen were subjected to one punitive expedition after another, largely carried out by their countrymen of the Highland Independent Companies who, now that the Jacobite field army was destroyed, came into their own at last. Elsewhere in Scotland, however, the process of "pacification"' was more lenient in character; and it is clear that much of the responsibility for the sufferings of their clansmen must be borne by Locheil and the other chiefs, for rejecting the amnesty and attempting to prolong the rebellion despite their decisive defeat and the flight of the Prince.

By July the Highlands were as secure as they were ever going to be, and Cumberland departed for the south, turning

View of the camp at Fort Augustus, by Thomas Sandby. The little group in the foreground is particularly interesting; the soldiers are wearing their coat skirts unhooked, but have discarded their gaiters. (The Royal Collection © 1994 Her Majesty The Queen)

over command of the army in Scotland to Lord Albemarle. Almost all the regular troops had now been withdrawn from the hills: Houghton's 24th (who had sat out the rebellion in Bristol) were in garrison at Fort William, with a rather lonely detachment of ten men under Captain Powell at Bernera. Two Culloden regiments – Blakeney's 27th and Battereau's 62nd – held Inverness. Five more – Handasyde's 16th, Mordaunt's 18th (both newly arrived), Dejean's (formerly Monro's) 37th, Fleming's 36th and Sackville's (formerly Bligh's) 20th – were spread out along the coast between Nairn and Dundee. Two battalions – the 2/Royals, and Skelton's newly arrived 12th – were in garrison at Perth; and two more – Price's 14th and Conway's (formerly Ligonier's) 59th – at Stirling. As for the rest: five companies of Barrell's were quartered in Linlithgow and the other five at nearby Bo'ness, the 21st Scots Fusiliers lay at Glasgow, and Lee's 55th remained in Edinburgh.

With the Argyll Militia disbanded, this left the Highlands to be policed by Lord Loudon's Regiment and 17 Highland Independent Companies. These were based at Fort Augustus but had numerous small detachments scattered throughout Badenoch and as far south as Blair, while the three Additional Companies of the 43rd Highlanders were deployed at Ruthven, Taybridge and Inveraray respectively.

By this time, too, the prisoners had all gone south to face trial. The limited amount of secure accommodation available in Inverness was soon exhausted, and after the first few days many of the wounded who were judged too badly injured to escape seem to have been farmed out to all sorts of unlikely places. Bellfinlay, for example, was billeted together with another wounded prisoner (Robert Nairn, of the Duke of Perth's Regiment) in a basement flat somewhere in the town. Even this expedient – and a high degree of mortality – failed to alleviate the growing problem of overcrowding; and the prisoners were first transferred to the transports which had accompanied the army along the coast, and then shipped southwards in the ungentle custody of the Vestry men from Handasyde's 16th and Mordaunt's 18th Foot.

The disposal of these and all the other prisoners taken at one time or another during the rebellion was a rather protracted affair, and some unfortunate individuals were still in custody two years later. An imperfect list compiled by Sir Bruce Gordon Seton and Jean Gordon Arnot in the 1920s came up with no fewer than 3,471 names. At least 43 others known to have been captured at Culloden are not included, but conversely upwards of 30 of those in the list have been counted twice. A further 566 came from the French service and were for the most part eventually repatriated as prisoners of war, though this figure is far from complete. Some 310 other men, women and children fall into a miscellaneous category best described as civil prisoners: individuals picked up on suspicion and more often than not released shortly afterwards; some military prisoners temporarily confined in local jails; and people who clearly had no connection with the

rebellion, but happened to be locked up at the time and were included in the lists by mistake.

As to their eventual fate: some 120 officers and men were executed (including 30 deserters taken at Culloden); 88 others are known to have died in custody; 936 were transported to the West Indies or to the American colonies (of which a fair number are known to have returned); and 58 managed to escape by one means or another – including James Miller, a trooper in Bagot's Hussars who calmly walked out of the Edinburgh Tolbooth two days before Culloden dressed in women's clothing.

No fewer than 1,585 of the prisoners, including some of those who were in the French service, were subsequently released, conditionally or otherwise; but the fate of some 700 others is uncertain. A good many of them, particularly the 43 whose names appear all too briefly on the Culloden lists, must have died in prison; the chances are that over 130 others, detained for the most part on suspicion, were equally casually released. The majority of those unaccounted for, ironically enough, probably ended up in the ranks of the British Army.

On 31 July 1746 it was ordered that 250 rebel prisoners were to be sent to Antigua to bring Dalzell's long-suffering 38th Foot back up to strength; 100 more were similarly to go to Trelawney's 63rd in Jamaica; and 200 each to Shirley's 65th and Pepperell's 66th at Cape Breton. In June 1747 at least two of the 12 Independent Companies being raised for Boscawen's expedition against Pondicherry in India were also ordered to be recruited from Jacobite prisoners. The extent to which these various quotas were actually filled is uncer-

tain, although the numbers of men thus enlisted clearly exceeded the 65 identified by Seton and Arnot. A number of the prisoners known to have been shipped out to Dalzell's, for example, were members of various Irish regiments who do not appear in Seton and Arnot's list.

Many of those who got away were also obliged to "go for soldiers", but in the French service. John William O'Sullivan, his reputation undiminished in that quarter at least, was again employed as a staff officer; he is known to have been with the French army at Lauffeldt in 1747, when Marechal Saxe fought Cumberland to a bloody draw. (Although he had materially assisted the Prince's escape after Culloden, they later became estranged when Charles Edward discovered that they had been sharing the affections of a certain Clementina Walkinshaw.) James Johnstone, too, having made his rather agreeable escape, served on General Montcalm's staff at Quebec in 1759, and thus had the unenviable experience of fighting on the losing side in two of the British Army's most famous 18th century victories.

If the second battalion of Drummond's Royal Ecossois was ever formed in the first place, it was disbanded after the rebellion. Instead two new Scottish regiments were raised, one commanded by Lord Ogilvy and the other, the Régiment d'Albany, raised for Prince Charles himself and given to Locheil in partial recompense for his financial losses. The Régiment d'Albany never saw action and, with the Prince banished from France, it was disbanded in 1748. The Royal Ecossois and the Régiment d'Ogilvy soldiered on until 1763, however, providing useful employment for a considerable number of Jacobite refugees. John Daniel, despite being

Sir William Gordon of Park (1712-1751). Originally Lieutenant Colonel of Lord Pitsligo's Horse, he appears to have fought with Lord Lewis Gordon's Regiment at Culloden. Escaping to France thereafter, he became Lieutenant Colonel of Ogilvy's Regiment, but died suddenly in June 1751. (Private Scottish collection)

court-martialled on the beach for an enterprising but unsuccessful attempt to steal some of the gold landed at Loch nan Uamh (the account given in his memoirs is quite untrue), served as a Captain in Ogilvy's Regiment; and another of its officers was John Cameron, the Presbyterian minister who furnished Robert Forbes with material on Culloden and afterwards for *The Lyon in Mourning*.

Perhaps one of the better known members of the Régiment d'Ogilvy was Alan Breck Stuart, generally held to have been the murderer of Colin Campbell of Glenure – Stevenson's fictional character is, however, rather more closely based upon John Roy Stuart, himself at one time an officer in the Royal Ecossois. The man actually hanged for the deed was one James Stewart "of the Glens", a sometime Captain of Ardshiel's Regiment; in one of history's grim little ironies, the prosecuting counsel in the case was none other than Simon Fraser, sometime Master of Lovat and once a Colonel in the Jacobite army. . . .

Simon Fraser had inherited his father's slippery character to the full, and his speedy rehabilitation in the eyes of the authorities was nothing short of astonishing. Ostensibly it was managed through the interest of the Duke of Argyll, but one cannot help but feel that his behaviour on 16 April 1746 was equivocal, to say the least. At any rate, having decisively declared for the Government, Simon went on to raise a Highland regiment which he led at Quebec in 1759.

Although Fraser's 78th Highlanders, and their sister regiment Montgomerie's 77th Highlanders, were preceded by the Black Watch and Loudon's ill-fated 64th, both of the earlier regiments had originally been formed as para-military police formations to be employed in a counter-insurgency

Contemporary and fairly undistinguished print of Lords Kilmarnock, Cromartie and Balmerino shortly before their executions; in the event Cromartie was reprieved. Its chief interest lies in the fact that Balmerino is known to have worn his Lifeguard uniform, and this may therefore be the only known illustration of its general appearance. (Author's collection)

Major Hugh Fraser of the 27th Foot. As a young Ensign he stood with his battalion at Culloden. (NMS)

role within Scotland itself. The 77th and 78th, raised in 1757, were the first Highland units to be specifically recruited for service overseas. This was the start of a long tradition, and significantly a considerable number of the officers and men serving in Fraser's 78th were, like their "hard and rapacious" Colonel, former rebel soldiers from the Jacobite heartland of the Great Glen. Where once upon a time bold young men would have sought service abroad in the mercenary regiments of Holland, France and Sweden, now increasingly they turned to the British Army instead; and made a significant part of it their own – to its later great benefit on a hundred battlefields.

In 1757 the chiefs' heritable powers of "Pit and Gallows" were stripped from them. No longer were they able to rule their people despotically, or to pull them out, willing or unwilling, on to the heather. This, it has been said, by destroying the paternalistic attachment of the chief and his clansmen, eventually paved the way for the Clearances. But it was the people themselves who first took the initiative, and the years which followed the "Forty-Five" were characterised above all by a growing independence on the part of many Highlanders.

Freed of the rigid hand of their chieftains, they sought their own destiny. To the impotent fury and despair of those who had once held the power of life and death over them, they turned their backs on their old masters and emigrated in their thousands, seeking a better life in the Americas or taking service with the mighty East India Company. Indeed, by 60 years after Culloden the Company was widely regarded as a Scottish mafia; and one of its most influential directors, Charles Grant, was the son of a clansman from Glen Urquhart who had stood in the ranks of Glengarry's Regiment on 16 April 1746. The bitter pain of the 19th century Clearances might capture our imagination, and justly excites our indignation; but by then far more people had already left the Highlands of their own free will than were ever evicted by force.

While the Highlands certainly changed after Culloden it was a gradual process, and it is questionable whether the terrible defeat of some of the Highland clans there was wholly

responsible for that change. It is perhaps too easy to draw a direct link between Culloden and the infamous Highland Clearances; the sad fact is that economic pressures upon the chiefs-turned-landlords would still have brought about the Clearances had the battle never been fought.

But on the chill afternoon of 16 April 1746 all that still lay far in the future. At that moment all that mattered was that the rebellion had at last been defeated; and many Scots – like Alexander Taylor of the Royals, and Edward Linn of the Fusiliers – thanked God for it.

APPENDICES

APPENDIX ONE:
The British Army – Morning State, 16 April 1746

A return of the officers and men in each battalion on the day of the battle of Culloden.

Regiments		Field Offs.	Capts.	Subs.	Serjs.	Drums.	R&F.
Royals	(1st)	2	5	19	29	25	401
Howard	(3rd)	2	4	10	21	14	413
Barrel	(4th)	2	5	13	18	10	325
Wolfe	(8th)	1	7	14	17	11	324
Pulteney	(13th)	2	6	14	23	19	410
Price	(14th)	2	7	14	21	11	304
Bligh	(20th)	2	5	13	22	13	412
Campbell	(21st)	1	5	13	21	14	358
Sempill	(25th)	3	5	15	20	14	420
Blakeney	(27th)	2	4	14	24	12	300
Cholmondley	(34th)	2	7	15	21	15	399
Fleming	(36th)	2	6	18	25	14	350
Monro	(37th)	2	6	15	23	19	426
Ligonier	(59th)	3	5	16	21	16	325
Battereau	(62nd)	1	7	19	24	18	354
Total		29	84	222	330	225	5,521

The "Guildhall List", (see *Origins* p429–434) generally quotes higher numbers for each battalion; but it relates to the distribution of money from a charitable fund raised in London, and actually includes men who were sick or on detachment from their battalions on 16 April. Like the morning state it omits the three cavalry regiments, but it does include the "Argyllshire Men": 32 sergeants, 30 corporals, nine drummers and 430 men. Money was also paid to named widows and orphans of men killed at both Falkirk and Culloden: eight officers' widows, two sergeants' widows, and those of 35 soldiers. Unfortunately none are identified by regiment except 19 belonging to the loyalist Glasgow Volunteers. However, as they accounted for over half the widows from both Falkirk and Culloden this confirms that the British Army actually lost very few men at Falkirk.

APPENDIX TWO:
British casualties at Culloden (inc. officers)

Regiment	Killed	Wounded
2/Royals	0	4
Howard's	1	2
Barrell's	17	108
Wolfe's	0	1
Pulteney's	0	0
Price's	1	9
Bligh's	4	17
Campbell's	0	7
Sempill's	1	13
Blakeney's	0	0
Cholmondley's	1	2
Fleming's	0	6
Monro's	14	68
Ligonier's	1	5
Battereau's	0	3
Loudon's	6	3
Argyll Militia	0	1
Artillery	0	6
Kingston's Horse	0	1
Cobham's Dragoons	1	0
Kerr's Dragoons	3	3
Horses:		
Kingston's	2	1
Cobham's	4	5
Kerr's	4	15

A fair number of those listed as wounded subsequently died of their wounds. All six Royal Artillerymen certainly did so; and a Lieutenant Dally of Monro's, included here amongst the wounded, had already died by 17 April.

APPENDIX THREE: Regimental Designations

Regiments are referred to in the text by the numbers which they bore in 1745/6; in some instances, given below, these changed after 1748:

43rd	Murray's (Highlanders)	: 42nd Highlanders
55th	Lee's	: 44th Foot
57th	Murray's	: 46th Foot
58th	Lascelles'	: 47th Foot
59th	Ligonier's	: 48th Foot
62nd	Battereau's	: Disbanded
64th	Loudon's (Highlanders)	: Disbanded

BIBLIOGRAPHY

Advice to the Officers of the British Army, with the addition of some hints to the drummer and private soldier. (1782) (2nd Edn. London 1946)

Allardyce, J. *Historical Papers relating to the Jacobite Period.* (2 vols. New Spalding Club 1895)

Anderson, Peter *Culloden Moor and the story of the battle* (2nd Edn. Stirling 1920)

Atkinson, C.T. *Jenkins Ear, The Austrian Succession War and The Forty-Five* (Journal of the Society for Army Historical Research vol.22 1943-4)

Bailey, D.W. *British Military Longarms 1715-1865* (London 1986)

Bell, R.F. *Memorials of John Murray of Broughton* (Scottish History Society 1898)

Blackmore, H.L. *British Military Firearms 1650-1850* (London 1961)

Blaikie, W.B.(Ed.) *Origins of the '45* (Scottish History Society 1916)

Blaikie, W.B.(Ed.) *Itinerary of Prince Charles Edward Stuart* (Scottish History Society 1897)

Black, Jeremy *Culloden and the '45* (Stroud 1990)

Bland, Humphrey *Treatise of Military Discipline* (London 1727)

Bruce, A. *The Purchase System in the British Army* (Royal Historical Society 1980)

Bulloch, J.M. *Territorial Soldiering in North-East Scotland* (New Spalding Club 1914)

Bumsted, J.M. *The People's Clearance: Highland Emigration to British North America 1770-1815* (Edinburgh 1982)

Caledonian Mercury 1745 & 1746

Campbell of Mamore papers (National Library of Scotland 3733-35)

Chambers, Robert *Jacobite Memoirs of the Rebellion of 1745* (Edinburgh 1834)

Chambers, Robert *History of the Rebellion in Scotland 1745* (1869)

Chandler, David *The Art of Warfare in the Age of Marlborough* (London 1976)

Charles, George *History of the Transactions in Scotland in the years 1715-16 and 1745-46* (2 vols. Leith 1817)

Darling, A.D. *Red Coat and Brown Bess* (Ottawa 1970)

Dennistoun, James *Memoirs of Sir Robert Strange . . .* (London 1855)

Elcho, David, Lord *A short Account of the Affairs of Scotland* (Ed. Hon. Evan Charteris 1907)

Fergusson, Sir Jas. of Kilkerran *Argyll in the Forty-five* (London 1951)

Forbes, Duncan *Culloden Papers* (1815)

Forbes, Rev. Robt. *The Lyon in Mourning: or, a Collection of Speeches, Letters, Journals etc., relative to the Affairs of Prince Charles Edward Stuart* (Ed. Henry Paton) (3 vols. Scottish History Society 1895)

General Wolfe's Instructions to Young Officers (London 1768)

Gentleman's Magazine 1745 & 1746

Gentleman Volunteer's Pocket Companion describing the various motions of the Foot Guards in the Manual Exercise (1745)

Gibson, John S. *Ships of the '45* (London 1967)

Gordon, Sir B. Seton & Arnot, J.G. *Prisoners of the '45* (Scottish History Society 1928-29)

Grant, George *The New Highland Discipline* (London 1757)

Guy, A.J. *Oeconomy and Discipline: Officership and administration in the British Army 1714-63* (Manchester 1985)

Guy, A.J. *Colonel Samuel Bagshawe and the Army of George II, 1731-1762* (Army Records Society 1990)

Henderson, Andrew *The History of the Rebellion, 1745 and 1746* (2nd Edn. 1748)

Home, John *The History of the Rebellion . . . 1745* (1802)

Houlding, J.A. *Fit for Service: The Training of the British Army 1715-1795* (Oxford 1981)

Hughes, B.P. *Firepower: Weapons Effectiveness on the Battlefield 1630-1850* (London 1974)

Jarvis, R.C. *Collected Papers on the Jacobite Risings* (2 vols. Manchester 1972)

Johnstone, James *Memoirs of the Rebellion in Scotland* (Folio Edn. 1970)

Leask, J.C. & McCance, H.M. *The Regimental Records of the Royal Scots* (Dublin 1915)

Lenman, Bruce *The Jacobite Clans of the Great Glen* (London 1984)

Lens, Bernard *The Granadiers Exercise 1735* (London 1967)

A List of the Colonels, Lieutenant Colonels, Majors, Captains, Lieutenants, and Ensigns of His Majesty's Forces (1740)

Livingstone, A., Aikman, W.H. & Hart, B.S. *Muster Roll of Prince Charles Edward Stuart's Army 1745-46* (Aberdeen 1984)

London Gazette 1745 & 1746

London Magazine 1745 & 1746

Mackay, W. *Urquhart and Glenmoriston* (Inverness 1914)

Mackintosh, Alex. *The Forfarshire or Lord Ogilvy's Regiment* (Inverness 1914)

McLynn, Frank *The Jacobite Army in England 1745* (Edinburgh 1983)

McLynn, Frank *France and the Jacobite Rising of 1745* (1981)

Miller, A.E. Haswell & Dawney, N.P. *Military Drawings and Paintings in the Collection of Her Majesty the Queen* (London 1970)

Miller, Diary of James (Journal of the Society for Army Historical Research 3 – 1902)

Murray, Lord George (see Chambers, R., & Charles, G.)

Newcastle Courant 1745 & 1746

Newcastle Gazette 1745 & 1746

Newcastle Journal 1745 & 1746

O'Callaghan, J. *History of the Irish Brigades in the Service of France* (Glasgow 1870)

Orderly Book of Lord Ogilvy's Regiment (JSAHR 2 – 1927)

O'Sullivan (see Tayler, A. & H.)

Peterkin, Ernest *The Exercise of Arms in the Continental Infantry* (Bloomfield Ontario 1989)

Prebble, John *Culloden* (London 1961)

Prebble, John *Mutiny* (London 1975)

Proceedings of the General Court Martial held for the Trial of Lieutenant Colonel James Durand the 15th and 16th of September 1746.

Public Record Office (Kew):
  W.O. 10/28-34: Royal Artillery muster rolls
  W.O. 120: Chelsea Pensions – Regimental Registers

Reid, Stuart *18th Century Highlanders* (London 1993)

The Report of the Proceedings and Opinion of the Board of General Officers, on the examination into the conduct, behaviour and proceedings of Lieutenant General Sir John Cope, Col. Peregrine Lascelles, and Brig. Gen. Thomas Fowke from the time of the breaking out of the rebellion in North Britain in the year 1745 til the action at Preston-Pans. (1749)

Rodgers, N.A.M. *The Wooden World: An Anatomy of the Georgian Navy* (London 1986)

Rosebery, Lord & Macleod, W. *List of Persons concerned in the Present Rebellion* (Scottish History Soc. 1890)

Scots Magazine 1745 & 1746

Scott-Moncrieff, L. *The '45: To gather an image whole.* (Edinburgh 1988)

Smith, Annette *Jacobite Estates of the Forty-Five* (Edinburgh 1982)

Speck, W.A. *The Butcher: The Duke of Cumberland and the Suppression of the 45* (Oxford 1981)

Stewart, David *Sketches of the Highlanders of Scotland* (Edinburgh 1822)

Tayler, A.& H. *1745 and After* (O'Sullivan's and Sir John McDonnell's narratives) (London 1938)

Tayler, A. & H. *Jacobites of Aberdeenshire and Banffshire in the Forty-five* (1928)

Tayler, A. & H. *Jacobite Letters to Lord Pitsligo* (1930)

Terry, C.S.(Ed.) *Albemarle Papers* (2 vols. New Spalding Club 1902)

Terry, C.S. *The Forty-five* (1922)

Thomson, J.P. *The Jacobite Rebellions 1689-1746* (London 1914)

Tomasson, K. & Buist, F. *Battles of the '45* (2nd Edn. London 1967)

Whitworth, Rex *William Augustus, Duke of Cumberland* (1992)

Willson, Beckles *Life and Letters of James Wolfe* (London 1909)

REFERENCES

Chapter One: Prestonpans

This is principally based on the verbal evidence and documents submitted to the 1746 inquiry into Cope's defeat. Johnstone's assessments of the Duke of Perth and Lord George Murray are in *Memoirs* p32-3, and his comments on Prestonpans on p34-43. Lord George Murray's version is in *Marches of the Highland Army* in Chambers' *Jacobite Memoirs* p36-43. The Jacobite official account appeared in most contemporary newspapers, and the well researched "impartial" account in the *Newcastle Journal* is also worth studying.

Chapter Two: Civil War

McLynn's *Jacobite Army in England* provides a useful, albeit strongly pro-Jacobite overview, and the proceedings of Durand's court-martial are useful for the siege of Carlisle – he was acquitted. Provincial newspaper reports usually contain fascinating details (including mention of the Indian chief accompanying the Georgia Rangers); and a letter from one of Cumberland's surgeons providing a complete list of casualties from Clifton is in *Newcastle Courant* 4 January 1746. Coverage of the second siege of Carlisle is particularly good in the *Newcastle Journal*. The British Army's movements prior to Falkirk, and Grossett's activities are usefully discussed in *Origins* p348-364. Lord George Murray's account of Falkirk is in *Marches* p82-95; a diary of the siege of Stirling forms a footnote on p96-97. Elcho, p372-379 and Johnstone, p85-93 also deal with it. Hawley's official account was published in the *London Gazette* and copied by most provincials. In the circumstances there seems no reason to doubt his casualty figures and attempts by pro-Jacobite writers to claim upwards of 400 dead appear to be founded on wishful thinking. A useful essay on Loudon and the Independent Companies by Alex. MacLean appears in Scott-Moncrieff p123-139; and details of the fighting at Dornoch and Inverurie can be found in *Origins* pp109-110 and 136-146 respectively.

Chapter Three: The British Army in 1745

This chapter is very largely based upon Houlding, and Guy. Details of Captain Hamilton Maxwell's company are taken from Bulloch p34-35. The purchase system is usefully described by Bruce, though Houlding has an interesting chapter. Bland's *Treatise of Military Discipline* is essential to understanding how an infantry battalion worked in combat. *Advice to Officers* provides some light relief.

Chapter Four: The Jacobite Army

The introductory essays in Seton & Arnot Vol. I, although dated, are still of considerable value, as are the succeeding volumes in gauging the social composition of the army. Livingstone, Aikman and Hart provide a useful register, though the individual essays on regiments are of limited value. John Daniel's account is in *Origins* p167-226. A surprising amount of information on individual Jacobites is in A. & H. Tayler's *Jacobites of Aberdeenshire & Banffshire*, and some important depositions are in Allardyce Vol.II. Useful insights into the everyday running of the army are to be found in the *Orderly Book of Lord Ogilvy's Regiment*.

Chapter Five: Advance to Contact

British Army dispositions and movements are recorded in Allardyce Vol.I p299-303, and there is a useful essay on the subject in A. & H.Tayler's *Jacobites*. Captain Stewart's narrative of the affair at Keith was originally included in *The Lyon in Mourning*, but a copy is also included in Chambers' *Jacobite Memoirs* p115-120. Identification of Lieutenant Campbell as an officer in Loudon's 64th comes from the Albemarle Papers Vol. I p207. John Daniel's account of his unmilitary adventures is in *Origins* p209, and the *Orderly Book of Lord Ogilvy's Regiment* has some useful details on Jacobite movements. O'Sullivan's account of the rearguard action at Nairn and his comments on the proposed battle-sites are to be found in Tayler, *1745 . . .* p150-153. Lord George Murray's contrasting views are in *Marches* p121-122.

Chapter Six: Alarums and Excursions

Lord Elcho's narrative p426-429 is useful, though Murray's version in *Marches* p121-2 is remarkably terse – a fuller account appears in Geo. Charles, *Transactions*. O'Sullivan *1745 . . .* covers the attack in p155-9. Ker's account in Chambers' *Jacobite Memoirs* adds little but atmosphere. Other useful memoirs are John Daniel p210-211, Johnstone p116-119, Lumisden (*Origins*) p415-416, and George Innes (*Lyon*) p288-90. On the British side, Alexander Taylor's letter is in Leask & McCance, and Campbell of Airds' narrative is in NLS 3735.

Chapter Seven: Culloden Moor

The description of the moor is based upon Thomas Sandby's invaluable maps and the current Ordnance Survey 1:2500 scale plan, supplemented by personal observation, and the comments of Peter Anderson. Elcho's plan needs to be treated with care since most of the dispositions appear to relate to 15 rather than 16 April. O'Sullivan relates how the Jacobite army was drawn up in *1745 . . .* p160-3. Lochgarry's narrative is in Blaikie *Itinerary* p120-1. D'Eguilles's figures for the French contingent are in *Origins* p178, and Captain John Hay's interrogation was widely reported in contemporary newspapers.

Chapter Eight: Dragoons and Cannonades

Hawley's thrust into the Jacobite rear is described by various Argyll Militia officers in NLS 3733-35, and by James Wolfe *Life and Letters* p62-5. The Jacobite response is chronicled in O'Sullivan p163, George Innes (*Lyon*) p291, John Cameron, ibid. p86-7, and Elcho p431-432. Details of British casualties are taken from Cumberland's official returns and from W.O.120. Sir Robert Strange's useful account of his troop's movements is in Denniston p60, and John Daniel's in *Origins* p214.

Chapter Nine: Like Hungry Wolves

British accounts are mainly taken from letters published in contemporary newspapers, most usefully the *Newcastle Journal* and *Newcastle Courant*, although Ashe Lee's account is in O'Callaghan p450 and Wolfe's *Life* p62-5. Cumberland's official report first appeared in the *London Gazette* and was widely reproduced. British casualties are again derived from returns and W.O.120. On the other side, Graden's account is in Chambers p140-143, O'Sullivan's p163-4 and Murray's *Marches* p124 – though see also the longer version in Charles *Transactions*.

Chapter Ten: A Most Glorious Victory

Campbell of Airds and other Argyll Militia narratives in NLS 3733-35 are invaluable, as are the letters published in the *Newcastle Journal* and *Newcastle Courant*. Wolfe op. cit. Trooper Bradshaw's account is in *Lyon* p380-3 and Captain Stewart's in Allardyce Vol. I p312-314; frustratingly, a much longer and more detailed letter to his sweetheart (Miss Willie) has been lost. The list of equipment captured was appended to the official account in the *London Gazette*, and the list of captured colours is reproduced in A.Warden *Angus or Forfarshire* (Dundee 1880) Vol. III p252. On the Jacobite side O'Sullivan p164-5, and Strange p60 are useful. Johnstone's adventures confusingly appear on pp124-126 and 135-139. John Daniel, *Origins* p214-5, Bellfinlay (*Lyon*) p4-6. Lord Kilmarnock's important account of the movements of the Royal Ecossois is in Allardyce Vol. I p322-3.

Chapter Eleven: Afterwards

A fairly full discussion of the "no quarter" order is in Speck p148-156, although the present writer's conclusions are his own. Accounts of alleged atrocities are to be found in *The Lyon in Mourning*, but these should be balanced against contrary reports in contemporary newspapers. Evidence as to the employment of Vestry men can be found in the Albemarle Papers Vol.I p206. Information on the final movements of the Jacobite army is taken from the *Orderly Book of Lord Ogilvy's Regiment*, Johnstone p140-142, John Daniel *Origins* p215-224 – and the true story of what happened to him on the beach is to be found in Chambers *History of the Rebellion* p522-523. John Cameron (*Lyon*) p88-9 is particularly useful on Locheil's attempt to keep the rebellion alive. Cumberland's amnesty offer is described in an essay by John S. Gibson in Scott-Moncrieff p154, and his *Ships of the 45* provides an excellent account of British and French naval activity on the west coast. Orders for the conscription of Jacobite prisoners into the British Army are summarised in Atkinson. As to the longer term effects, Lenman and Bumsted both provide measured discussions and Smith is also useful.